THE

POETICAL WORKS

OF

JOHN SKELTON:

PRINCIPALLY ACCORDING TO THE EDITION

OF THE

REV. ALEXANDER DYCE

IN THREE VOLUMES.

VOLUME II.

BOSTON:

LITTLE, BROWN AND COMPANY.

NEW YORK: BLAKEMAN AND MASON.

CINCINNATI: RICKEY AND CARROLL.

M.DCCC.LXIV.

CAMBRIDGE:

STEREOTYPED BY H. O. HOUGHTON.

Presswork by John Wilson & Son, Boston.

CONTENTS

OF VOLUME II.

THE

POETICAL WORKS

OF

JOHN SKELTON.

MAGNYFYCENCE,

A GOODLY INTERLUDE AND A MERY,

DEUYSED AND MADE BY

MAYSTER SKELTON, POET LAUREATE.*

These be the Names of the Players:

FELYCYTE.
LYBERTE.
MEASURE.
MAGNYFYCENCE.
FANSY.
COUNTERFET COUNTE-
[NAUNCE].
CRAFTY CONUEYAUNCE.
CLOKYD COLUSYON.
COURTLY ABUSYON.

FOLY.
ADUERSYTE.
POUERTE.
DYSPARE.
MYSCHEFE.
GOODHOPE.
REDRESSE.
[SAD] CYRCUMSPECCYON.
PERSEUERAUNCE.

* From the ed. printed by Rastell, n. d.;—in which the above list of characters is placed at the end of the drama.

POEMS OF SKELTON.

MAGNYFYCENCE.

Felicite. AL thyngys contryuyd by mannys
    reason,
The world enuyronnyd of hygh and low estate,
Be it erly or late, welth hath a season,
Welth is of wysdome the very trewe probate;
A fole is he ,with welth, that fallyth at ,debate:
But men nowe a dayes so vnhappely be vryd,
That nothynge than welth may worse be enduryd.
To tell you the cause me semeth it no nede,
The amense therof is far to call agayne;
For when men by welth, they haue lytyll drede 10
Of that may come after; experyence trewe and
    playne,
Howe after a drought there falleth a showre of
    rayne,

And after a hete oft cometh a stormy colde.

A man may haue welth, but not, as he wolde,

Ay to contynewe and styll to endure;

But yf prudence be proued with sad cyrcumspec-
cyon,

Welthe myght be wonne and made to the lure,

If noblenesse were aquayntyd with sober dyrec-
cyon;

But wyll hath reason so vnder subieccyon,

And so dysordereth this worlde ouer all,   20

That welthe and felicite is passynge small.

But where wonnys Welthe, and a man wolde wyt?

For welthfull Felicite truly is my name.

    Lyberte.[1] Mary, Welthe and I was apoynted to
mete,

And eyther I am dysseyued, or ye be the same.

    Fel. Syr, as ye say, I haue harde of your fame;

Your name is Lyberte, as I vnderstande.

    Lyb. Trewe you say, syr; gyue me your hande.

    Fel. And from whens come ye, and it myght
be askyd?

    Lyb. To tell you, syr, I dare not, leest I sholde
be maskyd   30

In a payre of fetters or a payre of stockys.

    Fel. Here you not howe this gentylman mockys?

    Lyb. Ye, to knackynge ernyst what and it
preue?

---

[1] *Lyberte*] Enters, probably, towards the end of the pre-
ceding speech.

Fel. Why, to say what he wyll, Lyberte hath
    leue.

Lyb. Yet Lyberte hath ben lockyd vp and kept
    in the mew.

Fel. In dede, syr, that lyberte was not worthe
    a cue :

Howe be it lyberte may somtyme be to large,

But yf reason be regent and ruler of your barge.

Lyb. To that ye say I can well condyssende :

Shewe forth, I pray you, here in what you intende.

Fel. Of that I intende to make demonstracyon,

It askyth lesure with good aduertysment.   41

Fyrst, I say, we owght to haue in consydera-
    cyon,

That lyberte be lynkyd with the chayne of coun-
    tenaunce,

Lyberte to let from all maner offence ;

For lyberte at large is lothe to be stoppyd,

But with countenaunce your corage must be
    croppyd.

Lyb. Then thus to you—

Fel. Nay, suffer me yet ferther to say,

And peraduenture I shall content your mynde.   50

Lyberte, I wot well, forbere no man there may,

It is so swete in all maner of kynde ;

Howe be it lyberte makyth many a man blynde ;

By lyberte is done many a great excesse ;

Lyberte at large wyll oft wax reklesse :

Perceyue ye this parcell ?

Lyb. Ye, syr, passyng well :

But, and you wolde me permyt
To shewe parte of my wyt,
Somwhat I coulde enferre,   60
Your consayte to debarre,
Vnder supportacyon
Of pacyent tolleracyon
   Fel. God forbyd ye sholde be let
Your reasons forth to fet ;
Wherfore at lyberte
Say what ye wyll to me.
    Lyb. Brefly to touche of my purpose the
      effecte ;
Lyberte is laudable and pryuylegyd from lawe,
Judycyall rygoure shall not me correcte—   70
    Fel. Softe, my frende ; herein your reason is
      but rawe.
    Lyb. Yet suffer me to say the surpluse of my
      sawe ;
What wote ye where vpon I wyll conclude ?
I say, there is no welthe where as lyberte is sub-
      dude ;
I trowe ye can not say nay moche to this ;
To lyue vnder lawe, it is captyuyte ;
Where drede ledyth the daunce, there is no ioy
    nor blysse ;
Or howe can you proue that there is felycyte,
And you haue not your owne fre lyberte
To sporte at your pleasure, to ryn and to ryde ?   80
Where lyberte is absent, set welthe asyde.

Hic intrat MEASURE.

Meas. Cryst you assyste in your altrycacyon!

Fel. Why, haue you harde of our dysputacyon?

Meas. I parceyue well howe eche of you doth
reason.

Lyb. Mayster Measure, you be come in good
season.

Meas. And it is wonder that your wylde in-
solence

Can be content with Measure presence.

Fel. Wolde it please you then—

Lyb. Vs to informe and ken—

Meas. A, ye be wonders men!   90

Your langage is lyke the penne

Of hym that wryteth to fast.

Fel. Syr, yf any worde haue past

Me other fyrst or last,

To you I arecte it, and cast

Therof the reformacyon.

Lyb. And I of the same facyon;

Howe be it, by protestacyon,

Dyspleasure that you none take,

Some reason we must make.   100

Meas. That wyll not I forsake,

So it in measure be:

Come of, therfore, let se;

Shall I begynne or ye?

Fel. Nay, ye shall begynne, by my wyll.

Lyb. It is reason and skyll,

We your pleasure fulfyll.

Meas. Then ye must bothe consent
You to holde content
With myne argument;   110
And I muste you requyre
Me pacyently to here.

Fel. Yes, syr, with ryght good chere.

Lyb. With all my herte intere.

Meas. Oracius to recorde, in his volumys olde,
With euery condycyon measure must be sought:
Welthe without measure wolde bere hymselfe to
    bolde,
Lyberte without measure proue a thynge of
    nought;
I ponder by nomber, by measure all thynge is
    wrought,
As at the fyrst orygynall by godly opynyon,   120
Whych prouyth well that measure shold haue
    domynyon:
Where measure is mayster, plenty dothe none
    offence;
Where measure lackyth, all thynge dysorderyd is;
Where measure is absent, ryot kepeth resydence;
Where measure is ruler, there is nothynge amysse;
Measure is treasure: howe say ye, is it not this?

Fel. Yes, questyonlesse, in myne opynyon,
Measure is worthy to haue domynyon.

Lyb. Vnto that same I am ryght well agrede,
So that lyberte be not lefte behynde.   130

Meas. Ye, lyberte with measure nede neuer
    drede.

Lyb. What, lyberte to measure then wolde ye
    bynde?

Meas. What ellys? for otherwyse it were
    agaynst kynde:

If lyberte sholde lepe and renne where he lyst,

It were no vertue, it were a thynge vnblyst;

It were a myschefe, yf lyberte lacked a reyne,

Where with to rule hym with the wrythyng of a
    rest:

All trebyllys and tenours be rulyd by a meyne;

Lyberte without measure is acountyd for a beste;

There is no surfet where measure rulyth the feste;

There is no excesse where measure hath his
    helthe;

Measure contynwyth prosperyte and welthe.   142

Fel. Vnto your rule I wyll annex my mynde.

Lyb. So wolde I, but I wolde be lothe,

That wonte was to be formyst, now to come be-
    hynde:

It were a shame, to God I make an othe,

Without I myght cut it out of the brode clothe,

As I was wonte euer at my fre wyll.

Meas. But haue ye not herde say, that wyll is
    no skyll?

Take sad dyreccyon, and leue this wantonnesse.   150

Lyb. It is no maystery.

Fel. Tushe, let Measure procede,

And after his mynde herdely your selfe adresse;

For, without measure, pouerte and nede

Wyll crepe vpon vs, and vs to myschefe lede;

For myschefe wyll mayster vs, yf measure vs
    forsake.

Lyb. Well, I am content your wayes to take.

Meas. Surely, I am ioyous that ye be myndyd
    thus.

Magnyfycence to mayntayne, your promosyon
    shalbe.

Fel. So in his harte he may be glad of vs.   160

Lyb. There is no prynce but he hath nede of
    vs thre,

Welthe, with Measure and plesaunt Lyberte.

Meas. Nowe pleasyth you a lytell whyle to
    stande ;

Me semeth Magnyfycence is comynge here at
    hande.

Hic intrat MAGNYFYCENCE.

Magn. To assure you of my noble porte and
    fame,

Who lyst to knowe, Magnyfycence I hyght.

But, Measure my frende, what hyght this mannys
    name ?

Meas. Syr, though ye be a noble prynce of
    myght,

Yet in this man you must set your delyght;

And, syr, this other mannys name is Lyberte.   170

Magn. Welcome, frendys, ye are bothe vnto me :

But nowe let me knowe of your conuersacyon.

Fel. Pleasyth your grace, Felycyte they me
    call.

Lyb. And I am Lyberte, made of in euery
nacyon.

Magn. Conuenyent persons for any prynce
ryall.

Welthe with Lyberte, with me bothe dwell ye
shall,

To the gydynge of my Measure you bothe com-
myttynge :

That Measure be mayster, vs semeth it is syttynge.

Meas. Where as ye haue, syr, to me them as-
sygned,

Suche order, I trust, with them for to take,   180

So that welthe with measure shalbe conbyned,

And lyberte his large with measure shall make.

Fel. Your ordenaunce, syr, I wyll not forsake.

Lyb. And I my selfe hooly to you wyll inclyne.

Magn. Then may I say that ye be seruauntys
myne,

For by measure, I warne you, we thynke to be
gydyd ;

Wherin it is necessary my pleasure you knowe,

Measure and I wyll neuer be deuydyd

For no dyscorde that any man can sawe ;   189

For measure is a meane, nother to hy nor to lawe,

In whose attemperaunce I haue suche delyght,

That measure shall neuer departe from my syght.

Fel. Laudable your consayte is to be acountyd ;

For welthe without measure sodenly wyll slyde.

Lyb. As your grace full nobly hath recountyd,

Measure with noblenesse sholde be alyde.

Magn. Then, Lyberte, se that Measure be your
    gyde,
For I wyll vse you by his aduertysment.
Fel. Then shall you haue with you prosperyte
    resydent.
Meas. I trowe, good fortune hath annexyd vs
    together,   200
To se howe greable we are of one mynde ;
There is no flaterer, nor losyll so lyther,
This lynkyd chayne of loue that can vnbynde.
Nowe that ye haue me chefe ruler assyngned,
I wyll endeuour me to order euery thynge
Your noblenesse and honour consernynge.
    Lyb. In ioy and myrthe your mynde shalbe in-
        largyd,
And not embracyd with pusyllanymyte ;
But plenarly all thought from you must be dys-
    chargyd,
If ye lyst to lyue after your fre lyberte :   210
All delectacyons aquayntyd is with me,
By me all persons worke what they lyste.
    Meas. Hem, syr, yet beware of Had I wyste !
Lyberte in some cause becomyth a gentyll mynde,
Bycause course of measure, yf I be in the way :
Who countyth without me, is caste to fer behynde
Of his rekenynge, as euydently we may
Se at our eye the worlde day by day ;
For defaute of measure all thynge dothe excede.
    Fel. All that ye say is as trewe as the Crede ;   220
For howe be it lyberte to welthe is conuenyent,

And from felycyte may not be forborne,
Yet measure hath ben so longe from vs absent,
That all men laugh at lyberte to scorne;
Welth and wyt, I say, be so threde bare worne,
That all is without measure, and fer beyonde the
   mone.
Magn. Then noblenesse, I se well, is almoste
   vndone,
But yf therof the soner amendys be made;
For dowtlesse I parceyue my magnyfycence
Without measure lyghtly may fade,   230
Of to moche lyberte vnder the offence:
Wherfore, Measure, take Lyberte with you hence,
And rule hym after the rule of your scole.
   Lyb. What, syr, wolde ye make me a poppynge
      fole?
   Meas. Why, were not your selfe agreed to the
      same,
And now wolde ye swarue from your owne ordyn-
   aunce?
   Lyb. I wolde be rulyd, and I myght for shame.
   Fel. A, ye make me laughe at your inconstaunce.
   Magn. Syr, without any longer delyaunce,
Take Lyberte to rule, and folowe myne entent. 240
   Meas. It shalbe done at your commaundement.

Itaque MEASURE *exeat locum cum* LIBERTATE, *et
   maneat* MAGNYFYCENCE *cum* FELICITATE.

   Magn. It is a wanton thynge this Lyberte;
Perceyue you not howe lothe he was to abyde

The rule of Measure, notwithstandynge we
Haue deputyd Measure hym to gyde?
By measure eche thynge duly is tryde:
Thynke you not thus, my frende Felycyte?

Fel. God forbede that it other wyse sholde be!

Magn. Ye coulde not ellys, I wote, with me
endure.

Fel. Endure? no, God wote, it were great
payne;   250
But yf I were orderyd by iust measure,
It were not possyble me longe to retayne.

Hic intrat FANSY.

Fan. Tusche, holde your pece, your langage is
vayne.
Please it your grace to take no dysdayne,
To shewe you playnly the trouth as I thynke.

Magn. Here is none forsyth whether you flete
or synke.

Fel. From whens come you, syr, that no man
lokyd after?

Magn. Or who made you so bolde to interrupe
my tale?

Fan. Nowe, *benedicite*, ye wene I were some
hafter,
Or ellys some iangelynge Jacke.of the vale;   260
Ye wene that I am dronken, bycause I loke
pale.

Magn. Me semeth that ye haue dronken more
than ye haue bled.

Fan. Yet amonge noble men I was brought vp
and bred.

Fel. Nowe leue this iangelynge, and to vs ex-
pounde

Why that ye sayd our langage was in vayne.

Fan. Mary, vpon trouth my reason I grounde,
That without largesse noblenesse can not rayne ;
And that I sayd ones, yet I say agayne,
I say without largesse wòrshyp hath no place, 269
For largesse is a purchaser of pardon and of grace.

Magn. Nowe, I beseche thé, tell me what is
thy name?

Fan. Largesse, that all lordes sholde loue, syr,
I hyght.

Fel. But hyght you, Largesse, encreace of
noble fame?

Fan. Ye, syr, vndoubted.

Fel. Then, of very ryght,
With Magnyfycence, this noble prynce of myght,
Sholde be your dwellynge, in my consyderacyon.

Magn. Yet we wyll therin take good delybera-
cyon.

Fan. As in that, I wyll not be agaynst your
pleasure.

Fel. Syr, hardely remembre what may your
name auaunce. 280

Magn. Largesse is laudable, so it be in measure.

Fan. Largesse is he that all prynces doth
auaunce ;
I reporte me herein to Kynge Lewes of Fraunce.

Fel. Why haue ye hym named, and all other
      refused?

Fan. For, syth he dyed, largesse was lytell
      vsed.

Plucke vp your mynde, syr; what ayle you to
      muse?

Haue ye not welthe here at your wyll?

It is but a maddynge, these wayes that ye vse:

What auayleth lordshyp, yourselfe for to kyll

With care and with thought howe Jacke shall
      haue Gyl?   290

Magn. What? I haue aspyed ye are a carles
      page.

Fan. By God, syr, ye se but fewe wyse men
      of myne age;

But couetyse hath blowen you so full of wynde,

That *colica passio* hath gropyd you by the guttys.

Fel. In fayth, broder Largesse, you haue a
      mery mynde.

Fan. In fayth, I set not by the worlde two
      Dauncaster cuttys.

Magn. Ye wante but a wylde flyeng bolte to
      shote at the buttes:

Though Largesse ye hyght, your langage is to
      large;

For whiche ende goth forwarde ye take lytell
      charge.

Fel. Let se, this checke yf ye voyde canne.   300

Fan. In faythe, els had I gone to longe to scole,

But yf I coulde knowe a gose from a swanne.

Magn. Wel, wyse men may ete the fysshe,
 when ye shal draw the pole.

Fan. In fayth, I wyll not say that ye shall
 proue a fole,

But ofte tymes haue I sene wyse men do mad
 dedys.

Magn. Go, shake the dogge,¹ hay, syth ye wyll
 nedys !

You are nothynge mete with vs for to dwell,

That with your lorde and mayster so pertly can
 prate :

Gete you hens, I say, by my counsell ;   309

I wyll not vse you to play with me checke mate.

Fan. Syr, yf I haue offended your noble estate,

I trow I haue brought you suche wrytynge of
 recorde,

That I shall haue you agayne my good lorde :

To you recommendeth Sad Cyrcumspeccyon,

And sendeth you this wrytynge closed vnder sele.

Magn. This wrytynge is welcome with harty
 affeccyon :

Why kepte you it thus longe ? howe dothe he ?
 wele ?

Fan. Syr, thanked be God, he hath his hele.

Magn. Welthe, gete you home, and commaunde
 me to Mesure ;   313

Byd hym take good hede to you, my synguler
 tresure.

---

¹ *the dogge*] Qy. " thé, dogge ? " but see notes.

Fel. Is there ony thynge elles your grace wyll
    commaunde me ?

Magn. Nothynge but fare you well tyll sone ;
And that he take good kepe to Lyberte.

Fel. Your pleasure, syr, shortely shall be done.

Magn. I shall come to you myselfe, I trowe,
    this afternone.[1]

I pray you, Larges, here to remayne,
Whylest I knowe what this letter dothe contayne.

*Hic faciat tanquam legeret litteras tacite. Interim
    superveniat cantando* COUNTERFET COUNTE-
    NAUNCE *suspenso gradu, qui, viso* MAGNYFY-
    CENCE, *sensim retrocedat ; at tempus post pusil-
    lum rursum accedat* COUNTERFET COUNTE-
    NAUNCE *prospectando et vocitando a longe ; et*
    FANSY *animat* [2] *silentium cum manu.*

C. Count. What, Fansy, Fansy !

Magn. Who is that that thus dyd cry ?
Me thought he called Fansy.   330

Fan. It was a Flemynge hyght Hansy.

Magn. Me thought he called Fansy me behynde.

Fan. Nay, syr, it was nothynge but your mynde :
But nowe, syr, as touchynge this letter—

Magn. I shall loke in it at leasure better :
And surely ye are to hym beholde ;
And for his sake ryght gladly I wolde
Do what I coude to do you good.

---

1 *after none*] Here Felycyte goes out.
2 *animat*] Qy. " animet ? "

Fan. I pray, God kepe you in that mood!

Magn. This letter was wryten ferre hence. 340

Fan. By lakyn, syr, it hathe cost me pence
And grotes many one, or I came to your presence.

Magn. Where was it delyuered you, shewe vnto
me.

Fan. By God, syr, beyonde the se.

Magn. At what place nowe, as you gesse?

Fan. By my trouthe, syr, at Pountesse;
This wrytynge was taken me there,
But neuer was I in gretter fere.

Magn. Howe so?

Fan. By God, at the see syde, 350
Had I not opened my purse wyde,
I trowe, by our lady, I had ben slayne,
Or elles I had lost myne eres twayne.

Magn.[1] By your soth?

Fan. Ye, and there is suche a wache,
That no man can scape but they hym cache.
They bare me in hande that I was a spye;
And another bade put out myne eye,
Another wolde myne eye were blerde,
Another bade shaue halfe my berde; 360
And boyes to the pylery gan me plucke,
And wolde haue made me Freer Tucke,
To preche out of the pylery hole,
Without an antetyme or a stole;

---

[1] *By your soth*] Ed. prefixes "*Fansy*" to these words, and
omits the prefix to the next speech.

And some bade sere hym with a marke:
To gete me fro them I had moche warke.

Magn. Mary, syr, ye were afrayde.

Fan. By my trouthe, had I not payde and
    prayde,
And made largesse as I hyght,
I had not ben here with you this nyght;   370
But surely largesse saued my lyfe,
For largesse stynteth all maner of stryfe.

Magn. It dothe so sure nowe and than,
But largesse is not mete for euery man.

Fan. No, but for you grete estates:
Largesse stynteth grete debates;
And he that I came fro to this place
Sayd I was mete for your grace;
And in dede, syr, I here men talke,
By the way as I ryde and walke,   380
Say howe you excede in noblenesse,
If you had with you largesse.

Magn. And say they so in very dede?

Fan. With ye, syr, so God me spede.

Magn. Yet mesure is a mery mene.

Fan. Ye, syr, a blannched almonde is no bene.
Measure is mete for a marchauntes hall,
But largesse becometh a state ryall.
What, sholde you pynche at a pecke of otes,
Ye wolde sone pynche at a pecke of grotes.   390
Thus is the talkynge of one and of oder,
As men dare speke it hugger mugger;
A lorde a negarde, it is a shame,
But largesse may amende your name.

Magn. In faythe, Largesse, welcome to me.
Fan. I pray you, syr, I may so be,
And of my seruyce you shall not mysse.
Magn. Togyder we wyll talke more of this :
Let vs departe from hens home to my place.
Fan. I folow euen after your noble grace. 400

Hic discedat MAGNIFICENS *cum* FANSY, *et intrat*[1]
COUNTERFET COUNTENAUNCE.

C. Count. What, I say, herke a worde.
Fan. Do away, I say, the deuylles torde!
C. Count. Ye, but how longe shall I here
   awayte ?
Fan. By Goddys body, I come streyte :
I hate this blurderyng that thou doste make.
C. Count. Nowe to the deuyll I thé betake,
For in fayth ye be well met.
Fansy hath cachyd in a flye net
This noble man Magnyfycence,
Of Largesse vnder the pretence. 410
They haue made me here to put the stone :
But nowe wyll I, that they be gone,
In bastarde ryme, after the dogrell gyse,
Tell you where of my name dothe ryse.
For Counterfet Countenaunce knowen am I ;
This worlde is full of my foly.

---

[1] *intrat*] Qy. " intret ? "—This stage-direction is not quite
correct, for *Count. Count.* enters as *Fansy* is going off, and
detains him till v. 406.

I set not by hym a fly,
That can not counterfet a lye,
Swere, and stare, and byde therby,
And countenaunce it clenly,   420
And defende it manerly.
A knaue wyll counterfet nowe a knyght,
A lurdayne lyke a lorde to fyght,[1]
A mynstrell lyke a man of myght,
A tappyster lyke a lady bryght:
Thus make I them wyth thryft to fyght,
Thus at the laste I brynge hym [2] ryght
To Tyburne, where they hange on hyght.
To counterfet I can by praty wayes:
Of nyghtys to occupy counterfet kayes,   430
Clenly to counterfet newe arayes,
Counterfet eyrnest by way of playes:
Thus am I occupyed at all assayes;
What so euer I do, all men me prayse,
And mekyll am I made of nowe adays:
Counterfet maters in the lawe of the lande,
Wyth golde and grotes they grese my hande,
In stede of ryght that wronge may stande,
And counterfet fredome that is bounde;
I counterfet [3] suger that is but founde;   440
Counterfet capytaynes by me are mande;
Of all lewdnesse I kyndell the brande;

---

[1] *to fyght*] Qy. " *to* flyght "—scold (a word used elsewhere
by Skelton), or " *to* syght? " see next line but two.
[2] *hym*] Compare v. 1275.
[3] *I counterfet, &c.*] This line seems to be corrupt.

Counterfet kyndnesse, and thynke dyscayte;
Counterfet letters by the way of sleyght;
Subtelly vsynge counterfet weyght;
Counterfet langage, fayty bone geyte.
Counterfetynge is a proper bayte;
A counte to counterfet in a resayte;
To counterfet well is a good consayte.
Counterfet maydenhode may well be borne,   45c
But counterfet coynes is laughynge to scorne;
It is euyll patchynge of that is torne;
Whan the noppe is rughe, it wolde be shorne;
Counterfet haltynge without a thorne;
Yet counterfet chafer is but euyll corne;
All thynge is worse whan it is worne.
What, wolde ye, wyues, counterfet
The courtly gyse of the newe iet?
An olde barne wolde be vnderset:
It is moche worthe that is ferre fet.   460
What, wanton, wanton, nowe well ymet!
What, Margery Mylke Ducke, mermoset!
It wolde be masked in my net;
It wolde be nyce, thoughe I say nay;
By Crede, it wolde haue fresshe aray,
And therfore shall my husbande pay;
To counterfet she wyll assay
All the newe gyse, fresshe and gaye,
And be as praty as she may,
And iet it ioly as a iay: 470
Counterfet prechynge, and byleue the contrary;
Counterfet conscyence, peuysshe pope holy;

Counterfet sadnesse, with delynge full madly;
Counterfet holynes is called ypocrysy;
Counterfet reason is not worth a flye;
Counterfet wysdome, and workes of foly;
Counterfet countenaunce euery man dothe occupy
Counterfet worshyp outwarde men may se;
Ryches rydeth out, at home is pouerte;
Counterfet pleasure is borne out by me: 480
Coll wolde go clenly, and it wyll not be,
And Annot wolde be nyce, and laughes, tehe
        wehe;
Your counterfet countenaunce is all of nysyte,
A plummed partrydge all redy to flye:
A knokylbonyarde wyll counterfet a clarke,
He wolde trotte gentylly, but he is to starke,
At his cloked counterfetynge dogges dothe
        barke;
A carter a courtyer, it is a worthy warke,
That with his whyp his mares was wonte to
        yarke;
A custrell to dryue the deuyll out of the derke, 490
A counterfet courtyer with a knaues marke.
To counterfet this freers haue lerned me;
This nonnes nowe and then, and it myght be,
Wolde take in the way of counterfet charyte
The grace of God vnder *benedicite;*
To counterfet thyr counsell they gyue me a fee;
Chanons can not counterfet but vpon thre,
Monkys may not for drede that men sholde
        them se.

Hic ingrediatur FANSY *properanter cum* CRAFTY
    CONUEYAUNCE, *cum famine multo adinvicem*
    garrulantes: tandem, viso COUNTERFET COUN-
    TENAUNCE, *dicat* CRAFTY CONUEYAUNCE.

Cr. Con. What, Counterfet Countenaunce!

C. Count. What, Crafty Conueyaunce!   500

Fan. What, the deuyll, are ye two of aquaynt-
    aunce?

God gyue you a very myschaunce!

Cr. Con. Yes, yes, syr, he and I haue met.

C. Count. We haue bene togyder bothe erly
    and late: [longe?

But, Fansy my frende, where haue ye bene so

Fan. By God, I haue bene about a praty
    pronge;

Crafty Conueyaunce, I sholde say, and I.

Cr. Con. By God, we haue made Magnyfycence
    to ete a flye.

C. Count. Howe coulde ye do that, and [I]
    was away?

Fan. By God, man, bothe his pagent and thyne
    he can play.

C. Count. Say trouth?   511

Cr. Con. Yes, yes, by lakyn, I shall thé warent,

As longe as I lyue, thou haste an heyre parent.

Fan. Yet haue we pyckyd out a rome for thé.

C. Count. Why, shall we dwell togyder all
    thre?

Cr. Con. Why, man, it were to great a wonder,

That we thre galauntes sholde be longe asonder.

C. Count. For Cockys harte, gyue me thy hande.

Fan. By the masse, for ye are able to dystroy
    an hole lande.

Cr. Con. By God, yet it muste begynne moche
    of thé.   520

Fan. Who that is ruled by vs, it shalbe longe
    or he thee.

C. Count. But, I say, kepest thou the olde name
    styll that thou had?

Cr. Con. Why, wenyst thou, horson, that I
    were so mad?

Fan. Nay, nay, he hath chaunged his, and I
    haue chaunged myne.

C. Count. Nowe, what is his name, and what
    is thyne?

Fan. In faythe, Largesse I hyght,
And I am made a knyght.

C. Count. A rebellyon agaynst nature,
So large a man, and so lytell of stature!
But, syr, howe counterfetyd ye?   530

Cr. Con. Sure Surueyaunce [1] I named me.

C. Count. Surueyaunce! where ye suruey,
Thryfte hathe lost her cofer kay.

Fan. But is it not well? howe thynkest thou?

C. Count. Yes, syr, I gyue God auowe,
Myselfe coude not counterfet it better.
But what became of the letter,
That I counterfeyted you vnderneath a shrowde?

---

[1] *Sure Surueyaunce, &c.*] Ed. gives this line to *C. Count.*,
and the next speech to *Cr. Con.* Compare v. 652.

Fan. By the masse, odly well alowde.

Cr. Con. By God, had not I it conuayed, 540
Yet Fansy had ben dysceyued.[1]

C. Count. I wote, thou arte false ynoughe for
one.

Fan. By my trouthe, we had ben gone :
And yet, in fayth, man, we lacked thé
For to speke with Lyberte.

C. Count. What is Largesse without Lyberte?

Cr. Con. By Mesure mastered yet is he.

C. Count. What, is your conueyaunce no better?

Fan. In faythe, Mesure is lyke a tetter,
That ouergroweth a mannes face, 550
So he ruleth ouer all our place.

Cr. Con. Nowe therfore, whylest we are to-
gyder,—
Counterfet Countenaunce, nay, come hyder,—
I say, whylest we are togyder in same—

C. Count. Tushe, a strawe, it is a shame
That we can no better than so.

Fan. We wyll remedy it, man, or we go;
For, lyke as mustarde is sharpe of taste,[2]
Ryght so a sharpe fansy must be founde
Wherwith Mesure to confounde. 560

Cr. Con. Can you a remedy for a tysyke,
That sheweth yourselfe thus spedde in physyke?

C. Count. It is a gentyll reason of a rake.

---

1 Qy. Dyscryued?
2 *taste*] Qy. a line wanting to rhyme with this?

Fan. For all these iapes yet that ye make—
Cr. Con. Your fansy maketh myne elbowe to
    ake.
Fan. Let se, fynde you a better way.
C. Count. Take no dyspleasure of that we say.
Cr. Con. Nay, and you be angry aud ouer-
    wharte,
A man may beshrowe your angry harte.
   Fan. Tushe, a strawe, I thought none yll.   570
   C. Count. What, shall we iangle thus all the
    day styll ?
Cr. Con. Nay, let vs our heddes togyder cast.
Fan. Ye, and se howe it may be compast,
That Mesure were cast out of the dores.
   C. Count. Alasse, where is my botes and my
    spores ?
Cr. Con. In all this hast whether wyll ye ryde ?
C. Count. I trowe, it shall not nede to abyde.
Cockes woundes, se, syrs, se, se !

Hic ingrediatur CLOKED COLUSYON *cum elato*
   aspectu, deorsum et sursum ambulando.

   Fan. Cockes armes, what is he ?
   Cr. Con. By Cockes harte, he loketh hye ;   580
He hawketh, me thynke, for a butterflye.
   C. Count. Nowe, by Cockes harte, well abyden,
For, had you not come, I had ryden.
   Cl. Col. Thy wordes be but wynde, neuer they
    haue no wayght ;
Thou hast made me play the iurde hayte.

C. Count. And yf ye knewe howe I haue
    mused,
I am sure ye wolde haue me excused.
    Cl. Col. I say, come hyder : what are these
      twayne?
    C. Count. By God, syr, this is Fansy small
      brayne ;
And Crafty Conuayaunce, knowe you not hym? 590
    Cl. Col. Know hym, syr! quod he ; yes, by
      Saynt Sym.
Here is a leysshe of ratches to renne an hare :
Woo is that purse that ye shall share!
    Fan. What call ye him, this?
    Cr. Con. I trowe, that he is.
    C. Count. Tushe, holde your pece.
Se you not how they prece
For to knowe your name?
    Cl. Col. Knowe they not me, they are to blame.
Knowe you not me, syrs?   600
    Fan. No, in dede.
    Cr. Con. Abyde, lette me se, take better hede ;
Cockes harte, it is Cloked Colusyon.
    Cl. Col. A, syr, I pray God gyue you con-
      fusyon!
    Fan. Cockes armes, is that your name?
    C. Count. Ye, by the masse, this is euen the
      same,
That all this matter must vnder grope.
    Cr. Con. What is this he wereth, a cope?
    Cl. Col. Cappe, syr ; I say you be to bolde.

Fan. Se, howe he is wrapped for the colde : 610
Is it not a vestment ?

    Cl. Col. A, ye wante a rope.

    C. Count. Tushe, it is Syr Johnn Double cloke.

    Fan. Syr, and yf ye wolde not be wrothe—

    Cl. Col. What sayst ?

    Fan. Here was to lytell clothe.

    Cl. Col. A, Fansy, Fansy, God sende thé
        brayne !

    Fan. Ye, for your wyt is cloked for the rayne.

    Cr. Con. Nay, lette vs not clatter thus styll.

    Cl. Col. Tell me, syrs, what is your wyll.   620

    C. Count. Syr, it is so that these twayne
With Magnyfycence in housholde do remayne ;
And there they wolde haue me to dwell,
But I wyll be ruled after your counsell.

    Fan. Mary, so wyll we also.

    Cl. Col. But tell me where aboute ye go.

    C. Count. By God, we wolde gete vs all thyder,
Spell the remenaunt, and do togyder.

    Cl. Col. Hath Magnyfycence ony tresure ?

    Cr. Con. Ye, but he spendeth it all in mesure. 630

    Cl. Col. Why, dwelleth Mesure where ye two
        dwell ?
In faythe, he were better to dwell in hell.

    Fan. Yet where we wonne, nowe there wonneth
        he.

    Cl. Col. And haue you not amonge you Ly-
        berte ?

    C. Count. Ye, but he is a captyuyte.

Cl. Col. What, the deuyll, howe may that be?

C. Count. I can not tell you: why aske you me?
Aske these two that there dothe dwell.

Cl. Col. Syr, the playnesse you tell me.[1]

Cr. Con. There dwelleth a mayster men calleth
Mesure—   640

Fan. Ye, and he hath rule of all his tresure.

Cr. Con. Nay, eyther let me tell, or elles tell ye.

Fan. I care not I, tell on for me.

C. Count. I pray God let you neuer to thee!

Cl. Col. What the deuyll ayleth you? can you
not agree?

Cr. Con. I wyll passe ouer the cyrcumstaunce,
And shortly shewe you the hole substaunce.
Fansy and I, we twayne,
With Magnyfycence in housholde do remayne,
And counterfeted our names we haue   650
Craftely all thynges vpryght to saue,
His name Largesse, Surueyaunce myne:
Magnyfycence to vs begynneth to enclyne
Counterfet Countenaunce to haue also,
And wolde that we sholde for hym go.

C. Count. But shall I haue myne olde name
styll?

Cr. Con. Pease, I haue not yet sayd what I
wyll.

---

[1] *Syr, the playnesse you tell me*] Ed. prefixes *Crafty Con.* to
these words, and omits the prefix to the next line.—Qy., for
the rhyme,—" you me tell? "

Fan. Here is a pystell of a postyke!

Cl. Col. Tusshe, fonnysshe Fansy, thou arte
    frantyke.

Tell on, syr, howe then?   660

Cr. Con. Mary, syr, he tolde vs, when

We had hym founde, we sholde hym brynge,

And that we fayled not for nothynge.

Cl. Col. All this ye may easely brynge aboute.

Fan. Mary, the better and Mesure were out.

Cl. Col. Why, can ye not put out that foule
    freke?

Cr. Con. No, in euery corner he wyll peke,

So that we haue no lyberte,

Nor no man in courte but he,

For Lyberte he hath in gydyng.   670

    C. Count. In fayth, and without Lyberte there
    is no bydyng.

    Fan. In fayth, and Lybertyes rome is there
    but small.

    Cl. Col. Hem! that lyke I nothynge at all.

    Cr. Con. But, Counterfet[1] Countenaunce, go
    we togyder,

All thre, I say.

    C. Count. Shall I go? whyder?

    Cr. Con.[2] To Magnyfycence with vs twayne,

And in his seruyce thé to retayne.

    C. Count. But then, syr, what shall I hyght?

---

[1] *But, Counterfet, &c.*] Ed. omits the prefix to this speech.

[2] *Cr. Con.*] Ed. " *Cl. Col.*"

Cr. Con. Ye and I talkyd therof to nyght.　680
Fan. Ye, my fansy, was out of owle flyght,
For it is out of my mynde quyght.
　Cr. Con. And nowe it cometh to my remem-
　　braunce:
Syr, ye shall hyght Good Demeynaunce.
　C. Count. By the armes of Calys, well con-
　　ceyued!
　Cr. Con. When we haue hym thyder con-
　　uayed,
What and I frame suche a slyght,
That Fansy with his fonde consayte
Put Magnyfycence in suche a madnesse,
That he shall haue you in the stede of sadnesse,　690
And Sober Sadnesse shalbe your name?
　Cl. Col. By Cockys body, here begynneth the
　　game!
For then shall we so craftely cary,
That Mesure shall not there longe tary.
　Fan. For Cockys harte, tary whylyst that I
　　come agayne.
　Cr. Con. We wyll se you shortly one of vs
　　twayne.
　C. Count. Now let vs go, and we shall, then.
　Cl. Col. Nowe let se quyte you lyke praty
　　men.[1]

　[1] *praty men*] Here *Fansy, Crafty Conueyaunce,* and *Counter
fet Countenaunce,* go out.

Hic deambulat.

To passe the tyme and order whyle a man may
    talke
Of one thynge and other to occupy the place; 700
Then for the season that I here shall walke,
As good to be occupyed as vp and downe to trace
And do nothynge; how be it full lytell grace
There cometh and groweth of my comynge,
For Clokyd Colusyon is a perylous thynge.
Double delynge and I be all one;
Craftynge and haftynge contryued is by me;
I can dyssemble, I can bothe laughe and grone;
Playne delynge and I can neuer agre; 709
But dyuysyon, dyssencyon, dyrysyon, these thre
And I am counterfet of one mynde and thought,
By the menys of myschyef to bryng all thynges
    to nought.
And though I be so odyous a geste,
And euery man gladly my company wolde
    - refuse,
In faythe yet am I occupyed with the best;
Full fewe that can themselfe of me excuse.
Whan other men laughe, than study I and muse,
Deuysynge the meanes and wayes that I can,
Howe I may hurte and hynder euery man:
Two faces in a hode couertly I bere, 720
Water in the one hande, and fyre in the other;
I can fede forth a fole, and lede hym by the eyre;
Falshode in felowshyp is my sworne brother.
By cloked colusyon, I say, and none other,

Comberaunce and trouble in Englande fyrst I
 began ;
From that lorde to that lorde I rode and I ran,
And flatered them with fables fayre before theyr
 face,
And tolde all the myschyef I coude behynde theyr
 backe,
And made as I had knowen nothynge of the case ;
I wolde begyn all myschyef, but I wolde bere no
 lacke :   730
Thus can I lerne you, syrs, to bere the deuyls
 sacke ;
And yet, I trowe, some of you be better sped
 than I
Frendshyp to fayne, and thynke full lytherly.
Paynte to a purpose good countenaunce I can,
And craftely can I grope howe euery man is
 mynded ;
My purpose is to spy and to poynte euery man ;
My tonge is with fauell forked and tyned :
By Cloked Colusyon thus many one is begyled.
Eche man to hynder I gape and I gaspe ;
My speche is all pleasure, but I stynge lyke a
 waspe :   740
I am neuer glad but whan I may do yll,
And neuer am I sory but whan that I se
I can not myne apyetyte accomplysshe and
 fulfyll
In hynderaunce of welthe and prosperyte ;
I laughe at all shrewdenes, and lye at lyberte.

I muster, I medle; amonge these grete estates
I sowe sedycyous sedes of dyscorde and de-
      bates:
To flater and to flery is all my pretence
Amonge all suche persones as I well vnder-
      stonde
Be lyght of byleue and hasty of credence;   750
I make them to startyll and sparkyll lyke a
      bronde,
I moue them, I mase them, I make them so
      fonde,
That they wyll here no man but the fyrst tale:
And so by these meanes I brewe moche bale.

Hic ingrediatur COURTLY ABUSYON *cantando.*
      Court. Ab. Huffa, huffa, taunderum, taunderum,
            tayné, huffa, huffa!
      Cl. Col. This was properly prated, syrs! what
            sayd a?
      Court. Ab. Rutty bully, ioly rutterkyn, heyda!
      Cl. Col. De que pays este vous?
            Et faciat tanquam exiat beretrum cronice. [1]
      Court. Ab. Decke your hofte and couer a
            lowce.
      Cl. Col. Say vous chaunter Venter tre dawce?
      Court. Ab. Wyda, wyda.   761
Howe sayst thou, man? am not I a ioly rutter?

---

[1] *exiat beretrum cronice*] Qy. " *exuat* (or rather, *exueret*)
barretum (*i. e.* pileum) *ironice?*

Cl. Col. Gyue this gentylman rome, syrs,
  stonde vtter!
By God, syr, what nede all this waste?
What is this, a betell, or a batowe,[1] or a buskyn
  lacyd?
Court. Ab. What, wenyst thou that I knowe
  thé not, Clokyd Colusyon?
Cl. Col. And wenyst thou that I knowe not
  thé, cankard Abusyon?
Court. Ab. Cankard Jacke Hare, loke thou be
  not rusty;
For thou shalt well knowe I am nother durty nor
  dusty.
Cl. Col. Dusty! nay, syr, ye be all of the lusty,
Howe be it of scape thryfte your clokes smelleth
  musty: 771
But whether art thou walkynge in faythe vn-
  faynyd?
Court. Ab. Mary, with Magnyfycence I wolde
  be retaynyd.
Cl. Col. By the masse, for the cowrte thou art
  a mete man:
Thy slyppers they swap it, yet thou fotys it lyke
  . a swanne.
Court. Ab. Ye, so I can deuyse my gere after
  the cowrtly maner.
Cl. Col. So thou arte personable to bere a
  prynces baner.

---

1 *batowe*] Qy. "batone?" [or "botowe," boot?]

By Goddes fote,[1] and I dare well fyght, for I
 wyll not start.
Court. Ab. Nay, thou art a man good inough
 but for thy false hart.
Cl. Col. Well, and I be a coward, ther is mo
 than I.   780
Court. Ab. Ye, in faythe, a bolde man and a
 hardy.
Cl. Col. A bolde man in a bole of newe ale in
 cornys.
Court. Ab. Wyll ye se this gentylman is all in
 his skornys?
Cl. Col. But are ye not auysed to dwell where
 ye spake?
Court. Ab. I am of fewe wordys, I loue not to
 barke.[2]
Beryst thou any rome, or cannyst thou do ought?
Cannyst thou helpe in fauer that I myght be
 brought?
Cl. Col. I may do somwhat, and more I thynke
 shall.

1 *By Goddes fote, &c.*] Here the prefixes to the speeches are
surely wrong: but as I am doubtful how they ought to be
assigned, I have not ventured to alter them. Qy.
 " *Court. Ab.* By Goddes fote, and I dare well fyght, for I
wyll not start.
 Cl. Col. Nay, thou art a man good inough but for thy false
hart.
 Court. Ab. Well, and I be a coward, ther is mo than I.
 Cl. Col. Ye, in faythe, a bolde man and a hardy;
A bolde man in a bole of newe ale in cornys.
 Court. Ab. Wyll ye se," &c

2 *barke*˥ Qy. " crake?" C.

Here cometh in CRAFTY CONUEYAUNCE, *poynt-*
yng with his fynger, and sayth, Hem,
Colusyon!

Court. Ab. Cockys harte, who is yonde that for
thé dothe call?

Cr. Con.[1] Nay, come at ones, for the armys of
the dyce!   790

Court. Ab. Cockys armys, he hath callyd for
thé twyce.

Cl. Col. By Cockys harte, and call shall agayne:
To come to me, I trowe, he shalbe fayne.

Court. Ab. What, is thy harte pryckyd with
such a prowde pynne?

Cl. Col. Tushe, he that hath nede, man, let
hym rynne.

Cr. Con. Nay, come away, man : thou playst
the cayser.

Cl. Col.[2] By the masse, thou shalt byde my
leyser.

Cr. Con. Abyde, syr, quod he! mary, so I
do.

Court. Ab. He wyll come, man, when he may
tende to.

Cr. Con. What the deuyll, who sent for thé? 800

Cl. Col. Here he is nowe, man; mayst thou
not sè?

---

[1] *Cr. Con.*] Ed. " *Cl. Col.*" Compare the next line, and
v. 796.

[2] *Cl. Col.*] Ed. " *Court. Ab.*"

Cr. Con. What the deuyll, man, what thou
    menyst?

Art thou so angry as thou semyst?

    Court. Ab. What the deuyll, can ye agre no
      better?

    Cr. Con. What the deuyll, where had we this
      ioly ietter?

    Cl. Col. What sayst thou, man? why dost thou
      not supplye,

And desyre me thy good mayster to be?

    Court. Ab. Spekest thou to me?

    Cl. Col. Ye, so I tell thé.

    Court. Ab. Cockes bones, I ne tell can   810

Whiche of you is the better man,

Or whiche of you can do most.

    Cr. Con. In fayth, I rule moche of the rost.

    Cl. Col. Rule the roste! ye, thou woldest[1]

As skante thou had no nede of me.

    Cr. Con. Nede! yes, mary, I say not nay.

    Court. Ab. Cockes ha[r]te, I trowe thou wylte
      make a fray.

    Cr. Con. Nay, in good faythe, it is but the gyse.

    Cl. Col. No, for, or we stryke, we wyll be ad-
      uysed twyse.

    Court. Ab. What the deuyll, vse ye not to
      drawe no swordes?   820

    Cr. Con. No, by my trouthe, but crake grete
      wordes.

---

[1] *ye, thou woldest*] Qy., for the rhyme, " thou woldest, ye?"

Court. Ab. Why, is this the gyse nowe adayes?

Cl. Col. Ye, for surety, ofte peas is taken for frayes.

But, syr, I wyll haue this man with me.

Cr. Con. Conuey yourselfe fyrst, let se.

Cl. Col. Well, tarry here tyll I for you sende.

Cr. Con. Why, shall he be of your bende?

Cl. Col. Tary here: wote ye what I say?

Court. Ab. I waraunt you, I wyll not go away.

Cr. Con. By Saynt Mary, he is a tawle man. 830

Cl. Col. Ye, and do ryght good seruyce he can ;
I knowe in hym no defaute
But that the horson is prowde and hawte.

>   *And so they*[1] *go out of the place.*

Court. Ab. Nay, purchace ye a pardon for the pose,
For pryde hath plucked thé by the nose,
As well as me : I wolde, and I durste,
But nowe I wyll not say the worste.

COURTLY ABUSYON *alone in the place.*

> What nowe, let se,
> Who loketh on me
> Well rounde aboute,   840
> Howe gay and howe stoute
> That I can were
> Courtly my gere :

---

[1] *they*] i. e. *Cloked Colusyon* and *Crafty Conueyaunce.*

My heyre bussheth
So plesauntly,
My robe russheth
So ruttyngly,
Me seme I flye,
I am so lyght,
To daunce delyght ;   850
Properly drest,
All poynte deuyse,
My persone prest
Beyonde all syse
Of the newe gyse,
To russhe it oute
In euery route :
Beyonde measure °
My sleue is wyde,
Al of pleasure,   860
My hose strayte tyde,
My buskyn wyde,
Ryche to beholde,
Gletterynge yn golde.
Abusyon
Forsothe I hyght :
Confusyon
Shall on hym lyght,
By day or by nyght
That vseth me ;   870
He can not thee.
A very fon,
A very asse,

Wyll take vpon
To compasse
That neuer was
Abusyd before;
A very pore
That so wyll do,
He doth abuse   880
Hym selfe to to,
He dothe mysse vse
Eche man take a fe [1]
To crake and prate;
I befoule his pate.
This newe fonne iet
From out of Fraunce
Fyrst I dyd set;
Made purueaunce
And suche ordenaunce,   890
That all men it founde
Through out Englonde:
All this nacyon
I set on fyre
In my facyon,
This theyr desyre,
This newe atyre;
This ladyes haue,
I it them gaue;
Spare for no coste;   900
And yet in dede

[1] *Eche man take a fe*] There seems to be some corruption of the text here. [Qy. " each man *to akuse,*? " C.]

It is coste loste
Moche more than nede
For to excede
In suche aray :
Howe be it, I say,
A carlys sonne,
Brought vp of nought,
Wyth me wyll wonne
Whylyst he hath ought ;   910
He wyll haue wrought
His gowne so wyde
That he may hyde
His dame and his syre
Within his slyue ;
Spende all his hyre,
That men hym gyue ;
Wherfore I preue,
A Tyborne checke
Shall breke his necke.   920

Here cometh in FANSY, *craynye,* Stow stow !
All is out of harre,
And out of trace,
Ay warre and warre
In euery place.
But what the deuyll art thou,
That cryest, Stow, stow ?
Fan. What, whom haue we here, Jenkyn
Joly ?
.Nowe welcom, by the God holy.

Court. Ab. What, Fansy, my frende! howe
doste thou fare?

Fan. By Cryst, as mery as a Marche hare. 930

Court. Ab. What the deuyll hast thou on thy
fyste? an owle?

Fan. Nay, it is a farly fowle.

Court. Ab. Me thynke she frowneth and lokys
sowre.

Fan. Torde, man, it is an hawke of the towre;
She is made for the malarde fat.

Court. Ab. Methynke she is well becked to
catche a rat.
But nowe what tydynges can you tell, let se.

Fan. Mary, I am come for thé.

Court. Ab. For me?

Fan. Ye, for thé, so I say. 940

Court. Ab. Howe so? tell me, I thé pray.

Fan. Why, harde thou not of the fray,
That fell amonge vs this same day

Court. Ab. No, mary, not yet.

Fan. What the deuyll, neuer a whyt?

Court. Ab. No, by the masse; what sholde I
swere?

Fan. In faythe, Lyberte is nowe a lusty spere.

Court. Ab. Why, vnder whom was he abydynge?

Fan. Mary, Mesure had hym a whyle in
gydynge,
Tyll, as the deuyll wolde, they fell a chydynge 950
With Crafty Conuayaunce.

Court. Ab. Ye, dyd they so?

Fan. Ye, by Goddes sacrament, and with
    other mo.

Court. Ab. What neded that, in the dyuyls date?

Fan. Yes, yes, he fell with me also at debate.

Court. Ab. With thé also? what, he playeth
    the state?

Fan. Ye, but I bade hym pyke out of the gate,
By Goddes body, so dyd I.

Court. Ab. By the masse, well done and boldely.

Fan. Holde thy pease, Measure shall frome vs
    walke.   960

Court. Ab. Why, is he crossed than with a
    chalke?

Fan. Crossed! ye, checked out of consayte.

Court. Ab. Howe so?

Fan. By God, by a praty slyght,
As here after thou shalte knowe more:
But I must tary here; go thou before.

Court. Ab. With whom shall I there mete?

Fan. Crafty Conueyaunce standeth in the strete,
Euen of purpose for the same.

Court. Ab. Ye, but what shall I call my name?

Fan. Cockes harte, tourne thé, let me se thyne
    aray: 971
Cockes bones, this is all of Johnn de gay.

Court. Ab. So I am poynted after my consayte.

Fan. Mary, thou iettes it of hyght.

Court. Ab. Ye, but of my name let vs be wyse.

Fan. Mary, Lusty Pleasure, by myne aduyse,
To name thyselfe, come of, it were done.

Court. Ab. Farewell, my frende.

Fan. Adue, tyll sone. [1]

Stowe, byrde, stowe, stowe! 980

It is best I fede my hawke now.

There is many euyll faueryd, and thou be foule;

Eche thynge is fayre when it is yonge : all hayle,
    owle!
        Lo, this is
        My fansy, I wys:
        Nowe Cryst it blysse!
        It is, by Jesse,
        A byrde full swete,
        For me full mete :
        She is furred for the hete 990
        All to the fete ;
        Her browys bent,
        Her eyen glent :
        Frome Tyne to Trent,
        From Stroude to Kent,
        A man shall fynde
        Many of her kynde,
        Howe standeth the wynde
        Before or behynde :
        Barbyd lyke a nonne, 1000
        For burnynge of the sonne ;
        Her fethers donne ;
        Well faueryd bonne.
        Nowe, let me se about,

---

[1] *tyll sone*] Here *Courtly Abusyon* goes out.

In all this rowte
Yf I can fynde out
So semely a snowte
Amonge this prese :
Euen a hole mese —
Pease, man, pease!   1010
I rede, we sease.
So farly fayre as it lokys,
And her becke so comely crokys,
Her naylys sharpe as tenter hokys!
I haue not kept her yet thre wokys,
And howe styll she dothe syt!
Teuyt, teuyt, where is my wyt?
The deuyll spede whyt!
That was before, I set behynde ;
Nowe to curteys, forthwith vnkynde ;   1020
Somtyme to sober, somtyme to sadde,
Somtyme to mery, somtyme to madde ;
Somtyme I syt as I were solempe prowde ;
Somtyme I laughe ouer lowde ;
Somtyme I wepe for a gew gaw ;
Somtyme I laughe at waggynge of a straw ;
With a pere my loue you may wynne,
And ye may lese it for a pynne.
I haue a thynge for to say,
And I may tende therto for play ;   1030
But in faythe I am so occupyed
On this halfe and on euery syde,
That I wote not where I may rest.
Fyrst to tell you what were best,

Frantyke Fansy-seruyce I hyght;
My wyttys be weke, my braynys are lyght:
For it is I that other whyle
Plucke downe lede, and theke with tyle;
Nowe I wyll this, and nowe I wyll that;
Make a wyndmyll of a mat;   1040
Nowe I wolde, and I wyst what;
Where is my cappe? I haue lost my hat;
And within an houre after,
Plucke downe an house, and set vp a rafter;
Hyder and thyder, I wote not whyder;
Do and vndo, bothe togyder;
Of a spyndell I wyll make a sparre;
All that I make, forthwith I marre;
I blunder, I blaster, I blowe, and I blother;
I make on the one day, and I marre on the other;
Bysy, bysy, and euer bysy,   1051
I daunce vp and downe tyll I am dyssy;
I can fynde fantasyes where none is;
I wyll not haue it so, I wyll haue it this.

Hic ingrediatur FOLY, *quatiendo crema*[1] *et
faciendo multum, feriendo tabulas
et similia.*

Fol. Maysters, Cryst saue euerychone!
What, Fansy, arte thou here alone?

---

[1] *crema*] If this be the right reading, I am unacquainted
with the word. It can hardly be a misprint for " cremia: "
qy. " crembalum ? " [Or,' crebro ?''C.]

Fan. What, fonnysshe Foly! I befole thy face.

Fol. What, frantyke Fansy in a foles case!
What is this, an owle or a glede?
By my trouthe, she hathe a grete hede.   1060

Fan. Tusshe, thy lyppes hange in thyne eye:
It is a Frenohe butterflye.

Fol. By my trouthe, I trowe well;
But she is lesse a grete dele
Than a butterflye of our lande.

Fan. What pylde curre ledest thou in thy
hande?

Fol. A pylde curre!

Fan. Ye so, I tell thé, a pylde curre.

Fol. Yet I solde his skynne to Mackemurre,
In the stede of a budge furre.   1070

Fan. What, fleyest thou his skynne euery yere?

Fol. Yes, in faythe, I thanke God I may here.

Fan. What, thou wylte coughe me a dawe for
forty pens?

Fol. Mary, syr, Cokermowthe is a good way
hens.

Fan. What? of Cokermowth spake I no worde.

Fol. By my faythe, syr, the frubyssher hath
my sworde.

Fan. A, I trowe, ye shall coughe me a fole.

Fol. In faythe, trouthe ye say, we wente to-
gyder to scole.

Fan. Ye, but I can somwhat more of the letter.

Fol. I wyll not gyue an halfepeny for to chose
the better.   1080

Fan. But, broder Foly, I wonder moche of one
    thynge,
That thou so hye fro me doth sprynge,
And I so lytell alway styll.
Fol. By God, I can tell thé, and I wyll.
Thou art so feble fantastycall,
And so braynsyke therwithall,
And thy wyt wanderynge here and there,
That thou cannyst not growe out of thy boyes
    gere ;
And as for me, I take but one folysshe way,
And therfore I growe more on one day   1090
Than thou can in yerys seuen.
Fan. In faythe, trouth thou sayst nowe, by God
    of heuen!
For so with fantasyes my wyt dothe flete,
That wysdome and I shall seldome mete.
Nowe, of good felowshyp, let me by thy dogge.
Fol. Cockys harte, thou lyest, I am no hogge.
Fan. Here is no man that callyd thé hogge noi
    swyne.
Fol. In faythe, man, my brayne is as good as
    thyne.
Fan. The deuyls torde for thy brayne!
Fol. By my syers soule, I fele no rayne.   1100
Fan. By the masse, I holde thé madde.
Fol. Mary, I knewe thé when thou waste a
    ladde.
Fan. Cockys bonys, herde ye euer syke an-
    other ?

Fol. Ye, a fole the tone, and a fole the tother.

Fan. Nay, but wotest thou what I do say?

Fol. Why, sayst thou that I was here yester-
day?

Fan. Cockys armys, this is a warke, I trowe.

Fol. What, callyst thou me a donnyshe crowe?

Fan. Nowe, in good faythe, thou art a fonde
gest.

Fol. Ye, bere me this strawe to a dawys nest.

Fan. What, wenyst thou that I were so folysshe
and so fonde?   1111

Fol. In faythe, ellys is there none in all Eng-
londe.

Fan. Yet for my fansy sake, I say,

Let me haue thy dogge, what soeuer I pay.

Fol. Thou shalte haue my purse, and I wyll
haue thyne.

Fan. By my trouth, there is myne.

Fol. Nowe, by my trouth, man, take, there is
myne;[1]

And I beshrowe hym that hath the worse.

Fan. Torde, I say, what haue I do?

Here is nothynge but the bockyll of a sho,   1120

And in my purse was twenty marke.

Fol. Ha, ha, ha! herke, syrs, harke!

For all that my name hyght Foly,

By the masse, yet art thou more fole than I.

Fan. Yet gyue me thy dogge, and I am content;

And thou shalte haue my hauke to a botchment.

[1] *myne*] Qy., for the rhyme, "my purse?"

Fol. That euer thou thryue, God it forfende!
For, Goddes cope, thou wyll spende.
Nowe take thou my dogge, and gyue me thy
    fowle.[1]
Fan. Hay, chysshe, come hyder!   1130
Fol. Nay, torde, take hym be tyme.
Fan. What callyst thou thy dogge?
Fol. Tusshe, his name is Gryme.
Fan. Come, Gryme, come, Gryme! it is my
    praty dogges.
Fol. In faythe, there is not a better dogge for
    hogges,
Not from Anwyke vnto Aungey.
Fan. Ye, but trowest thou that he be not
    maungey?
Fol. No, by my trouthe, it is but the scurfe and
    the scabbe.
Fan. What, he hathe ben hurte with a stabbe?
Fol. Nay, in faythe, it was but a strype   1140
That the horson had for etynge of a trype.
Fan. Where the deuyll gate he all these hurtes?
Fol. By God, for snatchynge of puddynges and
    wortes.
Fan. What, then he is some good poore mannes
    curre?
Fol. Ye, but he wyll in at euery mannes dore.
Fan. Nowe thou hast done me a pleasure grete.
Fol. In faythe, I wolde thou had a marmosete.

---

1 *fowle*] Qy. a line wanting to rhyme with this?

Fan. Cockes harte, I loue suche iapes.

Fol. Ye, for all thy mynde is on owles and apes.
But I haue thy pultre, and thou hast my catell.   1150

Fan. Ye, but thryfte and we haue made a
        batell.

Fol. Remembrest thou not the iapes and the
        toyes —

Fan. What, that we vsed whan we were boyes?

Fol. Ye, by the rode, euen the same.

Fan. Yes, yes, I am yet as full of game
As euer I was, and as full of tryfyls,
Nil, nihilum, nihil, anglice nyfyls.

Fol. What canest thou all this Latyn yet,
And hast so mased a wandrynge wyt?   1159

Fan. Tushe, man, I kepe some Latyn in store.

Fol. By Cockes harte, I wene thou hast no
        more.

Fan. No? yes, in faythe, I can versyfy.

Fol. Then, I pray thé hartely,
Make a verse of my butterfly;
It forseth not of the reason, so it kepe ryme.

Fan. But wylte thou make another on Gryme?

Fol. Nay, in fayth, fyrst let me here thyne.

Fan. Mary, as for that, thou shalte sone here
        myne:
Est snavi snago with a shrewde face *vilis imago.*[1]

Fol. Grimbaldus gredy, snatche a puddyng tyl
        the rost be redy.   1170

---

[1] *Est snavi, &c.*] Between this line and the next, ed. has
' *Versus.*"

Fan. By the harte of God, well done!

Fol. Ye, so redely and so sone!

Here cometh in CRAFTY CONUEYAUNCE.

Cr. Con. What, Fansy! Let me se who is the
    tother.

Fan. By God, syr, Foly, myne owne sworne
    brother.

Cr. Con. Cockys bonys, it is a farle freke :
Can he play well at the hoddypeke?

Fan. Tell by thy trouth what sport can thou
    make.

Fol. A, holde thy peas; I haue the tothe
    ake.

Cr. Con. The tothe ake! lo, a torde ye haue.

Fol. Ye, thou haste the four quarters of a
    knaue.   1180

Cr. Con. Wotyst thou, I say, to whom thou
    spekys?

Fan. Nay, by Cockys harte, he ne reckys,
For he wyll speke to Magnyfycence thus.

Cr. Con. Cockys armys, a mete man for vs.

Fol. What, wolde ye haue mo folys, and are so
    many?

Fan. Nay, offer hym a counter in stede of a
    peny.

Cr. Con. Why, thynkys thou he can no better
    skyll?

Fol. In fayth, I can make you bothe folys, and
    I wyll.

Cr. Con. What haste thou on thy fyst? a kes-
teryll?

Fol. Nay, I wys, fole, it is a doteryll.   1190

Cr. Con. In a cote thou can play well the
dyser.

Fol. Ye, but thou can play the fole without a
vyser.

Fan. Howe rode he by you? howe put he to
you?[1]

Cr. Con. Mary, as thou sayst, he gaue me a
blurre.

But where gatte thou that mangey curre?

Fan. Mary, it was his, and nowe it is myne.

Cr. Con. And was it his, and nowe it is thyne?

Thou must haue thy fansy and thy wyll,

But yet thou shalt holde me a fole styll.

Fol. Why, wenyst thou that I cannot make thé
play the fon?   1200

Fan. Yes, by my faythe, good Syr Johnn.

Cr. Con. For you bothe it were inough.

Fol. Why, wenyst thou that I were as moche
a fole as thou?

Fan. Nay, nay, thou shalte fynde hym another
maner of man.

Fol. In faythe, I can do mastryes, so I can.

Cr. Con. What canest thou do but play cocke
wat?

Fan. Yes, yes, he wyll make thé ete a gnat.

---

[1] *you*] Qy., for the rhyme, "*you* there?"

Fol. Yes, yes, by my trouth, I holde thé a grote,

That I shall laughe thé out of thy cote.

Cr. Con. Than wyll I say that thou haste no pere. 1210

Fan. Nowe, by the rode, and he wyll go nere.

Fol. Hem, Fansy! *regardes, voyes.*

> *Here* Foly *maketh semblaunt to take a lowse from* Crafty Conueyaunce *showlder.*

Fan. What hast thou founde there?

Fol. By God, a lowse.

Cr. Con. By Cockes harte, I trowe thou lyste.

Fol. By the masse, a Spaynysshe moght with a gray lyste.

Fan. Ha, ha, ha, ha, ha, ha!

Cr. Con. Cockes armes, it is not so, I trowe.

> *Here* Crafty Conu[ey]aunce *putteth of his gowne.*

Fol. Put on thy gowne agayne, for nowe thou hast lost.[1]

Fan. Lo, Johnn a Bonam, where is thy brayne?

Nowe put on, fole, thy cote agayne. 1221

Fol. Gyue me my grote, for thou hast lost.

> *Here* Foly *maketh semblaunt to take money of* Crafty Conueyaunce, *saynge to hym,*

Shyt thy purse, dawe, and do no cost.

---

[1] *for nowe thou hast lost*] Qy., for the rhyme, " for thou hast lost nowe? "

Fan. Nowe hast thou not a prowde mocke and
    a starke?

Cr. Con. With, yes, by the rode of Wodstocke
    Parke.

Fan. Nay, I tell thé, he maketh no dowtes
To tourne a fole out of his clowtes.

    Cr. Con. And for a fole a man wolde hym take.

    Fol. Nay, it is I that foles can make;

For, be he cayser or be he kynge,   1230
To felowshyp with Foly I can hym brynge.

    Fan. Nay, wylte thou here nowe of his scoles,
And what maner of people he maketh foles?

    Cr. Con. Ye, let vs here a worde or twayne.

    Fol. Syr, of my maner I shall tell you the
    playne.

Fyrst I lay before them my bybyll,
And teche them howe they sholde syt ydyll,
To pyke theyr fyngers all the day longe;
So in theyr eyre I synge them a songe,
And make them so longe to muse,   1240
That some of them renneth strayght to the stuse;
To thefte and bryboury I make some fall,
And pyke a locke and clyme a wall;
And where I spy a nysot gay,
That wyll syt ydyll all the day,
And can not set herselfe to warke,
I kyndell in her suche a lyther sparke,
That rubbed she must be on the gall
Bytwene the tappet and the wall.   1249

    Cr. Con. What, horson, arte thou such a one?

Fan. Nay, beyonde all other set hym alone.

Cr. Con. Hast thou ony more? let se, procede.

Fol. Ye, by God, syr, for a nede,

I haue another maner of sorte,

That I laugh at for my dysporte;

And those be they that come vp of nought,

As some be not ferre, and yf it were well sought:

Suche dawys, what soeuer they be,

That be set in auctorite,

Anone he waxyth so hy and prowde,　　　　1260

He frownyth fyersly, brymly browde,

The knaue wolde make it koy, and he cowde;

All that he dothe, muste be alowde;

And, This is not well done, syr, take hede;

And maketh hym besy where is no nede:

He dawnsys so longe, hey, troly loly,

That euery man lawghyth at his foly.

Cr. Con. By the good Lorde, truthe he sayth.

Fan. Thynkyst thou not so, by thy fayth?

Cr. Con. Thynke I not so, quod he! ellys haue

I shame,　　　　1270

For I knowe dyuerse that vseth the same.

Fol. But nowe, forsothe, man, it maketh no

mater;

For they that wyll so bysely smater,

So helpe me God, man, euer at the length

I make hym [1] lese moche of theyr strength;

---

[1] *hym*] Compare v. 427, p. 22. Perhaps these inconsisten
cies may have arisen from contractions in the MS.

For with foly so do I them lede,
That wyt he wantyth when he hath moste nede.
 Fan. Forsothe, tell on: hast thou any mo?
 Fol. Yes, I shall tell you, or I go,
Of dyuerse mo that hauntyth my scolys. 1280
 Cr. Con. All men beware of suche folys!
 Fol. There be two lyther, rude and ranke,
Symkyn Tytyuell and Pers Pykthanke; ·
Theys lythers I lerne them for to lere
What he sayth and she sayth to lay good ere,
And tell to his sufferayne euery whyt,
And then he is moche made of for his wyt;
And, be the mater yll more or lesse,
He wyll make it mykyll worse than it is:
But all that he dothe, and yf he reken well, 1290
It is but foly euery dell.
 Fan. Are not his wordys cursydly cowchyd?
 Cr. Con. By God, there be some that be
  shroudly towchyd:
But, I say, let se and yf thou haue any more.
 Fol. I haue an hole armory of suche haburdashe
  in store;
For there be other that foly dothe vse,
That folowe fonde fantasyes and vertu refuse.
 Fan. Nay, that is my parte that thou spekest
  of nowe.
 Fol. So is all the remenaunt, I make God
  auowe;
For thou fourmest suche fantasyes in theyr mynde,
That euery man almost groweth out of kynde. 1301

Cr. Con. By the masse, I am glad that I came
    hyder,
To here you two rutters dyspute togyder.
  Fan. Nay, but Fansy must be eyther fyrst or
    last.
  Fol. But whan Foly cometh, all is past.
  Fan. I wote not whether it cometh of thé or
    of me,
But all is foly that I can se.
  Cr. Con. Mary, syr, ye may swere it on a
    boke.
  Fol. Ye, tourne ouer the lefe, rede there and
    loke,
Howe frantyke Fansy fyrst of all   1310
Maketh man and woman in foly to fall.
  Cr. Con. A, syr, a, a! howe by that!
  Fan. A peryllous thynge, to cast a cat
Vpon a naked man, and yf she scrat.
  Fol. So how, I say, the hare is squat!
For, frantyke Fansy, thou makest men madde;
And I, Foly, bryngeth them to *qui fuit* gadde,
With *qui fuit* brayne seke I haue them brought
From *qui fuit aliquid* to shyre shakynge nought.
  Cr. Con. Well argued and surely on bothe
    sydes: 1320
But for thé, Fansy, Magnyfycence abydes.
  Fan. Why, shall I not haue Foly with me
    also?
  Cr. Con. Yes, perde, man, whether that ye
    ryde or go:

Yet for his name we must fynde a slyght.[1]

Fan. By the masse, he shall hyght Consayte.

Cr. Con. Not a better name vnder the sonne :
With Magnyfycence thou shalte wonne.

Fol. God haue mercy, good godfather.

Cr. Con. Yet I wolde that ye had gone rather;
For, as sone as you come in Magnyfycence syght,
All mesure and good rule is gone quyte.   1331

Fan. And shall we haue lyberte to do what
we wyll ?

Cr. Con. Ryot at lyberte russheth it out styll.

Fol. Ye, but tell me one thynge.

Cr. Con. What is that ?

Fol. Who is mayster of the masshe fat ?

Fan. Ye, for he hathe a full dry soule.

Cr. Con. Cockes armes, thou shalte kepe the
brewhouse boule.

Fol. But may I drynke therof whylest that I
stare ?

Cr. Con. When mesure is gone, what nedest
thou spare ?   1340

Whan mesure is gone, we may slee care.

Fol. Nowe then goo we hens, away the maré ![2]

CRAFTY CONUEYAUNCE *alone in the place.*

Cr. Con. It is wonder to se the worlde aboute,
To se what foly is vsed in euery place ;

---

[1] *slyght*] Ed. " shyfte." Compare v. 687, p. 33, and v. 964,
p. 46, where " slyght " (sleight) is the rhyme to " consayte."

[2] *the mare*] Here *Foly* and *Fansy* go out.

Foly hath a rome, I say, in euery route,
To put, where he lyst, Foly hath fre chace;
Foly and Fansy all where, euery man dothe face
    and brace;
Foly fotyth it properly, Fansy ledyth the dawnce;
And next come I after, Crafty Conueyaunce.
Who so to me gyueth good aduertence,   1350
Shall se many thyngys donne craftely:
By me conueyed is wanton insolence,
Pryuy poyntmentys conueyed so properly,
For many tymes moche kyndnesse is denyed
For drede that we dare not ofte lest we be spyed;
By me is conueyed mykyll praty ware,
Somtyme, I say, behynde the dore for nede;
I haue an hoby can make larkys to dare;
I knyt togyther many a broken threde.
It is great almesse the hungre to fede,   1360
To clothe the nakyd where is lackynge a smocke,
Trymme at her tayle, or a man can turne a socke:
What howe, be ye mery! was it not well con-
    ueyed?
As oft as ye lyst, so honeste be sauyd;
Alas, dere harte, loke that we be not perseyuyd!
Without crafte nothynge is well behauyd;
Though I shewe you curtesy, say not that I craue,[1]
Yet conuey it craftely, and hardely spare not for
    me,

---

[1] *aue*] Qy., for the rhyme, " craued? " unless something
be wanting.

So that there knowe no man but I and she.
Thefte also and pety brybery   1370
Without me be full oft aspyed;
My inwyt delynge there can no man dyscry,
Conuey it be crafte, lyft and lay asyde:
Full moche flatery and falsehode I hyde,
And by crafty conueyaunce I wyll, and I can,
Saue a stronge thefe and hange a trew man.
But some man wolde conuey, and can not skyll,
As malypert tauernars that checke with theyr
        betters,
Theyr conueyaunce weltyth the worke all by wyll;
And some wyll take vpon them to conterfet
        letters,   1380
And therwithall conuey hymselfe into a payre of
        fetters;
And some wyll conuey by the pretence of sad-
        nesse,
Tyll all theyr conueyaunce is turnyd into mad-
        nesse.
Crafty conueyaunce is no chyldlys game:
By crafty conueyaunce many one is brought vp
        of nought;
Crafty Conueyaunce can cloke hymselfe frome
        shame,
For by crafty conueyaunce wonderful thynges
        are wrought:
By conuayaunce crafty I haue brought
Vnto Magnyfyce[nce] a full vngracyous sorte,
For all hokes vnhappy to me haue resorte.   1390

Here cometh in MAGNYFYCENCE *with* LYBERTE
and FELYCYTE.

Magn. Trust me, Lyberte, it greueth me ryght
    sore
To se you thus ruled and stande in suche awe.
    Lyb. Syr, as by my wyll, it shall be so no more.
    Fel. Yet lyberte without rule is not worth a
      strawe.
    Magn. Tuske, holde your peas, ye speke lyke
      a dawe;
Ye shall be occupyed, Welthe, at my wyll. [skyll.
    Cr. Con. All that ye say, syr, is reason and
    Magn. Mayster Suruayour, where haue ye ben
      so longe?
Remembre ye not how my lyberte by mesure
    ruled was?
    Cr. Con. In good faythe, syr, me semeth he
      had the more wronge.   1400
    Lyb. Mary, syr, so dyd he excede and passe,
They droue me to lernynge lyke a dull asse.
    Fel. It is good yet that lyberte be ruled by
      reason.
    Magn. Tushe, holde your peas, ye speke out
      of season :
Yourselfe shall be ruled by lyberte and largesse.
    Fel. I am content, so it in measure be.
    Lyb. Must mesure, in the mares name, you
      furnysshe and dresse?
    Magn. Nay, nay, not so, my frende Felycyte.

Cr. Con. Not, and your grace wolde be ruled
  by me.

Lyb. Nay, he shall be ruled euen as I lyst. 1410

Fel. Yet it is good to beware of Had I wyst.

Magn. Syr, by lyberte and largesse I wyll that
  ye shall

Be gouerned and gyded: wote ye what I say?

Mayster Suruayour, Largesse to me call.

Cr. Con. It shall be done.

Magn. Ye, but byd hym come away

At ones, and let hym not tary all day.

  Here goth out CRAFTY CONUAYAUNCE.

Fel. Yet it is good wysdome to worke wysely
  by welth.

Lyb. Holde thy tonge, and thou loue thy helth.

Magn. What, wyll ye waste wynde, and prate
  thus in vayne?   1420

Ye haue eten sauce, I trowe, at the Taylers Hall.

Lyb. Be not to bolde, my frende; I counsell
  you, bere a brayne.

Magn. And what so we say, holde you content
  withall.

Fel. Syr, yet without sapyence your substaunce
  may be smal;

For, where is no mesure, howe may worshyp
  endure?

  Here cometh in FANSY.

Fan. Syr, I am here at your pleasure;

Your grace sent for me, I wene; what is **your**
  wyll?

Magn. Come hyther, Largesse, take here
 Felycyte.

Fan. Why, wene you that I can kepe hym longe
 styll?

Magn. To rule as ye lyst, lo, here is Lyberte!

Lyb. I am here redy.   1431

Fan. What, shall we haue welth at our gydynge
 to rule as we lyst?

Then fare well thryfte, by hym that crosse kyst!

Fel. I truste your grace wyll be agreabyll

That I shall suffer none impechment

By theyr demenaunce nor losse repryuable.

Magn. Syr, ye shall folowe myne appetyte and
 intent.

Fel. So it be by mesure I am ryght well con-
 tent.

Fan. What, all by mesure, good syr, and none
 excesse?

Lyb. Why, welth hath made many a man
 braynlesse.   1440

Fel. That was by the menys of to moche lyberte.

Magn. Whaͭ, can ye agree thus and appose?

Fel. Syr, as I say, there was no faute in me.

Lyb. Ye, of Jacke a thrommys bybyll can ye
 make a glose.

Fan. Sore sayde, I tell you, and well to the
 purpose:

What sholde a man do with you? loke you vnder
 kay?

Fel. I say, it is foly to gyue all welth away.

Lyb. Whether sholde welth be rulyd by lyberte,
Or lyberte by welth? let se, tell me that.   1449

    Fel. Syr, as me semeth, ye sholde be rulyd
       by me.

    Magn. What nede you with hym thus prate
       and chat?

    Fan. Shewe vs your mynde then, howe to do
       and what.

    Magn. I say, that I wyll ye haue hym in
       gydynge.

    Lyb. Mayster Felycyte, let be your chydynge,
And so as ye se it wyll be no better,
Take it in worthe suche as ye fynde.

    Fan. What the deuyll, man, your name shalbe
      the greter,
For welth without largesse is all out of kynde.

    Lyb. And welth is nought worthe, yf lyberte be
      behynde.

    Magn. Nowe holde ye content, for there is none
      other shyfte.   1460

    Fel. Than waste must be welcome, and fare
      well thryfte!

    Magn. Take of his substaunce a sure inuentory,
And get thou[1] home togyther; for Lyberte shall
      byde,
And wayte vpon me.

    Lyb. And yet for a memory,
Make indentures howe ye and I shal gyde.

---

[1] *thou*] Qy. " you? " see note on v. 1275, p. 59.

Fan. I can do nothynge but he stonde besyde.

Lyb. Syr, we can do nothynge the one without
the other.

Magn. Well, get you hens than, and sende me
some other.

Fan. Whom? lusty Pleasure, or mery Con-
sayte?   1470

Magn. Nay, fyrst lusty Pleasure is my desyre
to haue,

And let the other another [1] awayte,

Howe be it that fonde felowe is a mery knaue ;

But loke that ye occupye the auctoryte that I
you gaue.

[*Here goeth out* FELYCYTE, LYBERTE, *and* FANSY.

MAGNYFYCENCE *alone in the place.*

For nowe,[2] syrs, I am lyke as a prynce sholde be ;

I haue welth at wyll, largesse and lyberte :

Fortune to her lawys can not abandune me,

But I shall of Fortune rule the reyne ;

I fere nothynge Fortunes perplexyte ;

All honour to me must nedys stowpe and lene ;

I synge of two partys without a mene ;   1481

I haue wynde and wether ouer all to sayle,

No stormy rage agaynst me can peruayle.

Alexander, of Macedony kynge,

That all the oryent had in subieccyon,

---

1 *another*] Qy. " *another* time ? "

2 *For nowe, &c.*] In ed. this speech is given to *Fansy.*

Though al his conquestys were brought to reken-
    ynge,
Myght seem ryght wel vnder my proteccyon
To rayne, for all his marcyall affeccyon;
For I am prynce perlesse prouyd of porte,
Bathyd with blysse, embracyd with comforte. 1490
Syrus, that soleme syar of Babylon,
That Israell releysyd of theyr captyuyte,
For al his pompe, for all his ryall trone,
He may not be comparyd vnto me.
I am the dyamounde dowtlesse of dygnyte:
Surely it is I that all may saue and spyll;
No man so hardy to worke agaynst my wyll.
Porcenya, the prowde prouoste of Turky lande,
That ratyd the Romaynes and made them yll rest,
Nor Cesar July, that no man myght withstande,
Were neuer halfe so rychely as I am drest: 1501
No, that I assure you; loke who was the best.
I reyne in my robys, I rule as me lyst,
I dryue downe th[e]se dastardys with a dynt of
    my fyste.
Of Cato the counte acountyd the cane,
Daryus, the doughty cheftayn of Perse,
I set not by the prowdest of them a prane,
Ne by non other that any man can rehersse.
I folowe in felycyte without reue[r]sse,
I drede no daunger, I dawnce all in delyte; 1510
My name is Magnyfycence, man most of myght.
Hercules the herdy, with his stobburne clobbyd
    mase,

That made Cerberus to cache, the cur dogge of
      hell,
And Thesius, that prowde was Pluto to face,
It wolde not become them with me for to mell:
For of all barones bolde I bere the bell,
Of all doughty I am doughtyest duke, as I deme ;
To me all prynces to lowte man be sene.[1]
Cherlemayne, that mantenyd the nobles of Fraunce,
Arthur of Albyan, for all his brymme berde,   1520
Nor Basyan the bolde, for all his brybaunce,
Nor Alerycus, that rulyd the Gothyaunce by swerd,
Nor no man on molde can make me aferd.
What man is so maysyd with me that dare mete,
I shall flappe hym as a fole to fall at my fete.
Galba, whom his galantys garde for a gaspe,
Nor Nero, that nother set by God nor man,
Nor Vaspasyan, that bare in his nose a waspe,
Nor Hanyball agayne Rome gates that ranne,
Nor yet Cypyo, that noble Cartage wanne,   1530
Nor none so hardy of them with me that durste
      crake,
But I shall frounce them on the foretop, and gar
      them to quake.

Here cometh in COURTLY ABUSYON, *doynge
      reuerence and courtesy.*

Court. Ab. At your commaundement, syr, wyth
      all dew reuerence.

---

[1] *be sene*] Qy., " may beseme ? " C.

Magn. Welcom, Pleasure, to our magnyfycence.

Court. Ab. Plesyth it your grace to shewe what
I do shall?

Magn. Let vs here of your pleasure to passe
the tyme withall.

Court. Ab. Syr, then with the fauour of your
benynge sufferaunce

To shewe you my mynde myselfe I wyll auaunce,

If it lyke your grace to take it in degre.

Magn. Yes, syr, so good man in you I se,   1540

And in your delynge so good assuraunce,

That we delyte gretly in your dalyaunce.

Court. Ab. A, syr, your grace me dothe extole
and rayse,

And ferre beyond my merytys ye me commende
and prayse;

Howe be it, I wolde be ryght gladde, I you assure,

Any thynge to do that myght be to your pleasure.

Magn. As I be saued, with pleasure I am sup-
prysyd

Of your langage, it is so well deuysed;

Pullyshyd and fresshe is your ornacy.

Court. Ab. A, I wolde to God that I were halfe
so crafty,   1550

Or in electe vtteraunce halfe so eloquent,

As that I myght your noble grace content!

Magn. Truste me, with you I am hyghly
pleasyd,

For in my fauour I haue you feffyd and seasyd.

He is not lyuynge your maners can amend;

Mary, your speche is as pleasant as though it
    were pend ;
To here your comon, it is my hygh comforte ;
Poynt deuyse all pleasure is your porte.
    Court. Ab. Syr, I am the better of your noble
    reporte ;
But, of your pacyence vnder the supporte,   1560
If it wolde lyke you to here my pore mynde —
    Magn. Speke, I beseche thé, leue nothynge
    behynde.
    Court. Ab. So as ye be a prynce of great
    myght,
It is semynge your pleasure ye delyte,
And to aqueynte you with carnall delectacyon,
And to fall in aquayntaunce with euery newe
    facyon ;
And quyckely your appetytes to sharpe and
    adresse.
To fasten your fansy vpon a fayre maystresse,
That quyckly is enuyued with rudyes of the rose,
Inpurtured with fetures after your purpose,   1570
The streynes of her vaynes as asure inde blewe,
Enbudded with beautye and colour fresshe of
    hewe,
As lyly whyte to loke vpon her leyre,
Her eyen relucent as carbuncle so clere,
Her mouthe enbawmed, dylectable and mery,
Her lusty lyppes ruddy as the chery :
Howe lyke you? ye lacke, syr, suche a lusty
    lasse.

Magn. A, that were a baby to brace and to
    basse!
I wolde I had, by hym that hell dyd harowe,
With me in kepynge suche a Phylyp sparowe! 1580
I wolde hauke whylest my hede dyd warke,
So I myght hobby for suche a lusty larke.
These wordes in myne eyre they be so lustely
    spoken,
That on suche a female my flesshe wolde be
    wroken;
They towche me so thorowly, and tykyll my con-
    sayte,
That weryed I wolde be on suche a bayte:
A, Cockes armes, where myght suche one be
    founde?
    Court. Ab. Wyll ye spende ony money?
    Magn. Ye, a thousande pounde.
    Court. Ab. Nay, nay, for lesse I waraunt you
    to be sped,   1590
And brought home, and layde in your bed.
    Magn. Wolde money, trowest thou, make suche
    one to the call?
    Court. Ab. Money maketh marchauntes, I tell
    you, over all.
    Magn. Why, wyl a maystres be wonne for
    money and for golde?
    Court. Ab. Why, was not for money Troy bothe
    bought and solde?
Full many a stronge cyte and towne hath ben
    wonne

By the meanes of money without ony gonne.

A maystres, I tell you, is but a small thynge;

A goodly rybon, or a golde rynge,

May wynne with a sawte the fortresse of the
holde; 1600

But one thynge I warne you, prece forth and be
bolde.

 Magn. Ye, but some be full koy and passynge
  harde harted.

 Court. Ab. But, blessyd be our Lorde, they
  wyll be sone conuerted.

 Magn. Why, wyll they then be intreted, the
  most and the lest?

 Court. Ab. Ye, for *omnis mulier meretrix, si*
  celari potest.

 Magn. A, I haue spyed ye can moche broken
  sorowe.

 Court. Ab. I coude holde you with suche talke
  hens tyll to morowe;

But yf it lyke your grace, more at large

Me to permyt my mynde to dyscharge,

I wolde yet shewe you further of my consayte. 1610

 Magn. Let se what ye say, shewe it strayte.

 Court. Ab. Wysely let these wordes in your
  mynde be wayed:

By waywarde wylfulnes let eche thynge be con-
uayed;

What so euer ye do, folowe your owne wyll;

Be it reason or none, it shall not gretely skyll;

Be it ryght or wronge, by the aduyse of me,

Take your pleasure and vse free lyberte;
And yf you se ony thynge agaynst your mynde,
Then some occacyon of quarell ye must fynde,
And frowne it and face it, as thoughe ye wolde
    fyght,   1620
Frete yourselfe for anger and for dyspyte;
Here no man, what so euer they say,
But do as ye lyst, and take your owne way.
    Magn. Thy wordes and my mynde odly well
        accorde.
    Court. Ab. What sholde ye do elles? are not
        you a lorde?
Let your lust and lykynge stande for a lawe;
Be wrastynge and wrythynge, and away drawe.
And ye se a man that with hym ye be not pleased,
And that your mynde can not well be eased,   1629
As yf a man fortune to touche you on the quyke,
Then feyne yourselfe dyseased and make your-
    selfe seke:
To styre vp your stomake you must you forge,
Call for a candell and cast vp your gorge;
With, Cockes armes, rest shall I none haue
Tyll I be reuenged on that horson knaue!
A, howe my stomake wambleth! I am all in a
    swete!
Is there no horson that knaue that wyll bete?
    Magn. By Cockes woundes, a wonder felowe
        thou arte;

For ofte tymes suche a wamblynge goth ouer my
    harte ;
Yet I am not harte seke, but that me lyst   1640
For myrth I haue hym coryed, beten, and blyst,
Hym that I loued not and made hym to loute,
I am forthwith as hole as a troute ;
For suche abusyon I vse nowe and than.
    Court. Ab. It is none abusyon, syr, in a noble
    man,
It is a pryncely pleasure and a lordly mynde ;
Suche lustes at large may not be lefte behynde.

    Here cometh in CLOKED COLUSYON *with*
        MESURE.

    Cl. Col. Stande styll here, and ye shall se
That for your sake I wyll fall on my kne.
    Court. Ab. Syr, Sober Sadnesse cometh, wher-
    fore it be?   1650
    Magn. Stande vp, syr, ye are welcom to me.
    Cl. Col. Please it your grace, at the contem-
    placyon
Of my pore instance and supplycacyon,
Tenderly to consyder in your aduertence,
Of our blessyd Lorde, syr, at the reuerence,
Remembre the good seruyce that Mesure hath
    you done,
And that ye wyll not cast hym away so sone.
    Magn. My frende, as touchynge to this your
    mocyon,
I may say to you I haue but small deuocyon ;

Howe be it, at your instaunce I wyll the rather

Do as moche as for myne owne father.   1661

 Cl. Col. Nay, syr, that affeccyon ought to be
  reserued,

For of your grace I haue it nought deserued;

But yf it lyke you that I myght rowne in your
 eyre,

To shewe you my mynde I wolde haue the lesse
 fere.

 Magn. Stande a lytell abacke, syr, and let hym
  come hyder.

 Court. Ab. With a good wyll, syr, God spede
  you bothe togyder.

 Cl. Col. Syr, so it is, this man is here by,

That for hym to laboure he hath prayde me
 hartely;

Notwithstandynge to you be it sayde,   1670

To trust in me he is but dyssayued;

For, so helpe me God, for you he is not mete:

I speke the softlyer, because he sholde not wete.

 Magn. Come hyder, Pleasure, you shall here
  myne entent :

Mesure, ye knowe wel, with hym I can not be
 content,

And surely, as I am nowe aduysed,

I wyll haue hym rehayted and dyspysed.

Howe say ye, syrs? herein what is best?

 Court. Ab. By myne aduyse with you in fayth
  he shall not rest.

Cl. Col. Yet, syr, reserued your better aduyse-
    ment,   1680
It were better he spake with you or he wente,
That he knowe not but that I haue supplyed
All that I can his matter for to spede.
    Magn. Nowe, by your trouthe, gaue he you
        not a brybe?
    Cl. Col. Yes, with his hande I made hym to
        subscrybe
A byll of recorde for an annuall rent.
    Court. Ab. But for all that he is lyke to haue
        a glent.
    Cl. Col. Ye, by my trouthe, I shall waraunt
        you for me,
And he go to the deu[y]ll, so that I may haue
    my fee,
What care I?   1690
    Magn. By the masse, well sayd.
    Court. Ab. What force ye, so that ye be payde?
    Cl. Col. But yet, lo, I wolde, or that he wente,
Lest that he thought that his money were euyll
    spente,
That ye wolde loke on hym, thoughe it were not
    longe.
    Magn. Well cannest thou helpe a preest to
        synge a songe.
    Cl. Col. So it is all the maner nowe a dayes,
For to vse suche haftynge and crafty wayes.
    Court. Ab. He telleth you trouth, syr, as I you
        ensure.

Magn. Well, for thy sake the better I may en-
dure　　　　　　　　　　　　　　　　　1700
That he come hyder, and to gyue hym a loke
That he shall lyke the worse all this woke.

Cl. Col. I care not howe sone he be refused,
So that I may craftely be excused.

Court. Ab. Where is he?

Cl. Col. Mary, I made hym abyde,
Whylest I came to you, a lytell here besyde.

Magn. Well, call hym, and let vs here hym
reason,
And we wyll be comonynge in the mene season.

Court. Ab. This is a wyse man, syr, where so
euer ye hym had.　　　　　　　　　　　1710

Magn. An honest person, I tell you, and a sad.

Court. Ab. He can full craftely this matter
brynge aboute.

Magn. Whylest I haue hym, I nede nothynge
doute.

Hic introducat COLUSION MESURE, MAGNYFY-
CENCE *aspectant[e] vultu elatissimo.*

Cl. Col. By the masse, I haue done that I can,
And more than euer I dyd for ony man:
I trowe, ye herde yourselfe what I sayd.

Mes. Nay, indede; but I sawe howe ye prayed,
And made instance for me be lykelyhod.

Cl. Col. Nay, I tell you, I am not wonte to fode
Them that dare put theyr truste in me;　　1720
And therof ye shall a larger profe se.

Mes. Syr, God rewarde you as ye haue de-
serued :
But thynke you with Magnyfycence I shal be
reserued?

Cl. Col. By my trouth, I can not tell you that ;
But, and I were as ye, I wolde not set a gnat
By Magnyfycence, nor yet none of his,
For, go when ye shall, of you shall he mysse.

Mes. Syr, as ye say.

Cl. Col. Nay, come on with me :
Yet ones agayne I shall fall on my kne   1730
For your sake, what so euer befall ;
I set not a flye, and all go to all.

Mes. The Holy Goost be with your grace.

Cl. Col. Syr, I beseche you, let pety haue some
place
In your brest towardes this gentylman.

Magn. I was your good lorde tyll that ye be-
ganne
So masterfully vpon you for to take
With my seruauntys, and suche maystryes gan
make,
That holly my mynde with you is myscontente ;
Wherfore I wyll that ye be resydent   1740
With me no longer.

Cl. Col. Say somwhat nowe, let se, for your
selfe.[1]

---

[1] *let se, for your selfe*] Qy., for the rhyme, " for your selfe,
let se ? "—unless " for your selfe " was intended to form the
commencement of the next verse.

Mes. Syr, yf I myght permytted be,
I wolde to you say a worde or twayne.
    Magn. What, woldest thou, lurden, with me
        brawle agayne?
Haue hym hens, I say, out of my syght;
That day I se hym, I shall be worse all nyght.
            [*Here* MESURE *goth out of the place.*[1]
    Court. Ab. Hens, thou haynyarde, out of the
        dores fast!
    Magn. Alas, my stomake fareth as it wolde cast!
    Cl. Col. Abyde, syr, abyde, let me holde your
        hede.   1750
        Magn. A bolle or a basyn, I say, for Goddes
            brede!
A, my hede! But is the horson gone?
God gyue hym a myscheffe! Nay, nowe let me
        alone.
    Cl. Col. A good dryfte, syr, a praty fete:
By the good Lorde, yet your temples bete.
    Magn. Nay, so God me helpe, it was no grete
        vexacyon,
For I am panged ofte tymes of this same facyon.
    Cl. Col. Cockes armes, howe Pleasure plucked
        hym forth!

---

[1] *Here Mesure goth out of the place*] To this stage-direction
ought to be added—" *with Courtly Abusyon, who, as he carries
him off, exclaims.*" See what *Clokyd Colusyon* says a little
after,

    " Cockes armes, howe Pleasure plucked hym forth! "
Pleasure is the assumed name of *Courtly Abusyon.*

Magn. Ye, walke he must, it was no better
worth.

Cl. Col. Syr, rowe me thynke your harte is
well eased.   1760

Magn. Nowe Measure is gone, I am the better
pleased.

Cl. Col. So to be ruled by measure, it is a payne.

Magn. Mary, I wene he wolde not be glad to
come agayne.   ˒

Cl. Col. So I wote not what he sholde do here :
Where mennes belyes is mesured, there is no chere˒;
For I here but fewe men that gyue ony prayse ˷
Vnto measure, I say, nowe a days.

Magn. Measure, tut! what, the deuyll of hell!
Scantly one with measure that wyll dwell.

Cl. Col. Not amonge noble men, as the worlde
gothe :   1770
It is no wonder therfore thoughe ye be wrothe
With Mesure. Where as all noblenes is, there I
haue past :
They catche that catche may, kepe and holde fast,
Out of all measure themselfe to enryche ;
No force what thoughe his neyghbour dye in a
dyche.
With pollynge and pluckynge out of all measure,
Thus must ye stuffe and store your treasure.

Magn. Yet somtyme, parde, I must vse
largesse.

Cl. Col. Ye, mary, somtyme in a messe of
vergesse,

As in a tryfyll or in a thynge of nought,   1780
As gyuynge a thynge that ye neuer bought :
It is the gyse nowe, I say, ouer all ;
Largesse in wordes, for rewardes are but small :
To make fayre promyse, what are ye the worse?
Let me haue the rule of your purse.
   Magn. I haue taken it to Largesse and Lyberte.
   Cl. Col. Than is it done as it sholde be :
But vse your largesse by the aduyse of me,
And I shall waraunt you welth and lyberte.
   Magn. Say on ; me thynke your reasons be
     profounde.   1790
   Cl. Col. Syr, of my counsayle this shall be the
     grounde,
To chose out ii. iii. of suche as you loue best,
And let all your fansyes vpon them rest ;
Spare for no cost to gyue them pounde and peny,
Better to make iii. ryche than for to make many ;
Gyue them more than ynoughe and let them not
     lacke,
And as for all other let them trusse and packe ;
Plucke from an hundred, and gyue it to thre,
Let neyther patent scape them nor fee ;   1799
And where soeuer you wyll fall to a rekenynge,
Those thre wyll be redy euen at your bekenynge,
For then [1] shall you haue at lyberte to lowte ;
Let them haue all, and the other go without :
Thus ioy without mesure you shall haue.

---

[1] *then*] Qy. " them ? "

Magn. Thou sayst truthe, by the harte that
 God me gaue!
For, as thou sayst, ryght so shall it be :
And here I make thé vpon Lyberte
To be superuysour, and on Largesse also,
For as thou wylte, so shall the game go ;
For in Pleasure, and Surueyaunce, and also in
 thé,   1810
I haue set my hole felycyte,
And suche as you wyll shall lacke no promocyon.
 Cl. Col. Syr, syth that in me ye haue suche
  deuocyon,
Commyttynge to me and to my felowes twayne
Your welthe and felycyte, I trust we shall
 optayne
To do you seruyce after your appetyte.
 Magn. In faythe, and your seruyce ryght well
  shall I acquyte ;
And therfore hye you hens, and take this ouer-
 syght.
 Cl. Col. Nowe, Jesu preserue you, syr, prynce
  most of myght!

  Here goth CLOKED COLUSYON *awaye,*
   and leueth MAGNYFYCENCE *alone*
   in the place.

 Magn. Thus, I say, I am enuyronned with
  solace ;   1820
·I drede no dyntes of fatall desteny.
Well were that lady myght stande in my grace,
Me to enbrace and loue moost specyally :

A Lorde, so I wolde halse her hartely,
So I wolde clepe her, so I wolde kys her swete!

Here cometh in FOLY.

Fol. Mary, Cryst graunt ye catche no colde on
　　your fete!

Magn. Who is this?

Fol. Consayte, syr, your owne man.

Magn. What tydynges with you, syr? I befole
　　thy brayne pan.

Fol. By our lakyn, syr, I haue ben a hawkyng
　　for the wylde swan.　　　　　　　　　1830

My hawke is rammysshe, and it happed that she
　　ran,

Flewe I sholde say, in to an olde barne,

To reche at a rat, I coude not her warne;

She pynched her pynyon, by God, and catched
　　harme:

It was a ronner; nay, fole, I warant her blode
　　warme.

Magn. A, syr, thy iarfawcon and thou be
　　hanged togyder!

Fol. And, syr, as I was comynge to you hyder,

I sawe a fox sucke on a kowes ydder,

And with a lyme rodde I toke them bothe to-
　　gyder.

I trowe it be a frost, for the way is slydder:　1840

Se, for God auowe, for colde as I chydder.

Magn. Thy wordes hange togyder as fethers
　　in the wynde.

Fol. A, syr, tolde I not you howe I dyd fynde
A knaue and a carle, and all of one kynde?
I sawe a wethercocke wagge with the wynde;
Grete meruayle I had, and mused in my mynde;
The houndes ranne before, and the hare behynde;
I sawe a losell lede a lurden, and they were bothe
    blynde;
I sawe a sowter go to supper or euer he had
    dynde.
Magn. By Cockes harte, thou arte a fyne mery
    knaue.   1850
Fol. I make God auowe, ye wyll none other
    men [1] haue.
Magn. What sayst thou?
Fol. Mary, I pray God your maystershyp to
    saue:
I shall gyue you a gaude of a goslynge that I
    gaue,
The gander and the gose bothe grasynge on one
    graue;
Than Rowlande the reue ran, and I began to
    raue,
And with a brystell of a bore his berde dyd I
    shaue.
Magn. If euer I herde syke another, God gyue
    me shame.
Fol. Sym Sadylgose was my syer, and Daw-
    cocke my dame: 1859

----

[1] *men*] Qy. "man?"

I coude, and I lyst, garre you laughe at a game,
Howe a wodcocke wrastled with a larke that was
          lame:
The bytter sayd boldly that they were to blame;
The feldfare wolde haue fydled, and it wolde not
          frame;
The crane and the curlewe therat gan to grame;
The snyte snyueled in the snowte and smyled at
          the game.
      Magn. Cockes bones, herde you euer suche
          another?
      Fol. Se, syr, I beseche you, Largesse my
          brother.

              Here FANSY *cometh in.*

      Magn. What tydynges with you, syr, that you
          loke so sad?
      Fan. When ye knowe that I knowe, ye wyll
          not be glad.   1870
      Fol. What, brother braynsyke, how farest thou?
      Magn. Ye, let be thy iapes, and tell me howe
The case requyreth.
      Fan. Alasse, alasse, an heuy metynge!
I wolde tell you, and yf I myght for wepynge.
      Fol. What, is all your myrthe nowe tourned to
          sorowe?
Fare well tyll sone, adue tyll to morowe.
                    Here goth FOLY *away.*
      Magn. I pray thé, Largesse, let be thy sob-
          bynge.

Fan. Alasse, syr, ye are vndone with stelyng
 and robbynge!
Ye sent vs a superuysour for to take hede: 1879
Take hede of your selfe, for nowe ye haue nede.
Magn. What, hath Sadnesse begyled me so?
Fan. Nay, madnesse hath begyled you and
 many mo;
For Lyberte is gone and also Felycyte.
Magn. Gone? alasse, ye haue vndone me!
Fan. Nay, he that ye sent vs, Clokyd Colusyon,
And your payntyd Pleasure, Courtly Abusyon,
And your demenour with Counterfet Counten-
 aunce,
And your suruayour,[1] Crafty Conueyaunce,
Or euer we were ware brought vs in aduersyte,
And had robbyd you quyte from all felycyte. 1890
Magn. Why, is this the largesse that I haue
 vsyd?
Fan. Nay, it was your fondnesse that ye haue
 vsyd.
Magn. And is this the credence that I gaue to
 the letter?
Fan. Why, coulde not your wyt serue you no
 better?
Magn. Why, who wolde haue thought in you
 suche gyle?

1 *suruayour*] Ed. "superuysour:" compare v. 1414, p. 66:
v. 652, p. 31, &c. *Cl. Col.* has just been made "superuy-
sour:" see v. 1808, p. 85.

Fan. What? yes, by the rode, syr, it was I all
    this whyle
That you trustyd, and Fansy is my name;
And Foly, my broder, that made you moche game.

Here cometh in ADUERSYTE.

Magn. Alas, who is yonder, that grymly lokys?
Fan. Adewe, for I wyll not come in his clokys.[1]
Magn. Lorde, so my flesshe trymblyth nowe
    for drede!   1901
       Here MAGNYFYCENCE *is beten downe,*
          and spoylyd from all his goodys
          and rayment.

Aduer. I am Aduersyte, that for thy mysdede
From God am sent to quyte thé thy mede.
Vyle velyarde, thou must not nowe my dynt with-
    stande,
Thou must not abyde the dynt of my hande:
Ly there, losell, for all thy pompe and pryde;
Thy pleasure now with payne and trouble shalbe
    tryde.
The stroke of God, Aduersyte I hyght;
I pluke downe kynge, prynce, lorde, and knyght,
I rushe at them rughly, and make them ly full
    lowe,   1910
And in theyr moste truste I make them ouer-
    throwe.
Thys losyll was a lorde, and lyuyd at his lust,
And nowe, lyke a lurden, he lyeth in the dust:

    [1] *clokys*] Here *Fansy* goes out.

He knewe not hymselfe, his harte was so hye;
Nowe is there no man that wyll set by hym a flye:
He was wonte to boste, brage, and to brace;
Nowe dare he not for shame loke one in the face:
All worldly welth for hym to lytell was;
Nowe hath he ryght nought, naked as an asse:
Somtyme without measure he trusted in golde, 1920
And now without mesure he shal haue hunger
    and colde.
Lo, syrs, thus I handell them all
That folowe theyr fansyes in foly to fall:
Man or woman, of what estate they be,
I counsayle them beware of Aduersyte.
Of sorowfull seruauntes I haue many scores:
I vysyte them somtyme with blaynes and with
    sores;
With botches and carbuckyls in care I them knyt;
With the gowte I make them to grone where
    they syt;
Some I make lyppers and lazars full horse; 1930
And from that they loue best some I deuorse;
Some with the marmoll to halte I them make;
And some to cry out of the bone ake;
And some I vysyte with brennynge of fyre;
Of some I wrynge of the necke lyke a wyre;
And some I make in a rope to totter and walter;
And some for to hange themselfe in an halter;
And some I vysyte to[1] batayle, warre, and mur-
    ther,

[1] *to*] Qy. " with ? " compare vv. 1927, 1934. [Rather change
" vysyte " to *ynsyte*, incite. C.]

And make eche man to sle other;
To drowne or to sle themselfe with a knyfe; 1940
And all is for theyr vngracyous lyfe.
Yet somtyme I stryke where is none offence,
Bycause I wolde proue men of theyr pacyence.
But, nowe a dayes, to stryke I haue grete cause,
Lydderyns so lytell set by Goddes lawes.
Faders and moders, that be neclygent,
And suffre theyr chyldren to haue theyr entent,
To gyde them vertuously that wyll not remembre,
Them or theyr chyldren ofte tymes I dysmembre;
Theyr chyldren, bycause that they haue no
  mekenesse; 1950
I vysyte theyr faders and moders with sekenesse;
And yf I se therby they wyll not amende,
Then myschefe sodaynly I them sende;
For there is nothynge that more dyspleaseth God
Than from theyr chyldren to spare the rod
Of correccyon, but let them haue theyr wyll;
Some I make lame, and some I do kyll;
And some I stryke with a fransey;
Of some of theyr chyldren I stryke out the eye;
And where the fader by wysdom worshyp hath
  wonne, 1960
I sende oft tymes a fole to his sonne.
Wherfore of Aduersyte loke ye be ware,
For when I come, comyth sorowe and care:
For I stryke lordys of realmes and landys,
That rule not by mesure that they haue in theyr
  handys,

That sadly rule not theyr howsholde men ;
I am Goddys preposytour, I prynt them with a
 pen ;
Because of theyr neglygence and of theyr wanton
 vagys,
I vysyte them and stryke them with many sore
 plagys.
To take, syrs, example of that I you tell,   1970
And beware of aduersyte by my counsell,
Take hede of this caytyfe that lyeth here on
 grounde ;
Beholde, howe Fortune of [1] hym hath frounde !
For though we shewe you this in game and play,
Yet it proueth eyrnest, ye may se, euery day.
For nowe wyll I from this caytyfe go,
And take myscheffe and vengeaunce of other mo,
That hath deseruyd it as well as he.
Howe, where art thou? come hether, Pouerte ;
Take this caytyfe to thy lore.   1980

Here cometh in POUERTE.[2]

Pouer. A, my bonys ake, my lymmys be sore ;
Alasse, I haue the cyatyca full euyll in my hyppe !
Alasse, where is youth that was wont for to skyppe ?
I am lowsy, and vnlykynge, and full of scurffe,
My colour is tawny, colouryd as a turffe :
I am Pouerte, that all men doth hate,
I am baytyd with doggys at euery mannys gate :

  [1] *of*] Qy. " on ? "
  [2] *Pouerte*] And *Aduersyte* goes out.

I am raggyd and rent, as ye may se ;
Full fewe but they haue enuy at me.
Nowe must I this carcasse lyft vp :　　　1990
He dynyd with delyte, with Pouerte he must sup.
Ryse vp, syr, and welcom vnto me.

> *Hic accedat ad levandum* MAGNYFYCENCE,
> *et locabit eum super locum stratum.*

　Magn. Alasse, where is nowe my golde and fe ?
Alasse, I say, where to am I brought ?
Alasse, alasse, alasse, I dye for thought !
　Pouer. Syr, all this wolde haue bene thought
　　on before :
He woteth not what welth is that neuer was sore.
　Magn. Fy, fy, that euer I sholde be brought in
　　this snare !
I wenyd ones neuer to haue knowen of care.
　Pouer. Lo, suche is this worlde ! I fynd it wryt,
In welth to beware, and that is wyt.　　　2001
　Magn. In welth to beware, yf I had grace,
Neuer had I bene brought in this case.
　Pouer. Nowe, syth it wyll no nother be,
Ali that God sendeth, take it in gre ;
For, thoughe you were somtyme a noble estate,
Nowe must you lerne to begge at euery mannes gate.
　Magn. Alasse, that euer I sholde be so shamed !
Alasse, that euer I Magnyfycence was named !
Alasse, that euer I was so harde happed,　　　2010
In mysery and wretchydnesse thus to be lapped !
Alasse, that I coude not myselfe no better gyde !
Alasse, in my cradell that I had not dyde !

Pouer. Ye, syr, ye, leue all this rage,
And pray to God your sorowes to asswage :
It is foly to grudge agaynst his vysytacyon.
With harte contryte make you supplycacyon
Vnto your Maker, that made bothe you and me,
And, whan it pleaseth God, better may be.
 Magn. Alasse, I wote not what I sholde pray!
 Pouer. Rem[e]mbre you better, syr, beware
  what ye say,   2021
For drede ye dysplease the hygh deyte.
Put your wyll to his wyll, for surely it is he
That may restore you agayne to felycyte,
And brynge you agayne out of aduersyte.
Therfore pouerte loke pacyently ye take,
And remembre he suffered moche more for your
  sake,
Howe be it of all synne he was innocent,
And ye haue deserued this punysshment.
 Magn. Alasse, with colde my lymmes shall be
  marde!   2030
 Pouer. Ye, syr, nowe must ye lerne to lye
  harde,
That was wonte to lye on fetherbeddes of
  downe;
Nowe must your fete lye hyer than your
  crowne :
Where you were wonte to haue cawdels for your
  hede,
Nowe must you monche mamockes and lumpes
  of brede;

And where you had chaunges of ryche aray,
Nowe lap you in a couerlet full fayne that you
    may ;
And where that ye were pomped with what that
    ye wolde,
Nowe must ye suffre bothe hunger and colde :
With courtely sylkes ye were wonte to be drawe ;
Nowe must ye lerne to lye on the strawe ;   2041
Your skynne that was wrapped in shertes of
    Raynes,
Nowe must ye be stormy beten[1] with showres
    and raynes ;
Your hede that was wonte to be happed moost
    drowpy and drowsy,
Now shal ye be scabbed, scuruy, and lowsy.
   Magn. Fye on this worlde, full of trechery,
That euer noblenesse sholde lyue thus wretchydly !
   Pouer. Syr, remembre the tourne of Fortunes
    whele,
That wantonly can wynke, and wynche with her
    hele.   2049
Nowe she wyll laughe, forthwith she wyll frowne ;
Sodenly set vp, and sodenly pluckyd downe :
She dawnsyth varyaunce with mutabylyte ;
Nowe all in welth, forthwith in pouerte :
In her promyse there is no sykernesse ;
All her delyte is set in doublenesse.
   Magn. Alas, of Fortune I may well complayne !

---

1 *stormy beten*] Perhaps " storm ybeten."

Pouer. Ye, syr, yesterday wyll not be callyd
 agayne:
But yet, syr, nowe in this case,
Take it mekely, and thanke God of his grace;
For nowe go I wyll begge for you some mete; 2060
It is foly agaynst God for to plete;
I wyll walke nowe with my beggers baggys,
And happe you the whyles with these homly
 raggys.
      Discedendo dicat ista verba.
A, howe my lymmys be lyther and lame!
Better it is to begge than to be hangyd with
 shame;
Yet many had leuer hangyd to be,
Then for to begge theyr mete for charyte:
They thynke it no shame to robbe and stele,
Yet were they better to begge a great dele;
For by robbynge they rynne to *in manus tuas*
 quecke,   2070
But beggynge is better medecyne for the necke;
Ye, mary, is it, ye, so mote I goo:
A Lorde God, howe the gowte wryngeth me by
 the too!

Here MAGNYFYCENCE *dolorously maketh his*
 mone.

Magn. O feble fortune, O doulfull destyny!
O hatefull happe, O carefull cruelte!
O syghynge sorowe, O thoughtfull mysere!
O rydlesse rewthe, O paynfull pouerte!

O dolorous herte, O harde aduersyte!

O odyous dystresse, O dedly payne and woo!   2079

For worldly shame I wax bothe wanne and bloo.

Where is nowe my welth and my noble estate?

Where is nowe my treasure, my landes, and my
    rent?

Where is nowe all my seruauntys that I had here
    a late?

Where is nowe my golde vpon them that I spent?

Where is nowe all my ryche abylement?

Where is nowe my kynne, my frendys, and my
    noble blood?

Where is nowe all my pleasure and my worldly
    good?

Alasse, my foly! alasse, my wanton wyll!

I may no more speke, tyll I haue wept my fyll.

[*Here cometh in* LYBERTE.]

Lyb. With ye, mary, syrs, thus sholde it be.   2090

I kyst her swete, and she kyssyd me;

I daunsed the darlynge on my kne;

I garde her gaspe, I garde her gle,

With, daunce on the le, the le!

I bassed that baby with harte so free;

She is the bote of all my bale:

A, so, that syghe was farre fet!

To loue that louesome I wyll not let;

My harte is holly on her set:

I plucked her by the patlet;   2100

At my deuyse I with her met;

My fansy fayrly on her I set;
So merely syngeth the nyghtyngale!
In lust and lykynge my name is Lyberte:
I am desyred with hyghest and lowest degre;
I lyue as me lyst, I lepe out at large;
Of erthely thynge I haue no care nor charge;
I am presydent of prynces, I prycke them with
      pryde:[1]
What is he lyuynge that lyberte wolde lacke?
A thousande pounde with lyberte may holde no
      tacke;   2110
At lyberte a man may be bolde for to brake;
Welthe without lyberte gothe all to wrake.
But yet, syrs, hardely one thynge lerne of me:
I warne you beware of to moche lyberte,
For *totum in toto* is not worth an hawe;
To hardy, or to moche, to free of the dawe;
To sober, to sad, to subtell, to wyse;
To mery, to mad, to gyglynge, to nyse;
To full of fansyes, to lordly, to prowde;
To homly, to holy, to lewde, and to lowde;   2120
To flatterynge, to smatterynge, to to out of harre,
To claterynge, to chaterynge, to shorte, and to
      farre;
To iettynge, to iaggynge, and to full of iapes;
To mockynge, to mowynge, to lyke a iackenapes:
Thus *totum in toto* groweth vp, as ye may se,
By meanes of madnesse, and to moche lyberte.;

----

[1] *pryde*] Qy. a line wanting to rhyme with this?

For I am a vertue, yf I be well vsed,
And I am a vyce where I am abused.

 Magn. A, woo worthe thé, Lyberte, nowe thou
  sayst full trewe!

That I vsed thé to moche, sore may I rewe.   2130

 Lyb. What, a very vengeaunce, I say, who is
  that?

What brothell, I say, is yonder bounde in a mat?

 Magn. I am Magnyfycence, that somtyme thy
  mayster was.

 Lyb. What, is the worlde thus come to passe?

Cockes armes, syrs, wyll ye not se
Howe he is vndone by the meanes of me?
For yf Measure had ruled Lyberte as he began,
This lurden that here lyeth had ben a noble man.
But he abused so his free lyberte,
That nowe he hath loste all his felycyte,   2140
Not thorowe largesse of lyberall expence,
But by the way of fansy insolence;
For lyberalyte is most conuenyent
A prynce to vse with all his hole intent,
Largely rewardynge them that haue deseruyd,
And so shall a noble man nobly be seruyd:
But nowe adayes as huksters they hucke and they
  stycke,
And pynche at the payment of a poddynge prycke;
A laudable largesse, I tell you, for a lorde,
To prate for the patchynge of a pot sharde!   2150
Spare for the spence of a noble, that his honour
  myght saue,

And spende c. s̃. for the pleasure of a knaue!
But so longe they rekyn with theyr reasons amysse,
That they lose theyr lyberte and all that there is.
Magn. Alasse, that euer I occupyed suche
  abusyon!
Lyb. Ye, for nowe it hath brought thé to con-
  fusyon :
For, where I am occupyed and vsyd wylfully,
It can not contynew longe prosperyously ;
As euydently in retchlesse youth ye may se,   2159
Howe many come to myschefe for to moche lyberte;
And some in the worlde theyr brayne is so ydyll,
That they set theyr chyldren to rynne on the
  brydyll,
In youth to be wanton and let them haue theyr
  wyll ;
And they neuer thryue in theyr age, it shall not
  gretly skyll :
Some fall to foly them selfe for to spyll,
And some fall ¹ prechynge at the Toure Hyll ;
Some hath so moche lyberte of one thynge and
  other,
That nother they set by father and mother ;
Some haue so moche lyberte that they fere no
  synne,
Tyll, as ye se many tymes, they shame all theyr
  kynne.   2170
I am so lusty to loke on, so freshe, and so fre,

   ¹ *fall*] Qy. " fall to ? "

That nonnes wyll leue theyr holynes, and ryn
    after me ;
Freers with foly I make them so fayne,
They cast vp theyr obedyence to cache me agayne,
At lyberte to wander and walke ouer all,
That lustely they lepe somtyme theyr cloyster
    wall.
> *Hic aliquis buccat in cornu a retro*
> *post populum.*

Yonder is a horson for me doth rechate :
Adewe, syrs, for I thynke leyst that I come to late.[1]
   Magn. O good Lorde, howe long shall I indure
This mysery, this carefull wrechydnesse ?   2180
Of worldly welthe, alasse, who can be sure ?
In Fortunys frendshyppe there is no stedfast-
    nesse :
She hath dyssayuyd me with her doublenesse.
For to be wyse all men may lerne of me,
In welthe to beware of herde aduersyte.

  Here cometh in CRAFTY CONUEYAUNCE, [*and*]
    CLOKED COLUSYON, *with a lusty laughter.*
    Cr. Con. Ha, ha, ha ! for laughter I am lyke
      to brast.
    Cl. Col. Ha, ha, ha! for sporte I am lyke to
      spewe and cast.
    Cr. Con. What hast thou gotted in faythe to
      thy share ?

---

[1] *late*] Here *Lyberte* goes out.

Cl. Col. In faythe, of his cofers the bottoms are
  bare.

Cr. Con. As for his plate of syluer, and suche,
  trasshe,   2190

I waraunt you, I haue gyuen it a lasshe.

Cl. Col. What, then he may drynke out of a
  stone cruyse?

Cr. Con. With, ye, syr, by Jesu that slayne
  was with Jewes!

He may rynse a pycher, for his plate is to wed.

Cl. Col. In faythe, and he may dreme on a
  daggeswane for ony fether bed.

Cr. Con. By my trouthe, we haue ryfled hym
  metely well.

Cl. Col. Ye, but thanke me therof euery dele.

Cr. Con. Thanke thé therof, in the deuyls date!

Cl. Col. Leue thy pratynge, or els I shall lay
  thé on the pate.

Cr. Con. Nay, to wrangle, I warant thé, it is
  but a stone caste.   2200

Cl. Col. By the messe, I shall cleue thy heed to
  the waste.

Cr. Con. Ye, wylte thou clenly cleue me in the
  clyfte with thy nose?

Cl. Col. I shall thrust in thé my dagger —

Cr. Con. Thorowe the legge in to the hose.

Cl. Col. Nay, horson, here is my gloue; take
  it vp, and thou dare.

Cr. Con. Torde, thou arte good to be a man
  of warre.

Cl. Col. I shall skelpe thé on the skalpe ; lo,
　　seest thou that?

Cr. Con. What, wylte thou skelpe me? thou
　　dare not loke on a gnat.

Cl. Col. By Cockes bones, I shall blysse thé,
　　and thou be to bolde.

Cr. Con. Nay, then thou wylte dynge the
　　deuyll, and thou be not holde.　　　2210

Cl. Col. But wottest thou, horson? I rede thé
　　to be wyse.

Cr. Con. Nowe I rede thé beware, I haue
　　warned thé twyse.

Cl. Col. Why, wenest thou that I forbere thé
　　for thyne owne sake?

Cr. Con. Peas, or I shall wrynge thy be in a
　　brake.

Cl. Col. Holde thy hande, dawe, of thy dagger,
　　and stynt of thy dyn,

Or I shal fawchyn thy flesshe, and scrape thé on
　　the skyn.

Cr. Con. Ye, wylte thou, ha[n]gman? I say,
　　thou cauell!

Cl. Col. Nay, thou rude rauener, rayne beten
　　iauell!

Cr. Con. What, thou Colyn cowarde, knowen
　　and tryde!

Cl. Col. Nay, thou false harted dastarde, thou
　　dare not abyde!　　　2220

Cr. Con. And yf there were none to dysplease
　　but thou and I,

Thou sholde not scape, horson, but thou sholde
    dye.
Cl. Col. Nay, iche shall wrynge thé, horson,
    on the wryst.
Cr. Con. Mary, I defye thy best and thy worst.

[*Here cometh in* COUNTERFET COUNTENAUNCE.[1]]
  C. Count. What, a very vengeaunce, nede all
    these wordys?
Go together by the heddys, and gyue me your
    swordys.
  Cl. Col. So he is the worste brawler that euer
    was borne.
  Cr. Con. In fayth, so to suffer thé, it is but a
    skorne.
  C. Count. Now let vs be all one, and let vs
    lyue in rest,
For we be, syrs, but a fewe of the best.   2230
  Cl. Col. By the masse, man, thou shall fynde
    me resonable.
  Cr. Con. In faythe, and I wyll be to reason
    agreable.
  C. Count. Then truste I to God and the holy
    rode,
Here shalbe not great sheddynge of blode.
  Cl. Col. By our lakyn, syr, not by my wyll.
  Cr. Con. By the fayth that I owe to God, and
    I wyll syt styll.

1 *Here cometh, &c.*] Ed., besides omitting this stage-direc-
tion, leaves the two following lines unappropriated.

C. Count. Well sayd: but, in fayth, what was
    your quarell?

Cl. Col. Mary, syr, this gentylman called me
    iauell.

Cr. Con. Nay, by Saynt Mary, it was ye called
    me knaue.

Cl. Col. Mary, so vngoodly langage you me
    gaue.   2240

C. Count. A, shall we haue more of this maters
    yet?

Me thynke ye are not gretly acomberyd with wyt.

Cr. Con. Goddys fote, I warant you, I am a
    gentylman borne,

And thus to be facyd I thynke it great skorne.

C. Count. I can not well tell of your dysposy-
    cyons;

And ye be a gentylman, ye haue knauys condy-
    cyons.

Cl. Col. By God, I tell you, I wyll not be out
    facyd.

Cr. Con. By the masse, I warant thé, I wyll
    not be bracyd.

C. Count. Tushe, tushe, it is a great defaute:

The one of you is to proude, the other is to haute.

Tell me brefly where vpon ye began.   2251

Cl. Col. Mary, syr, he sayd that he was the
    pratyer man

Then I was, in opynynge of lockys;

And, I tell you, I dysdayne moche of his mockys.

Cr. Con. Thou sawe neuer yet but I dyd my
    parte,

The locke of a caskyt to make to starte.

   C. Count. Nay, I know well inough ye are
      bothe well handyd

To grope a gardeuyaunce, though it be well
      bandyd.

   Cl. Col. I am the better yet in a bowget.

   Cr. Con. And I the better in a male.   2260

   C. Count. Tushe, these maters that ye moue
      are but soppys in ale:

Your trymynge and tramynge by me must be
      tangyd,

For, had I not bene, ye bothe had bene hangyd,

When we with Magnyfycence goodys made cheuy-
      saunce.

   Magn. And therfore our Lorde sende you a
      very wengaunce!

   C. Count. What begger art thou that thus doth
      banne and wary?

   Magn. Ye be the theuys, I say, away my
      goodys dyd cary.

   Cl. Col. Cockys bonys, thou begger, what is
      thy name?

   Magn. Magnyfycence I was, whom ye haue
      brought to shame.

   C. Count. Ye, but trowe you, syrs, that this is
      he?   2270

   Cr. Con. Go we nere, and let vs se.

   Cl. Col. By Cockys bonys, it is the same.

   Magn. Alasse, alasse, syrs, ye are to blame!

I was your mayster, though ye thynke it skorne,

And nowe on me ye gaure and sporne.

    C. Count. Ly styll, ly styll nowe, with yll
       hayle!

    Cr. Con. Ye, for thy langage can not thé auayle.

    Cl. Col. Abyde, syr, abyde, I shall make hym
       to pysse.[1]

    Magn. Nowe gyue me somwhat, for God sake
       I craue!

    Cr. Con. In faythe, I gyue thé four quarters
       of a knaue.   2280

    C. Count. In faythe, and I bequethe hym the
       tothe ake.

    Cl. Col. And I bequethe hym the bone ake.

    Cr. Con. And I bequethe hym the gowte and
       the gyn.

    Cl. Col. And I bequethe hym sorowe for his
       syn.

    C. Count. And I gyue hym Crystys curse,
With neuer a peny in his purse.

    Cr. Con. And I gyue hym the cowghe, the
       murre, and the pose.

    Cl. Col. Ye, for *requiem æternam* groweth forth
       of his nose:
But nowe let vs make mery and good chere.

    C. Count. And to the tauerne let vs drawe
       nere.   2290

    Cr. Con. And from thens to the halfe strete,
To get vs there some freshe mete.

---

[1] *pysse*] Qy. a line wanting to rhyme with this?

Cl. Col. Why, is there any store of rawe
    motton?
C. Count. Ye, in faythe, or ellys thou arte to
    great a glotton.
Cr. Con. But they say it is a queysy mete;
It wyll stryke a man myscheuously in a hete.
Cl. Col. In fay, man, some rybbys of the mot-
    ton be so ranké,
That they wyll fyre one vngracyously in the
    flanke.
C. Count. Ye, and when ye come out of the
    shoppe,
Ye shall be clappyd with a coloppe,   2300
That wyll make you to halt and to hoppe.
Cr. Con. Som be wrestyd there that they
    thynke on it froty dayes,
For there be horys there at all assayes.
Cl. Col. For the passyon of God let vs go
    thyther![1]
        Et cum festinatione discedant a loco.
Magn. Alas, myne owne seruauntys to shew me
    such reproche,
Thus to rebuke me, and haue me in dyspyght!
So shamfully to me theyr mayster to aproche,
That somtyme was a noble prynce of myght!
Alasse, to lyue longer I haue no delyght!
For to lyue in mysery it is herder than dethe: 2310

---

[1] *thyther*] Qy. a line wanting to rhyme with this?

I am wery of the worlde, for vnkyndnesse me
    sleeth.

Hic intrat DYSPARE.

Dys. Dyspare is my name, that aduersyte doth
    folowe :
In tyme of dystresse I am redy at hande ;
I make heuy hertys with eyen full holowe ;
Of faruent charyte I quenche out the bronde ;
Faythe and goodhope I make asyde to stonde ;
In Goddys mercy I tell them is but foly to truste ;
All grace and pyte I lay in the duste.
What lyest thou there lyngrynge, lewdly and
    lothsome ?
It is to late nowe thy synnys to repent ;   2320
Thou hast bene so waywarde, so wranglyng, and
    so wrothsome,
And so fer thou arte behynde of thy rent,
And so vngracyously thy dayes thou hast spent,
That thou arte not worthy to loke God in the face.
    Magn. Nay, nay, man, I loke neuer to haue
        parte of his grace ;
For I haue so vngracyously my lyfe mysusyd,
Though I aske mercy, I must nedys be refusyd.
    Dys. No, no, for thy synnys be so excedynge
        farre,
So innumerable and so full of dyspyte,
And agayne thy Maker thou hast made suche
    warre,   2330
That thou canst not haue neuer mercy in hys syght.

Magn. Alasse, my wyckydnesse, that may I
 wyte!
But nowe I se well there is no better rede,
But sygh and sorowe, and wysshe my selfe
 dede.
Dys. Ye, ryd thy selfe, rather than this lyfe for
 to lede ;
The worlde waxyth wery of thé, thou lyuest to
 longe.

   Hic intrat MYSCHEFE.

Mys. And I, Myschefe, am comyn at nede,
Out of thy lyfe thé for to lede :
And loke that it be not longe
Or that thy selfe thou go honge   2340
With this halter good and stronge ;
Or ellys with this knyfe cut out a tonge
Of thy throte bole, and ryd thé out of payne :
Thou arte not the fyrst hymselfe hath slayne.
Lo, here is thy knyfe and a halter ! and, or we go
 ferther,
Spare not thy selfe, but boldly thé murder.
Dys. Ye, haue done at ones without delay.
Magn. Shall I myself hange with an halter ?
 nay ;
Nay, rather wyll I chose to ryd me of this
 lyue
In styckynge my selfe with this fayre knyfe.   2350
 Here MAGNYFYCENCE *wolde slee hymselfe*
  with a knyfe.

Mys.[1] Alarum, alarum! to longe we abyde!

Dys. Out, harowe, hyll burneth! where shall I
     me hyde?

Hic intrat GOODHOPE, *fugientibus* DYSPAYRE *et*
MYSCHEFE: *repente* GOODHOPE *surripiat illi*
gladium, et dicat.

Good. Alas, dere sone, sore combred is thy
     mynde,
Thyselfe that thou wolde sloo agaynst nature and
     kynde!

Magn. A, blessyd may ye be, syr! what shall
     I you call?

Good. Goodhope, syr, my name is; remedy
     pryncypall
Agaynst all sautes of your goostly foo:
Who knoweth me, hymselfe may neuer sloo.

Magn. Alas, syr, so I am lapped in aduersyte,
That dyspayre well nyghe had myscheued me! 2360
For, had ye not the soner ben my refuge,
Of dampnacyon I had ben drawen in the luge.

Good. Vndoubted ye had lost yourselfe eter-
     nally:
There is no man may synne more mortally
Than of wanhope thrughe the vnhappy wayes,
By myschefe to breuyate and shorten his dayes:
But, my good sonne, lerne from dyspayre to
     flee,

---

[1] *Mys.*] Ed. "*Magn.*"

Wynde you from wanhope, and aquaynte you
    with me.
A grete mysaduenture, thy Maker to dysplease,
Thyselfe myscheuynge to thyne endlesse dysease!
There was neuer so harde a storme of mysery, 2371
But thrughe goodhope there may come remedy.
  Magn. Your wordes be more sweter than ony
    precyous narde,
They molefy so easely my harte that was so
    harde;
There is no bawme, ne gumme of Arabe,
More delectable than your langage to me.
  Good. Syr, your fesycyan is the grace of God,
That you hath punysshed with his sharpe rod.
Goodhope, your potecary assygned am I:
That Goddes grace hath vexed you sharply, 2380
And payned you with a purgacyon of odyous
    pouerte,
Myxed with bytter alowes of herde aduersyte;
Nowe must I make you a lectuary softe,
I to mynyster it, you to receyue it ofte,
With rubarbe of repentaunce in you for to rest;
With drammes of deuocyon your dyet must be
    drest;
With gommes goostly of glad herte and mynde,
To thanke God of his sonde, and comforte ye shal
    fynde.
Put fro you presumpcyon and admyt humylyte,
And hartely thanke God of your aduersyte; 2390
And loue that Lorde that for your loue was dede,
  VOL. II.   8

Wounded from the fote to the crowne of the
    hede :
For who loueth God can ayle nothynge but good;
He may helpe you, he may mende your mode :
Prosperyte to [1] hym is gyuen solacyusly to man,
Aduersyte to hym therwith nowe and than ;
Helthe of body his besynesse to acheue,
Dysease and sekenesse his conscyence to dys-
    cryue,
Afflyccyon and trouble to proue his pacyence,
Contradyccyon to proue his sapyence,   2400
Grace of assystence his measure to declare,
Somtyme to fall, another tyme to beware :
And nowe ye haue had, syr, a wonderous fall,
To lerne you hereafter for to beware withall.
Howe say you, syr? can ye these wordys
    grope?
   Magn. Ye, syr, nowe am I armyd with good-
    hope,
And sore I repent me of my wylfulnesse :
I aske God mercy of my neglygence,[2]
Vnder goodhope endurynge euer styll,
Me humbly commyttynge vnto Goddys wyll.   2410
   Good. Then shall you be sone delyuered from
    dystresse,
For nowe I se comynge to youwarde Redresse.

---

  1 *to*] Qy. " by? "
  2 *neglygence*] Qy., did Skelton write, for the rhyme, " neg-
lygesse ? "

Hic intrat REDRESSE.

Red. Cryst be amonge you and the Holy
    Goste!

Good. He be your conducte, the Lorde of
    myghtys moste!

Red. Syr, is your pacyent any thynge a-
    mendyd?

Good. Ye, syr, he is sory for that he hath
    offendyd.

Red. How fele you your selfe, my frend? how
    is your mynde?

Magn. A wrechyd man, syr, to my Maker
    vnkynde.

Red. Ye, but haue ye repentyd you with harte
    contryte?

Magn. Syr, the repentaunce I haue, no man
    can wryte.   2420

Red. And haue ye banyshed from you all
    dyspare?

Magn. Ye, holly to goodhope I haue made my
    repare.

Good. Questyonlesse he doth me assure
In goodhope alway for to indure.

Red. Than stande vp, syr, in Goddys name!
And I truste to ratyfye and amende your fame.
Goodhope, I pray you with harty affeccyon
To sende ouer to me Sad Cyrcumspeccyon.

Good. Syr, your requeste shall not be delayed.

                  Et exeat.

Red. Now surely, Magnyfycence, I am ryght
    well apayed   2430
Of that I se you nowe in the state of grace;
Nowe shall ye be renewyd with solace :
Take nowe vpon you this abylyment,
And to that I say gyue good aduysement.
        MAGNYFYCENCE *accipiat indumentum.*
Magn. To your requeste I shall be confyrm-
    able.
Red. Fyrst,[1] I saye, with mynde fyrme and
    stable
Determyne to amende all your wanton excesse,
And be ruled by me, whiche am called Redresse :
Redresse my name is, that lytell am I vsed
As the worlde requyreth, but rather I am re-
    fused :   2440
Redresse sholde be at the rekenynge in euery
    accompte,
And specyally to redresse that were out of ioynte :
Full many thynges there be that lacketh redresse,
The whiche were to longe nowe to expresse ;
But redresse is redlesse, and may do no correc-
    cyon.
Nowe welcome forsoth, Sad Cyrcumspeccyon.

Here cometh in SAD CYRCUMSPECCYON, *sayenge,*
    Sad Cyr. Syr, after your message I hyed me
      hyder streyght,

---

[1] *Fyrst, &c.*] Ed. leaves this speech unappropriated.

For to vnderstande your pleasure and also your
    mynde.

Red. Syr, to accompte you the contynewe of
    my consayte,

Is from aduersyte Magnyfycence to vnbynde. 2450

Sad Cyr. How fortuned you, Magnyfycence,
    so far to fal behynde?

Magn. Syr, the longe absence of you, Sad Cyr-
    cumspeceyon,

Caused me of aduersyte to fall in subieccyon.

Red. All that he sayth, of trouthe doth pro-
    cede;

For where sad cyrcumspeccyon is longe out of
    the way,

Of aduersyte it is to stande in drede.

Sad Cyr. Without fayle, syr, that is no nay ;

Cyrcumspeccyon inhateth all rennynge astray.

But, syr, by me to rule fyrst ye began. 2459

Magn. My wylfulnesse, syr, excuse I ne can.

Sad Cyr. Then ye repent you of foly in tymes
    past?

Magn. Sothely, to repent me I haue grete
    cause :

Howe be it from you I receyued a letter,[1]

Whiche conteyned in it a specyall clause

That I sholde vse largesse.

Sad Cyr. Nay, syr, there a pause.

---

[1] *a letter*] Qy. some corruption? This line ought to rhyme
with the preceding line but one.

Red. Yet let vs se this matter thorowly in-
grossed.

Magn. Syr, this letter ye sent to me, at Pountes
was enclosed.

Sad Cyr. Who brought you that letter, wote
ye what he hyght?

Magn. Largesse, syr, by his credence was his
name.   2470

Sad Cyr. This letter ye speke of, neuer dyd I
wryte.

Red. To gyue so hasty credence ye were moche
to blame.

Magn. Truth it is, syr; for after he wrought
me moch shame,

And caused me also to vse to moche lyberte,

And made also mesure to be put fro me.

Red. Then welthe with you myght in no wyse
abyde.

Sad Cyr. A ha! fansy and foly met with you,
I trowe.

Red. It wolde be founde so, yf it were well
tryde.

Magn. Surely my welthe with them was ouer-
throw.

Sad Cyr. Remembre you, therfore, howe late
ye were low.   2480

Red. Ye, and beware of vnhappy abusyon.

Sad Cyr. And kepe you from counterfaytynge
of clokyd colusyon.

Magn. Syr, in goodhope I am to amende.

Red. Vse not then your countenaunce for to
counterfet.

Sad Cyr. And from crafters and hafters I you
forfende.

Hic intrat PERSEUERAUNCE.

Magn. Well, syr, after your counsell my mynde
I wyll set.

Red. What, brother Perceueraunce! surely
well met.

Sad Cyr. Ye com hether as well as can be
thought.

Per. I herde say that Aduersyte with Magny-
fycence had fought.

Magn. Ye, syr, with aduersyte I haue bene
vexyd;   2490
But goodhope and redresse hath mendyd myne
estate,
And sad cyrcumspeccyon to me they haue
annexyd.

Red. What this man hath sayd, perceyue ye
his sentence? [1]

Magn. Ye, syr, from hym my corage shall
neuer flyt.

Sad Cyr. Accordynge to treuth they be well
deuysyd.

Magn. Syrs, I am agreed to abyde your orde-
naunce,

---

[1] *sentence*] Qy. some corruption? This line ought to rhyme
with the preceding line but one. [Qy. " consayte? " C.]

Faythfull assuraunce with good peraduertaunce.

Per. Yf you be so myndyd, we be ryght glad.

Red. And ye shall haue more worshyp then
euer ye had.

Magn. Well, I perceyue in you there is moche
sadnesse,   2500

Grauyte of counsell, prouydence, and wyt;

Your comfortable aduyse and wyt excedyth all
gladnesse.

But frendly I wyll refrayne you ferther, or we
flyt,

Whereto were most metely my corage to knyt:

Your myndys I beseche you here in to expresse,

Commensynge this processe at mayster Redresse.

Red. Syth vnto me formest this processe is
erectyd,

Herein I wyll aforse me to shewe you my mynde.

Fyrst, from your magnyfycence syn must be
abiectyd,

In all your warkys more grace shall ye fynde; 2510

Be gentyll then of corage, and lerne to be kynde,

For of noblenesse the chefe poynt is to be lyberall,

So that your largesse be not to prodygall.

Sad Cyr. Lyberte to a lorde belongyth of
ryght,

But wylfull waywardnesse muste walke out of the
way;

Measure of your lustys must haue the ouersyght,

And not all the nygarde nor the chyncherde to
play;

Let neuer negarshyp your noblenesse affray;
In your rewardys vse suche moderacyon   2519
That nothynge be gyuen without consyderacyon.
    Per. To the increse of your honour then arme
        you with ryght,
And fumously adresse you with magnanymyte;
And euer let the drede of God be in your syght;
And knowe your selfe mortall, for all your dyg-
        nyte;
Set not all your affyaunce in Fortune full of gyle;
Remember this lyfe lastyth but a whyle.
    Magn. Redresse, in my remembraunce your
        lesson shall rest,
And Sad Cyrcumspeccyon I marke in my mynde;
But, Perseueraunce, me semyth your probleme
      was best;
I shall it neuer forget nor leue it behynde,   2530
But hooly to perseueraunce my selfe I wyll bynde,
Of that I haue mysdone to make a redresse,
And with sad cyrcumspeccyon correcte my van-
        tonnesse.
    Red. Vnto this processe brefly compylyd,
Comprehendyng the worlde casuall and transytory,
Who lyst to consyder shall neuer be begylyd,
Yf it be regystryd well in memory;
A playne example of worldly vaynglory,
Howe in this wcrlde there is no seke[r]nesse,   2539
But fallyble flatery enmyxyd with bytternesse;
Nowe well, nowe wo, nowe hy, nowe lawe degre,
Nowe ryche, nowe pore, nowe hole, nowe in
        dysease,

Nowe pleasure at large, nowe in captyuyte,
Nowe leue, nowe lothe, now please, nowe dys-
 please,
Now ebbe, now flowe, nowe increase, now dys-
 crease ;
So in this worlde there is no sykernesse,
But fallyble flatery enmyxyd with bytternesse.

Sad Cyr. A myrrour incleryd is this interlude,
This lyfe inconstant for to beholde and se ;
Sodenly auaunsyd, and sodenly subdude,   2550
Sodenly ryches, and sodenly pouerte,
Sodenly comfort, and sodenly aduersyte ;
Sodenly thus Fortune can bothe smyle and frowne,
Sodenly set vp, and sodenly cast downe ;
Sodenly promotyd, and sodenly put backe,
Sodenly cherysshyd, and sodenly cast asyde,
Sodenly commendyd, and sodenly fynde a lacke,
Sodenly grauntyd, and sodenly denyed,
Sodenly hyd, and sodenly spyed ;
Sodenly thus Fortune can bothe smyle and frowne,
Sodenly set vp, and sodenly cast downe.   2561

Per. This treatyse, deuysyd to make you dys-
 porte,
Shewyth nowe adayes howe the worlde com-
 beryd is,
To the pythe of the mater who lyst to resorte ;
To day it is well, to morowe it is all amysse,
To day in delyte, to morowe bare of blysse,
To day a lorde, to morowe ly in the duste ;
Thus in this worlde there is no erthly truste ;

To day fayre wether, to morowe a stormy rage,
To day hote, to morowe outragyous colde,   2570
To day a yoman, to morowe made of page,
To day in surety, to morowe bought and solde,
To day maysterfest, to morowe he hath no holde,
To day a man, to morowe he lyeth in the duste;
Thus in this worlde there is no erthly truste.

Magn. This mater we haue mouyd, you myrthys
  to make,
Precely purposyd vnder pretence of play,
Shewyth wysdome to them that wysdome can
  take,
Howe sodenly worldly welth dothe dekay,
How wysdom thorowe wantonnesse vanysshyth
  away,   2580
How none estate lyuynge of hymselfe can be sure,
For the welthe of this worlde can not indure ;
Of the terestre rechery we fall in the flode,
Beten with stormys of many a frowarde blast,
Ensordyd with the wawys sauage and wode,
Without our shyppe be sure, it is lykely to brast,
Yet of magnyfycence oft made is the mast ;
Thus none estate lyuynge of hym can be sure,
For the welthe of this worlde can not indure. ✓

Red. Nowe semeth vs syttynge that ye then
  resorte   2590
Home to your paleys with ioy and ryalte.

Sad Cyr. Where euery thyng is ordenyd after
  your noble porte.

Per. There to indeuer with all felycyte.

Magn. I am content, my frendys, that it so be.
Red. And ye that haue harde this dysporte
and game,
Jhesus preserue you frome endlesse wo and
shame!

Amen.

COLYN CLOUTE.*

HERE AFTER FOLOWETH A LITEL BOKE CALLED COLYN
CLOUTE, COMPYLED BY MAYSTER SKELTON, POETE
LAUREATE.

Quis consurget mecum adversus malignantes?
aut quis stabit mecum adversus operantes iniqui-
tatem? Nemo, Domine!

WHAT can it auayle
To dryue forth a snayle,
Or to make a sayle
Of an herynges tayle ;
To ryme or to rayle,
To wryte or to indyte,
Eyther for delyte
Or elles for despyte ;
Or bokes to compyle
Of dyuers maner style,   10
Vyce to reuyle
And synne to exyle ;
To teche or to preche,
As reason wyll reche ?

* From the ed. by Kele, n. d., collated with the ed. by
Kytson, n. d., with Marshe's ed. of Skelton's *Workes*, 1568,
and with a MS. in the Harleian Collection, 2252. fol. 147.

Say this, and say that,
His hed is so fat,
He wotteth neuer what
Nor wherof he speketh ;
He cryeth and he creketh,
He pryeth and he peketh,   20
He chydes and he chatters,
He prates and he patters,
He clytters and he clatters,
He medles and he smatters,
He gloses and he flatters ;
Or yf he speake playne,
Than he lacketh brayne,
He is but a fole ;
Let hym go to scole,
On a thre foted stole   30
That he may downe syt,
For he lacketh wyt ;
And yf that he hyt
The nayle on the hede,
It standeth in no stede ;
The deuyll, they say, is dede,
The deuell is dede.
    It may well so be,
Or els they wolde se
Otherwyse, and fle   40
From worldly vanyte,
And foule couetousnesse,
And other wretchednesse,
Fyckell falsenesse,

Varyablenesse,
With vnstablenesse.
And if ye stande in doubte
Who brought this ryme aboute,
My name is Colyn Cloute.
I purpose to shake oute   50
All my connyng bagge,
Lyke a clerkely hagge ;
For though my ryme be ragged,
Tattered and iagged,
Rudely rayne beaten,
Rusty and moughte eaten,
If ye take well therwith,
It hath in it some pyth.
For, as farre as I can se,
It is wronge with eche degre :   60
For the temporalte
Accuseth the spiritualte ;
The spirituall agayne
Dothe grudge and complayne
Vpon the temporall men :
Thus eche of other blother
The tone agayng the tother :
Alas, they make me shoder !
For in hoder moder
The Churche is put in faute ;   70
The prelates ben so haut,
They say, and loke so hy,
As though they wolde fly
Aboue the sterry skye.

Laye men say indede
How they take no hede
Theyr sely shepe to fede,
But plucke away and pull
The fleces of theyr wull,
Vnethes they leue a locke   80
Of wull amonges theyr flocke ;
And as for theyr connynge,
A glommynge and a mummynge,
And make therof a iape ;
They gaspe and they gape
All to haue promocyon,
There is theyr hole deuocyon,
With money, if it wyll hap,
To catche the forked cap :
Forsothe they are to lewd   90
To say so, all beshrewd !
    What trow ye they say more
Of the bysshoppes lore ?
How in matters they be rawe,
They lumber forth the lawe,
To herken Jacke and Gyll,
Whan they put vp a byll,
And iudge it as they wyll,
For other mennes skyll,
Expoundyng out theyr clauses,   100
And leue theyr owne causes :
In theyr prouynciall cure
They make but lytell sure,
And meddels very lyght
In the Churches ryght ;

But *ire* and *venire*,
And selfa so alamyre,
That the premenyre
Is lyke to be set a fyre
In theyr iurisdictions   110
Through temporall afflictions :
Men say they haue prescriptions
Agaynst spirituall contradictions,
Accomptynge them as fyctions.
And whyles the heedes do this,
The remenaunt is amys
Of the clergy all,
Bothe great and small.
I wot neuer how they warke,
But thus the people barke ;[1]   120
And surely thus they say,
Bysshoppes, if they may,
Small houses wolde kepe,
But slumbre forth and slepe,
And assay to crepe
Within the noble walles
Of the kynges halles,
To fat theyr bodyes full,
Theyr soules lene and dull,
And haue full lytell care   130
How euyll theyr shepe fare.
  The temporalyte say playne,
Howe bysshoppes dysdayne
Sermons for to make,

[1] *barke*] So MS. Eds. " carke." Qy. " carpe ? " Compare
v. 540.

Or suche laboure to take;
And for to say trouth,
A great parte is for slouth,
But the greattest parte
Is for they haue but small arte
And ryght sklender connyng   140
Within theyr heedes wonnyng.
But this reason they take '
How they are able to make
With theyr golde and treasure
Clerkes out of measure,
And yet that is a pleasure.
Howe be it some there be,
Almost two or thre,
Of that dygnyte,
Full worshypfull clerkes,   150
As appereth by theyr werkes,
Lyke Aaron and Ure,
The wolfe from the dore
To werryn and to kepe
From theyr goostly shepe,
And theyr spirituall lammes
Sequestred from rammes
And from the berded gotes
With theyr heery cotes;
Set nought by golde ne grotes,   160
Theyr names if I durst tell.
    But they are loth to mell,
And loth to hang the bell
Aboute the cattes necke,
For drede to haue a checke;

They ar fayne to play deuz decke,
They ar made for the becke.
How be it they are good men,
Moche herted lyke an hen :
Theyr lessons forgotten they haue   176
That Becket them gaue :
Thomas *manum mittit ad fortia,*
Spernit damna, spernit opprobria,
Nulla Thomam frangit injuria.
But nowe euery spirituall father,
Men say, they had rather
Spende moche of theyr share
Than to be combred with care :
Spende! nay, nay, but spare ;
For let se who that dare   180
Sho the mockysshe mare ;
They make her wynche and keke,
But it is not worth a leke :
Boldnesse is to seke
The Churche for to defend.
Take me as I intende,   {
For lothe I am to offende
In this that I haue pende :
I tell you as men say ;
Amende whan ye may,   190
For, *usque ad montem Sare,*[1]
Men say ye can not appare ;
For some say ye hunte in parkes,
And hauke on hobby larkes,
And other wanton warkes,

[1] *Sare*] Other eds. "fare." MS. "sciire." (Perhaps Skel-
ton wrote "Seir"—and in the next line "appeire."

Whan the nyght darkes.
　What hath lay men to do
The gray gose for to sho?
Lyke houndes of hell,
They crye and they yell,　　　　　　200
Howe that ye sell
The grace of the Holy Gost:
Thus they make theyr bost
Through owte euery cost,
Howe some of you do eate
In Lenton season fleshe mete,
Fesauntes, partryche, and cranes;
Men call you therfor prophanes;
Ye pycke no shrympes nor pranes,
Saltfysshe, stocfysshe, nor heryng,　　210
It is not for your werynge;
Nor in holy Lenton season
Ye wyll netheyr benes ne peason,
But ye loke to be let lose
To a pygge or to a gose,
Your gorge not endewed
Without a capon stewed,
Or a stewed cocke,
To knowe whate ys a clocke
Vnder her surfled smocke,　　　　　　220
And her wanton wodicocke.
　And howe whan ye gyue orders
In your prouinciall borders,
As at *Sitientes,*
Some are *insufficientes,*
Some *parum sapientes,*

Some *nihil intelligentes,*
Some *valde negligentes,*
Some *nullum sensum habentes,*
But bestiall and vntaught;   230
But whan thei haue ones caught
Dominus vobiscum by the hede,
Than renne they in euery stede,
God wot, with dronken nolles;
Yet take they cure of soules,
And woteth neuer what thei rede,
Paternoster, Ave, nor Crede;
Construe not worth a whystle
Nether Gospell nor Pystle;
Theyr mattyns madly sayde,   240
Nothynge deuoutly prayde;
Theyr lernynge is so small,
Theyr prymes and houres fall
And lepe out of theyr lyppes
Lyke sawdust or drye chyppes.
I speke not nowe of all,
But the moost parte in generall.
Of suche vagabundus
Speketh *totus mundus;*
Howe some synge *Lætabundus*   250
At euery ale stake,
With, welcome hake and make!
By the brede that God brake,
I am sory for your sake.
I speke not of the good wyfe,
But of theyr apostles lyfe;

Cum ipsis vel illis
Qui manent in villis
Est uxor vel ancilla,
Welcome Jacke and Gylla!   260
My prety Petronylla,
And you wyll be stylla,
You shall haue your wylla.
Of suche Paternoster pekes
All the worlde spekes.

In you the faute is supposed,
For that they are not apposed
By iust examinacyon
In connyng and conuersacyon ;
They haue none instructyon   270
To make a true constructyon :
A preest without a letter,
Without his vertue be gretter,
Doutlesse were moche better
Vpon hym for to take
A mattocke or a rake.
Alas, for very shame !
Some can not declyne their name ;
Some can not scarsly rede,
And yet he wyll not drede   280
For to kepe a cure,
And in nothyng is sure ;
This *Dominus vobiscum,*
As wyse as Tom a thrum,
A chaplayne of trust
Layth all in the dust.

Thus I, Colyn Cloute,
As I go aboute,
And wandrynge as I walke,
I here the people talke.   290
Men say, for syluer and golde
Myters are bought and solde ;
There shall no clergy appose
A myter nor a crose,
But a full purse :
A strawe for Goddes curse !
What are they the worse ?
For a symonyake
Is but a hermoniake ;
And no more ye make   300
Of symony, men say,
But a chyldes play.
    Ouer this, the foresayd laye
Reporte howe the Pope may
An holy anker call
Out of the stony wall,
And hym a bysshopp make,
If he on hym dare take
To kepe so harde a rule,
To ryde vpon a mule   310
With golde all betrapped,
In purple and paule belapped ;
Some hatted and some capped,
Rychely and warme bewrapped,
God wot to theyr great paynes,
In rotchettes of fyne Raynes,

Whyte as morowes mylke ;
Theyr tabertes of fyne silke,
Theyr styrops of myxt gold begared ;
There may no cost be spared ;   320
Theyr moyles golde dothe eate,
Theyr neyghbours dye for meate.
    What care they though Gil sweate,
Or Jacke of the Noke?
The pore people they yoke
With sommons and citacyons
And excommunycacyons,
About churches and market :
The bysshop on his carpet
At home full softe dothe syt.   330
This is a farly fyt,
To here the people iangle,
Howe warely they wrangle :
Alas, why do ye not handle
And them all to-mangle?
Full falsely on you they lye,
And shamefully you ascrye,
And say as vntruely,
As the butterflye
A man myght saye in mocke   340
Ware the[1]wethercocke
Of the steple of Poules ;
And thus they hurte theyr soules
In sclaunderyng you for truthe :
Alas, it is great ruthe !
Some say ye syt in trones,
                1 MS. " Wasa."

Lyke prynces *aquilonis*,
And shryne your rotten bones
With perles and precyous stones ;
But how the commons grones,   355
And the people mones
For prestes and for lones
Lent and neuer payd,
But frcm day to day delayoe,
The commune welth decayde,
Men say ye are tonge tayde,
And therof speke nothynge
But dyssymulyng and glosyng.
Wherfore men be supposyng
That ye gyue shrewd counsell   360
Agaynst the commune well,
By poollynge and pyllage
In cytyes and vyllage,
By taxyng and tollage,
Ye make monkes to haue the culerage
For couerynge of an olde cottage,
That commytted is a collage
In the charter of dottage,
Tenure par seruyce de sottage,
And not *par seruyce de socage*,   370
After olde seygnyours,
And the lerning of Lytelton tenours :
Ye haue so ouerthwarted,
That good lawes are subuerted,
And good reason peruerted.
    Relygous men are fayne
For to tourne agayne

In secula seculorum,
And to forsake theyr corum,
And *vagabundare per forum,*   380
And take a fyne *meritorum,*
Contra regulam morum,
Aut blacke *monachorum,*
Aut canonicorum,
Aut Bernardinorum,
Aut crucifixorum,
And to synge from place to place,
Lyke apostataas.

And the selfe same game
Begone ys nowe with shame   390
Amongest the sely nonnes :
My lady nowe she ronnes,
Dame Sybly our abbesse,
Dame Dorothe and lady Besse,
Dame Sare our pryoresse,
Out of theyr cloyster and quere
With an heuy chere,
Must cast vp theyr blacke vayles,
And set vp theyr fucke sayles,
To catch wynde with their ventales—   400
What, Colyne, there thou shales !
Yet thus with yll hayles
The lay fee people rayles.

And all the fawte they lay
On you, prelates, and say
Ye do them wrong and no ryght
To put them thus to flyght;

No matyns at mydnyght,
Boke and chalys gone quyte;
And plucke awaye the leedes   410
Evyn ouer theyr heedes,
And sell away theyr belles,
And all that they haue elles:
Thus the people telles,
Rayles lyke rebelles,
Redys shrewdly and spelles,
And with foundacyons melles,
And talkys lyke tytyuelles,
Howe ye brake the dedes wylles,
Turne monasteris into water milles,   420
Of an abbay ye make a graunge;
Your workes, they saye, are straunge;
So that theyr founders soules
Haue lost theyr beade rolles,
The mony for theyr masses
Spent amonge wanton lasses;
The *Diriges* are forgotten;
Theyr founders lye theyr rotten,
But where theyr soules dwell,
Therwith I wyll not mell.   430
What coulde the Turke do more
With all his false lore,
Turke, Sarazyn, or Jew?
I reporte me to you,
O mercyfull Jesu,
You supporte and rescue,.
My style for to dyrecte,

It may take some effecte!
For I abhorre to wryte
Howe the lay fee dyspyte   440
You prelates, that of ryght
Shulde be lanternes of lyght.
Ye lyue, they say, in delyte,
Drowned *in deliciis*,
In gloria et divitiis,
In admirabili honore,
In gloria, et splendore
Fulgurantis hastæ,
Viventes parum caste:
Yet swete meate hath soure sauce,   450
For after *gloria, laus,*
Chryst by cruelte
Was nayled vpon a tre;
He payed a bytter pencyon
For mannes redemcyon,
He dranke eysell and gall
To redeme vs withall;
But swete ypocras ye drynke,
With, Let the cat wynke!
Iche wot what yche other thynk;   460
Howe be it *per assimile*
Some men thynke that ye
Shall haue penalte
For your iniquyte.
Nota what I say,
And bere it well away;
If it please not theologys,

It is good for astrologys ;
For Ptholome tolde me
The sonne somtyme to be   470
In Ariete,
Ascerdent a degre,[1]
Whan Scorpion descendynge,
Was so then pretendynge
A fatall fall of one
That shuld syt on a trone,
And rule all thynges alone.
Your teth whet on this bone
Amongest you euerychone,
And let Collyn Cloute haue none [2]   480

---

[1] *Ascendent a degre*] This passage seems to be corrupted.
MS. "Assendente a *dextre :*" (and compare the Lansdown
MS. quoted below.)

[2] *haue none*] MS. has "alone;" and omits the seventy-
eight lines which follow. Among the *Lansdown MSS.* (762.
fol. 75) I find the subjoined fragment:

> " Som men thynke that ye
> shall haue penaltie
> for your Inyquytie
> Note well what to saye
> yf yt please the not onely
> yt is good for astrollogy
> ffor tholomy tolde me
> the sonn somtyme to be
> In a Signe called ariotte
> assendam ad dextram
> when Scorpio is descendyng
> affatuall fall of one
> that syttys now on trone
> and rewles all thynge alone

Maner of cause to mone :
Lay salue to your owne sore,
For els, as I sayd before,
After *gloria, laus,*
May come a soure sauce ;
Sory therfore am I,
But trouth can neuer lye.
  With language thus poluted
Holy Churche is bruted
And shamfully confuted.   490
My penne nowe wyll I sharpe,
And wrest vp my harpe
With sharpe twynkyng trebelles,
Agaynst all suche rebelles
That laboure to confounde
And bryng the Churche to the grounde ;
As ye may dayly se
Howe the lay fee
Of one affynyte
Consent and agre   500
Agaynst the Churche to be,
And the dygnyte
Of the bysshoppes see.

        your tethe whet on this bone
        Amonge you euery chone
        And lett colen clowte alone.
                The profecy of Skelton
                        1529."
(The name originally written " *Skylton.*"

And eyther ye be to bad,
Or els they ar mad
Of this to reporte :
But, vnder your supporte,
Tyll my dyenge day
I shall bothe wryte and say,
And ye shall do the same,   510
Howe they are to blame
You thus to dyffame :
For it maketh me sad
Howe that the people are glad
The Churche to depraue ;
And some there are that raue,
Presumynge on theyr wyt,
Whan there is neuer a whyt,
To maynteyne argumentes
Agaynst the sacramentes.   520
  Some make epylogacyon
Of hyghe predestynacyon ;
And of resydeuacyon
They make interpretacyon
Of an aquarde facyon ;
And of the prescience
Of dyuyne essence ;
And what ipostacis
Of Christes manhode is.
Suche logyke men wyll chop,   530
And in theyr fury hop,
When the good ale sop
Dothe daunce in theyr fore top ;

Bothe women and men,
Suche ye may well knowe and ken,
That agaynst preesthode
Theyr malyce sprede abrode,
Raylynge haynously
And dysdaynously
Of preestly dygnytes,   540
But theyr malygnytes.
    And some haue a smacke
Of Luthers sacke,
And a brennyng sparke
Of Luthers warke,
And are somewhat suspecte
In Luthers secte ;
And some of them barke,
Clatter and carpe
Of that heresy arte   550
Called Wicleuista,
The deuelysshe dogmatista ;
And some be Hussyans,
And some be Arryans,
And some be Pollegians,
And make moche varyans
Bytwene the clergye
And the temporaltye,
Howe the Church [1] hath to mykel,
And they haue to lytell,   560

[1] *Howe the Church, &c.*] This passage in MS. stands thus:
    " Some sey holy chyrche haue to mykell
    Som sey they haue tryalytes

And bryng in materialites
And qualyfyed qualytes;
Of pluralytes,
Of tryalytes,
And of tot quottes,
They commune lyke sottes,
As commeth to theyr lottes;
Of prebendaries and deanes,
Howe some of them gleanes
And gathereth vp the store   570
For to catche more and more;
Of persons and vycaryes
They make many outcryes;
They cannot kepe theyr wyues
From them for theyr lyues;
And thus the loselles stryues,
And lewdely sayes by Christ
Agaynst the sely preest.
Alas, and well away,
What ayles them thus to say?   580
They mought be better aduysed
Then to be so dysgysed:
But they haue enterprysed,
And shamfully surmysed,

And some sey they brynge pluralites
And qualifie qualites
And also tot cotte
They talke lyke sottes
Makynge many owte cryes
That they cannot kepe ther wyffes
And thus the losselles stryvys."

Howe prelacy is solde and bought,
And come vp of nought;
And where the prelates be
Come of lowe degre,
And set in maieste
And spirituall dyngnyte,   590
Farwell benygnyte,
Farwell symplicite,
Farwell humylyte,
Farwell good charyte!
  Ye are so puffed wyth pryde,
That no man may abyde
Your hygh and lordely lokes:.
Ye cast vp then your bokes,
And vertue is forgotten;
For then ye wyll be wroken   600
Of euery lyght quarell,
And call a lorde a iauell,
A knyght a knaue ye make;
Ye bost, ye face, ye crake,
And vpon you ye take
To rule bothe kynge and kayser;
And yf ye may haue layser,
Ye wyll brynge all to nought,
And that is all your thought:
For the lordes temporall,   610
Theyr rule is very small,
Almost nothyng at all.
Men saye howe ye appall
The noble blode royall:

In ernest and in game,
Ye are the lesse to blame,
For lordes of noble blode,
If they well vnderstode
How connyng myght them auaunce,
They wold pype you another daunce :   620
But noble men borne
To lerne they haue scorne,
But hunt and blowe an horne,
Lepe ouer lakes and dykes,
Set nothyng by polytykes ;
Therfore ye kepe them bace,
And mocke them to theyr face :
This is a pyteous case,
To you that ouer the whele
Grete lordes must crouche and knele,   630
And breke theyr hose at the kne,
As dayly men may se,
And to remembraunce call,
Fortune so turneth the ball
And ruleth so ouer all,
That honoure hath a great fall.
    Shall I tell you more ? ye, shall.
I am loth to tell all ;
But the communalte yow call
Ydolles of Babylon,   640
De terra Zabulon,
De terra Neptalym ;
For ye loue to go trym,
Brought vp of poore estate,

With pryde inordinate,
Sodaynly vpstarte
From the donge carte,
The mattocke and the shule,
To reygne and to rule;
And haue no grace to thynke   650
Howe ye were wonte to drynke
Of a lether bottell
With a knauysshe stoppell,
Whan mamockes was your meate,
With moldy brede to eate;
Ye cowde none other gete
To chewe and to gnawe,
To fyll therwith your mawe;
Loggyng in fayre strawe,
Couchyng your drousy heddes   660
Somtyme in lousy beddes.
Alas, this is out of mynde!
Ye growe nowe out of kynde:
Many one ye haue vntwynde,
And made the commons blynde.
But *qui se existimat stare*,
Let hym well beware
Lest that his fote slyp,
And haue suche a tryp,
And falle in suche dekay,   670
That all the worlde may say,
Come downe, in the deuyll way!
    Yet, ouer all that,
Of bysshops they chat,

That though ye round your hear
An ynche aboue your ear,
And haue *aures patentes*
And *parum intendentes,*
And your tonsors be croppyd,
Your eares they be stopped;   680
For maister *Adulator,*
And doctour *Assentator,*
And *Blandior blandiris,*
With *Mentior mentiris,*
They folowe your desyres,
And so they blere your eye,
That ye can not espye
Howe the male dothe wrye.
 Alas, for Goddes wyll,
Why syt ye, prelates, styll,   690
And suffre all this yll?
Ye bysshops of estates
Shulde open the brode gates
Of your spirituall charge,
And com forthe at large,
Lyke lanternes of lyght,
In the peoples syght,
In pullpettes awtentyke,
For the wele publyke
Of preesthode in this case;   700
And alwayes to chase
Suche maner of sysmatykes
And halfe heretykes,
That wolde intoxicate,

That wolde conquinate,
That wolde contaminate,
And that wolde vyolate,
And that wolde derogate,
And that wolde abrogate
The Churchis hygh estates,   710
After this maner rates,
The which shulde be
Both franke and free,
And haue theyr lyberte,
As of antiquyte
It was ratefyed,
And also gratifyed,
By holy synodalles
And bulles papalles,
As it is *res certa*   720
Conteyned in *Magna Charta.*
    But maister Damyan,
Or some other man,
That clerkely is and can
Well scrypture expounde
And hys textes grounde,
His benefyce worthe ten pounde,
Or skante worth twenty marke,
And yet a noble clerke,
He must do this werke ;   730
As I knowe a parte,
Some maisters of arte,
Some doctours of lawe,
Some lernde in other sawe,

As in dyuynyte,
That hath no dygnyte
But the pore degre
Of the vnyuersyte ;
Or els frere Frederycke,
Or els frere Dominike,   740
Or frere Hugulinus,
Or frere Agustinus,
Or frere Carmelus,
That gostly can heale vs ;
Or els yf we may
Get a frere graye,
Or els of the order
Vpon Grenewyche border,
Called Obseruaunce,
Or a frere of Fraunce ;   750
Or else the poore Scot,
It must come to his lot
To shote forthe his shot ;
Or of Babuell besyde Bery,
To postell vpon a kyry,
That wolde it shulde be noted
Howe scripture shulde be coted,
And so clerkley promoted ;
And yet the frere doted.
But men sey your awtoryte,   760
And your noble se,
And your dygnyte,
Shulde be imprynted better
Then all the freres letter ;
For if ye wolde take payne

To preche a worde or twayne,
Though it were neuer so playne,
With clauses two or thre,
So as they myght be
Compendyously conueyde,   770
These wordes shuld be more weyd,
And better perceyued,
And thankfullerlye receyued,
And better shulde remayne
Amonge the people playne,
That wold your wordes retayne
And reherce them agayne,
Than a thousand thousande other,
That blaber, barke, and blother,
And make a Walshmans hose   780
Of the texte and of the glose.

    For protestatyon made,
That I wyll not wade
Farther in this broke,
Nor farther for to loke
In deuysynge of this boke,
But answere that I may
For my selfe alway,
Eyther *analogice*
Or els *categorice*,   790
So that in diuinite
Doctors that lerned be,
Nor bachelers of that faculte
That hath taken degre
In the vniuersite,
Shall not be obiecte at by me.

But doctour Bullatus,
Parum litteratus,
Dominus doctoratus
At the brode gatus,   806
Doctour Daupatus,
And bacheler *bacheleratus,*
Dronken as a mouse,
At the ale house,
Taketh his pyllyon and his cap
At the good ale tap,
For lacke of good wyne;
As wyse as Robyn swyne,
Vnder a notaryes sygne
Was made a dyuyne ;   810
As wyse as Waltoms calfe,
Must preche, a Goddes halfe,
In the pulpyt solempnely ;
More mete in the pyllory,
For, by saynt Hyllary,
He can nothyng smatter
Of logyke nor scole matter,
Neyther *syllogisare,*
Nor *enthymemare,*
Nor knoweth his elenkes,   820
Nor his predicamens ;
And yet he wyll mell
To amend the gospell,
And wyll preche and tell
What they do in hell ;
And he dare not well neuen

What they do in heuen,
Nor how farre Temple barre is
From the seuen starrys.

Nowe wyll I go 830
And tell of other mo,
Semper protestando
De non impugnando
The foure ordores of fryers,
Though some of them be lyers;
As Lymyters at large
Wyll charge and dyscharge;
As many a frere, God wote,
Preches for his grote,
Flatterynge for a newe cote 840
And for to haue his fees;
Some to gather chese;
Loth they are to lese
Eyther corne or malte;
Somtyme meale and salte,
Somtyme a bacon flycke,
That is thre fyngers thycke
Of larde and of greace,
Theyr couent to encreace.

I put you out of doute, 850
This can not be brought aboute
But they theyr tonges fyle,
And make a plesaunt style
To Margery and to Maude,
Howe they haue no fraude;
And somtyme they prouoke

Bothe Gyll and Jacke at Noke
Their dewtyes to withdrawe,
That they ought by the lawe
Theyr curates to content   860
In open tyme and in Lent :
God wot, they take great payne
To flatter and to fayne ;
But it is an olde sayd sawe,
That nede hath no lawe.
Some walke aboute in melottes,
In gray russet and heery cotes ;
Some wyl neyther golde ne grotes ;
Some plucke a partrych in remotes,
And by the barres of her tayle   870
Wyll knowe a rauen from a rayle,
A quayle, the raile, and the olde rauen :
Sed libera nos a malo ! Amen.
And by *Dudum,* theyr Clementine,
Agaynst curates they repyne ;
And say propreli they ar *sacerdotes,*
To shryue, assoyle, and reles
Dame Margeries soule out of hell :
But when the freare fell in the well,
He coud not syng himselfe therout   880
But by the helpe of Christyan Clout.
Another Clementyne also,[1]

---

[1] *Another Clementyne also, &c.*] I suspect some corruption
here. In MS. the passage stands thus ;

  " *Another clementyn how frere* faby and *mo*
  Exivit," &c.

How frere Fabian, with other mo,
Exivit de Paradiso ;
Whan they agayn theder shal come,
De hoc petimus consilium :
And through all the world they go
With *Dirige* and *Placebo.*

But nowe my mynd ye vnderstand,
For they must take in hande   890
To prech, and to withstande
Al maner of abiections ;
For bysshops haue protections,
They say, to do corrections,
But they haue no affections
To take the sayd dyrections ;
In such maner of cases,
Men say, they bere no faces
To occupye suche places,
To sowe the sede of graces :   900
Theyr hertes are so faynted,
And they be so attaynted
With coueytous and ambycyon,
And other superstycyon,
That they be deef and dum,
And play scylens and glum,
Can say nothynge but mum.
   They occupye them so
With syngyng *Placebo,*
They wyll no farther go :   910
They had leuer to please,
And take their worldly ease,

Than to take on hande
Worsshepfully to withstande
Such temporall warre and bate,
As nowe is made of late
Agaynst holy Churche estate,
Or to maynteyne good quarelles.
The lay men call them barrelles
Full of glotony   920
And of hypocrysy,
That counterfaytes and payntes
As they were very sayntes:
In matters that them lyke
They shewe them polytyke,
Pretendyng grauyte
And sygnyoryte,
With all solempnyte,
For theyr indempnyte;
For they wyll haue no losse   930
Of a peny nor of a crosse
Of theyr predyall landes,
That cometh to theyr handes,
And as farre as they dare set,
All is fysshe that cometh to net:
Buyldyng royally
Theyr mancyons curyously,
With turrettes and with toures,
With halles and with boures,
Stretchynge to the starres,   940
With glasse wyndowes and barres;
Hangynge aboute the walles

Clothes of golde and palles,
Arras of ryche aray,
Fresshe as flours in May;
Wyth dame Dyana naked;
Howe lusty Venus quaked,
And howe Cupyde shaked
His darte, and bent his bowe
For to shote a crowe   950
At her tyrly tyrlowe;
And howe Parys of Troy
Daunced a lege de moy,
Made lusty sporte and ioy
With dame Helyn the quene;
With suche storyes bydene
Their chambres well besene;
With triumphes of Cesar,
And of Pompeyus war,
Of renowne and of fame   960
By them to get a name:
Nowe all the worlde stares,
How they ryde in goodly chares,
Conueyed by olyphantes,
With lauryat garlantes,
And by vnycornes
With their semely hornes;
Vpon these beestes rydynge,
Naked boyes strydynge,
With wanton wenches winkyng.   970
Nowe truly, to my thynkynge,
That is a speculacyon

And a mete meditacyon
For prelates of estate,
Their courage to abate
From worldly wantonnesse,
Theyr chambres thus to dresse
With suche parfetnesse
And all suche holynesse ;
How be it they let downe fall   980
Their churches cathedrall.
  Squyre, knyght, and lorde,
Thus the Churche remorde ;
With all temporall people
They rune agaynst the steple,
Thus talkynge and tellyng
How some of you are mellyng ;
Yet softe and fayre for swellyng,
Beware of a quenes yellyng.
It is a besy thyng   990
For one man to rule a kyng
Alone and make rekenyng,
To gouerne ouer all
And rule a realme royall
By one mannes verrey wyt ;
Fortune may chaunce to flyt,
And whan he weneth to syt,
Yet may he mysse the quysshon:
For I rede a preposycyon,
Cum regibus amicare,   1000
Et omnibus dominari,
Et supra te pravare ;

Wherfore he hathe good vre
That can hymselfe assure
Howe fortune wyll endure.
Than let reason you supporte,
For the communalte dothe reporte
That they haue great wonder
That ye kepe them so vnder;
Yet they meruayle so moche lesse,   1010
For ye play so at the chesse,
As they suppose and gesse,
That some of you but late
Hath played so checkemate
With lordes of great estate,
After suche a rate,
That they shall mell nor make,
Nor vpon them take,
For kynge nor kayser sake,
But at the playsure of one .   1020
That ruleth the roste alone.
  Helas, I say, helas!
Howe may this come to passe,
That a man shall here a masse,
And not so hardy on his hede
To loke on God in forme of brede,
But that the parysshe clerke
There vpon must herke,
And graunt hym at his askyng
For to se the sacryng?   1030
  And howe may this accorde,
No man to our souerayne lorde

So hardy to make sute,
Nor yet to execute
His commaundement,
Without the assent
Of our presydent,
Nor to expresse to his person,
Without your consentatyon
Graunt hym his lycence 1040
To preas to his presence,
Nor to speke to hym secretly,
Openly nor preuyly,
Without his presydent be by,
Or els his substytute
Whom he wyll depute?
Neyther erle ne duke
Permytted? by saynt Luke,
And by swete saynt Marke,
This is a wonderous warke! 1050
That the people talke this,
Somewhat there is amysse:
The deuil cannot stop their mouthes,
But they wyl talke of such vncouthes,
All that euer they ken
Agaynst all spirituall men.
   Whether it be wrong or ryght,
Or els for dyspyght,
Or howe euer it hap,
Theyr tonges thus do clap, 1060
And through suche detractyon
They put you to your actyon;

And whether they say trewly
As they may abyde therby,
Or els that they do lye,
Ye knowe better then I.
But nowe *debetis scire,*
And groundly *audire,*
In your *convenire,*
Of this premenire,   1070
Or els in the myre
They saye they wyll you cast;
Therfore stande sure and fast.
  Stande sure, and take good fotyng,
And let be all your motyng,
Your gasyng and your totyng,
And your parcyall promotyng
Of those that stande in your grace ;
But olde seruauntes ye chase,
And put them out of theyr place.   1080
Make ye no murmuracyon,
Though I wryte after this facion ;
Though I, Colyn Cloute,
Among the hole route
Of you that clerkes be,
Take nowe vpon me
Thus copyously to wryte,
I do it for no despyte.
Wherfore take no dysdayne
At my style rude and playne ;   1090
For I rebuke no man
That vertuous is : why than

Wreke ye your anger on me?
For those that vertuous be
Haue no cause to say
That I speke out of the way.
    Of no good bysshop speke I,
Nor good preest I escrye,
Good frere, nor good chanon,
Good nonne, nor good canon,   1100
Good monke, nor good clercke,
Nor yette of no good werke:
But my recountyng is
Of them that do amys,
In speking and rebellyng,
In hynderyng and dysauaylyng
Holy Churche, our mother,
One agaynst another;
To vse suche despytyng
Is all my hole wrytyng;   1110
To hynder no man,
As nere as I can,
For no man haue I named:
Wherfore sholde I be blamed?
Ye ought to be ashamed,
Agaynst me to be gramed,
And can tell no cause why,
But that I wryte trewly.
    Then yf any there be
Of hygh or lowe degre   1120
Of the spiritualte,
Or of the temporalte,

That dothe thynke or wene
That his conscyence be not clene,
And feleth hymselfe sycke,
Or touched on the quycke,
Suche grace God them sende
Themselfe to amende,
For I wyll not pretende
Any man to offende.   1130
   Wherfore, as thynketh me,
Great ydeottes they be,
And lytell grace they haue,
This treatyse to depraue;
Nor wyll here no prechyng,
Nor no vertuous techyng,
Nor wyll haue no resytyng
Of any vertuous wrytyng;
Wyll knowe none intellygence
To refourme theyr neglygence,   1140
But lyue styll out of facyon,
To theyr owne dampnacyon.
To do shame they haue no shame,
But they wold no man shulde them blame:
They haue an euyl name,
But yet they wyll occupy the same.
   With them the worde of God
Is counted for no rod;
They counte it for a raylyng,
That nothyng is auaylyng;   1150
The prechers with euyll hayling:
Shall they daunt vs prelates,

That be theyr prymates?
Not so hardy on theyr pates!
Herke, howe the losell prates,
With a wyde wesaunt!
Auaunt, syr Guy of Gaunt!
Auaunt, lewde preest, auaunt!
Auaunt, syr doctour Deuyas!
Prate of thy matyns and thy masse,   1160
And let our maters passe:
Howe darest thou, daucocke, mell?
Howe darest thou, losell,
Allygate the gospell
Agaynst vs of the counsell?
Auaunt to the deuyll of hell!
Take hym, wardeyne of the Flete,
Set hym fast by the fete!
I say, lyeutenaunt of the Toure,
Make this lurdeyne for to loure;   1170
Lodge hym in Lytell Ease,
Fede hym with beanes and pease!
The Kynges Benche or Marshalsy,
Haue hym thyder by and by!
The vyllayne precheth openly,
And declareth our vyllany;
And of our fre symplenesse
He sayes that we are rechelesse,
And full of wylfulnesse,
Shameles and mercylesse,   1180
Incorrigible and insaciate;
And after this rate
Agaynst vs dothe prate.

At Poules Crosse or els where,
Openly at Westmynstere,
And Saynt Mary Spyttell,
They set not by vs a whystell :
At the Austen fryers
They count vs for lyers :
And at Saynt Thomas of Akers   1190
They carpe vs lyke crakers,
Howe we wyll rule all at wyll
Without good reason or skyll;
And say how that we be
Full of parcyalyte ;
And howe at a pronge
We tourne ryght into wronge,
Delay causes so longe
That ryght no man can fonge ;
They say many matters be born   1200
By the ryght of a rambes horne.
Is not this a shamfull scorne,
To be teared thus and torne
    How may we thys indure ?
Wherfore we make you sure,
Ye prechers shall be yawde ;
And some shall be sawde,
As noble Isaias,
The holy prophet, was ;
And some of you shall dye,   1210
Lyke holy Jeremy ;
Some hanged, some slayne,
Some beaten to the brayne ;

And we wyll rule and rayne,
And our matters mayntayne
Who dare say there agayne,
Or who dare dysdayne
At our pleasure and wyll :
For, be it good or be it yll,
As it is, it shall be styll,   1220
For all master doctour of Cyuyll,
Or of Diuine, or doctour Dryuyll,
Let hym cough, rough, or sneuyll ;
Renne God, renne deuyll,
Renne who may renne best,
And let take all the rest !
We set not a nut shell
The way to heuen or to hell.
　　Lo, this is the gyse now a dayes !
It is to drede, men sayes,   1230
Lest they be Saduces,
As they be sayd sayne
Whiche determyned playne
We shulde not ryse agayne
At dredefull domis day ;
And so it semeth they play,
Whiche hate to be corrected
Whan they be infected,
Nor wyll suffre this boke
By hoke ne by croke   1240
Prynted for to be,
For that no man shulde se
Nor rede in any scrolles

Of theyr dronken nolles,
Nor of theyr noddy polles,
Nor of theyr sely soules,
Nor of some wytles pates
Of dyuers great estates,
As well as other men.

Now to withdrawe my pen,   1250
And now a whyle to rest,
Me semeth it for the best.

The forecastell of my shyp
Shall glyde, and smothely slyp
Out of the wawes wod
Of the stormy flod;
Shote anker, and lye at rode,
And sayle not farre abrode,
Tyll the cost be clere,
And the lode starre appere: 1260
My shyp nowe wyll I stere
Towarde the porte salu
Of our Sauyour Jesu,
Suche grace that he vs sende,
To rectyfye and amende
Thynges that are amys,
Whan that his pleasure is.
                    Amen!
In opere imperfecto,
In opere semper perfecto,
Et in opere plusquam perfecto!   1270

*Colinus Cloutus, quanquam mea carmina multis
Sordescunt stultis,* sed puevinate *sunt* rare *cultis,*
Pue vinatis altisem *divino flamine flatis.*

*Unde meâ refert tanto minus, invida quamvis
Lingua nocere parat, quia, quanquam rustica
canto,
Undique cantabor tamen et celebrabor ubique,
Inclita dum maneat gens Anglica. Laurus honoris,
Quondam regnorum regina et gloria regum,
Heu, modo marcescit, tabescit, languida torpet!
Ah pudet, ah miseret! vetor hic ego pandere plura
Pro gemitu et lacrimis: præstet peto præmia
pæna.**

* These verses, not in eds., follow the poem of *Colyn Cloute* in the Harleian MS. The corruptions in the second and third lines (distinguished by Roman letter) have baffled the ingenuity of the several scholars to whom I submitted them.

A reviewer in the *Gentleman's Magazine* (Sept. 1844, p. 246,) would cure this corrupted passage as follows:

*Colinus Cloutus, quanquam mea carmina multis
Sordescunt stultis;* sed paucis *sunt* data *cultis,*
Paucis ante alios *divino flamine flatis.*

A RYGHT DELECTABLE TRATYSE VPON A GOODLY

GARLANDE OR CHAPELET OF LAURELL,*

BY MAYSTER SKELTON, POETE LAUREAT, STUDYOUSLY
DYUYSED AT SHERYFHOTTON CASTELL, IN THE FORESTE
OF GALTRES, WHEREIN AR COMPRYSYDE MANY AND
DYUERS SOLACYONS AND RYGHT PREGNANT ALLECTYUES
OF SYNGULAR PLEASURE, AS MORE AT LARGE IT DOTH
APERE IN THE PROCES FOLOWYNGE.

Eterno mansura die dum sidera fulgent,
Æquora dumque tument, hæc laurea nostra virebit:
Hinc nostrum celebre et nomen referetur ad astra,
Undique Skeltonis memorabitur alter Adonis.

ARECTYNG my syght towarde the zodyake,
  The sygnes xii for to beholde a farre,
When Mars retrogradant reuersyd his bak,
  Lorde of the yere in his orbicular,
  Put vp his sworde, for he cowde make no warre,
And whan Lucina plenarly did shyne,
Scorpione ascendynge degrees twyse nyne;

---

* From Faukes's ed. 1523, collated with Marshe's ed. of
Skelton's *Workes*, 1568, (in which it is entitled *The Crowne
of Lawrell*,) and with fragments of the poem among the Cot-
tonian MSS. *Vit.* E.X. fol. 200. The prefatory Latin lines
are from Faukes's ed., where they are given on the back of
the title-page, and below a woodcut portrait headed " *Skelton
Poeta*," (see *List of Editions*, in Appendix to *Account of Skel-
ton*, &c.): they are not in Marshe's ed. nor in MS.

In place alone then musynge in my thought
  How all thynge passyth as doth the somer
    flower,
On euery halfe my reasons forthe I sought,   10
  How oftyn fortune varyeth in an howre,
  Now clere wether, forthwith a stormy showre ;
All thynge compassyd, no perpetuyte,
But now in welthe, now in aduersyte.

So depely drownyd I was in this dumpe,
  Encraumpysshed so sore was my conceyte,
That, me to rest, I lent me to a stumpe
  Of an oke, that somtyme grew full streyghte,
  A myghty tre and of a noble heyght,
Whose bewte blastyd was with the boystors
    wynde,   20
His leuis loste, the sappe was frome the rynde.

Thus stode I in the frytthy forest of Galtres,
  Ensowkid with sylt of the myry mose,
Where hartis belluyng, embosyd with distres,
  Ran on the raunge so longe, that I suppose
  Few men can tell now where the hynde calfe
    gose ;
Faire fall that forster that so well can bate his
    hownde !
But of my purpose now torne we to the grownde.

Whylis I stode musynge in this medytatyon,
  In slumbrynge I fell and halfe in a slepe ;   30

And whether it were of ymagynacyon,
  Or of humors superflue, that often wyll crepe
  Into the brayne by drynkyng ouer depe,
Or it procedyd of fatall persuacyon,
I can not wele tell you what was the occasyon;

But sodeynly at ones, as I me aduysed,
  As one in a trans or in an extasy,
I sawe a pauylyon wondersly disgysede,
  Garnysshed fresshe after my fantasy,
  Enhachyde with perle and stones preciously, 45
The grounde engrosyd and bet with bourne golde,
That passynge goodly it was to beholde:

Within it, a prynces excellente of porte;
  But to recount her ryche abylyment,
And what estates to her did resorte,
  Therto am I full insuffycyent;
  A goddesse inmortall she dyd represente;
As I harde say, dame Pallas was her name;
To whome supplyed the royall Quene of Fame.[1]

The Quene of Fame to Dame Pallas.

Prynces moost pusant, of hygh preemynence, 50
  Renownyd lady aboue the sterry heuyn,
All other transcendyng, of very congruènce

----

[1] *Quene of Fame*] Opposite this line MS. has a marginal
note, partly illegible, and partly cut off, " *Egida concussit*
p . . . dea pectore porta . . ."

Madame regent of the scyence seuyn,
　To whos astate all noblenes most lenen,
My supplycacyon to you I arrect,
Whereof I beseche you to tender the effecte.

Not vnremembered it is vnto your grace,
　How you gaue me a ryall commaundement
That in my courte Skelton shulde haue a place,
　Bycause that his tyme he studyously hath
　　　spent　　　　　　　　　　　　　　60
　In your seruyce; and, to the accomplysshe-
　　　ment
Of your request, regestred is his name
With laureate tryumphe in the courte of Fame.

But, good madame, the accustome and vsage
　Of auncient poetis, ye wote full wele, hath bene
Them selfe to embesy with all there holl corage,
　So that there workis myght famously be sene,
　In figure wherof they were the laurell grene;
But how it is, Skelton is wonder slake,
And, as we dare, we fynde in hym grete lake: 70

For, ne were onely he hath your promocyon,
　Out of my bokis full sone I shulde hym rase;
But sith he hath tastid of the sugred pocioun
　Of Elyconis well, refresshid with your grace,
　And wyll not endeuour hymselfe to purchase
The fauour of ladys with wordis electe,
It is sittynge that ye must hym correct.

Dame Pallas to the Quene of Fame.

The sum of your purpose, as we ar aduysid,
    Is that our seruaunt is sum what to dull;
Wherin this answere for hym we haue comprisid,
    How ryuers rin not tyll the spryng be full;   81
    Better a dum mouthe than a brainles scull;
For if he gloryously pullishe his matter,
Then men wyll say how he doth but flatter;

And if so hym fortune to wryte true and plaine,
    As sumtyme he must vyces remorde,
Then sum wyll say he hath but lyttill brayne,
    And how his wordes with reason wyll not
        accorde;
    Beware, for wrytyng remayneth of recorde;
Displease not an hundreth for one mannes
    pleasure;   90
Who wryteth wysely hath a grete treasure.

Also, to furnisshe better his excuse,
    Ouyde was bannisshed for suche a skyll,
And many mo whome I cowde enduce;
    Iuuenall was thret parde for to kyll
    For certayne enuectyfys, yet wrote he none ill,
Sauynge he rubbid sum vpon the gall;
It was not for hym to abyde the tryall.

In generrall wordes, I say not gretely nay,
    A poete somtyme may for his pleasure taunt,   100

Spekyng in parablis, how the fox, the grey,
   The gander, the gose, and the hudge oliphaunt,
   Went with the pecok ageyne the fesaunt;
The lesarde came lepyng, and sayd that he must,
With helpe of the ram, ley all in the dust.

Yet dyuerse ther be, industryous of reason,
   Sum what wolde gadder in there coniecture
Of suche an endarkid chapiter sum season;
   How be it, it were harde to construe this
      lecture;
Sophisticatid craftely is many a confecture; 110
Another manes mynde diffuse is to expounde;
Yet harde is to make but sum fawt be founde.

The Quene of Fame to Dame Pallas.

Madame, with fauour of your benynge sufferaunce,
   Vnto your grace then make I this motyue;
Whereto made ye me hym to auaunce
   Vnto the rowme of laureat promotyue?
   Or wherto shulde he haue that prerogatyue,
But if he had made sum memoryall,
Wherby he myght haue a name inmortall?

To pas the tyme in slowthfull ydelnes,   120
   Of your royall palace it is not the gyse,
But to do sumwhat iche man doth hym dres:
   For how shulde Cato els be callyd wyse,
   But that his bokis, whiche he did deuyse,
Recorde the same? or why is had in mynde
Plato, but for that he left wrytynge behynde,

For men to loke on? Aristotille also,
  Of phylosophers callid the princypall,
Olde Diogenes, with other many mo,
  Demostenes, that oratour royall,   130
  That gaue Eschines suche a cordyall,
That bannisshed was he by his proposicyoun,
Ageyne whome he cowde make no contradic-
     cyoun?

Dame Pallas to the Quene of Fame.

Soft, my good syster, and make there a pawse:
  And was Eschines rebukid as ye say?
Remembre you wele, poynt wele that clause;
  Wherfore then rasid ye not away
  His name? or why is it, I you praye,
That he to your courte is goyng and commynge,
Sith he is slaundred for defaut of konnyng? 140

The Quene of Fame to Dame Pallas.

Madame, your apposelle is wele inferrid,
  And at your auauntage quikly it is
Towchid, and hard for to be debarrid;
  Yet shall I answere your grace as in this,
  With your reformacion, if I say amis,
For, but if your bounte did me assure,
Myne argument els koude not longe endure.

As towchyng that Eschines is remembred,
  That he so sholde be, me semith it sittyng,
All be it grete parte he hath surrendred 150

Of his onour, whos dissuasyue in wrytyng
To corage Demostenes was moche excitynge,
In settyng out fresshely his crafty persuacyon,
From whiche Eschines had none euacyon.

The cause why Demostenes so famously is brutid,
Onely procedid for that he did outray
Eschines, whiche was not shamefully confutid
But of that famous oratour, I say,
Whiche passid all other ; wherfore I may
Among my recordes suffer hym namyd,   160
For though he were venquesshid, yet was he not
    shamyd :

As Ierome, in his preamble *Frater Ambrosius,*
Frome that I haue sayde in no poynt doth vary,
Wherein he reporteth of the coragius
Wordes that were moch consolatory
By Eschines rehersed to the grete glory
Of Demostenes, that was his vtter foo :
Few shall ye fynde or none that wyll do so.

    Dame Pallas to the Quene of Fame.
A thanke to haue, ye haue well deseruyd,
Your mynde that can maynteyne so apparently ;
But a grete parte yet ye haue reseruyd   171
Of that most fclow then conseqently,
Or els ye demeane you inordinatly ;
For if ye laude hym whome honour hath opprest,
Then he that doth worste is as good as the best.

But whome that ye fauoure, I se well, hath a
    name,
    Be he neuer so lytell of substaunce,
And whome ye loue not ye wyll put to shame;
    Ye counterwey not euynly your balaunce;
    As wele foly as wysdome oft ye do avaunce: 180
For reporte ryseth many deuerse wayes:
Sume be moche spokyn of for makynge of frays;

Some haue a name for thefte and brybery;
    Some be called crafty, that can pyke a purse;
Some men be made of for their mokery;
    Some carefull cokwoldes, some haue theyr
        wyues curs;
    Some famous wetewoldis, and they be moche
        wurs;
Some lidderons, some losels, some noughty
    packis;
Some facers, some bracers, some make great
    crackis;

Some dronken dastardis with their dry soules; 190
    Some sluggyssh slouyns, that slepe day and
        nyght;
Ryot and Reuell be in your courte rowlis;
    Maintenaunce and Mischefe, theis be men of
        myght;
    Extorcyon is counted with you for a knyght;
Theis people by me haue none assignement,
Yet they ryde and rinne from Carlyll to Kente.

But lytell or nothynge ye shall here tell
  Of them that haue vertue by reason of cunnyng,
Whiche souerenly in honoure shulde excell;   199
  Men of suche maters make but a mummynge,
  For wysdome and sadnesse be set out a sun-
      nyng;
And suche of my seruauntes as I haue promotyd,
One faute or other in them shalbe notyd:

Eyther they wyll say he is to wyse,
  Or elles he can nought bot whan he is at scole;
Proue his wytt, sayth he, at cardes or dyce,
  And ye shall well fynde he is a very fole;
  Twyshe, set hym a chare, or reche hym a
      stole,
To syt hym vpon, and rede Iacke a thrummis
      bybille,
For truly it were pyte that he sat ydle.   210

The Quene of Fame to Dame Pallas.

To make repungnaunce agayne that ye haue
      sayde,
  Of very dwte it may not well accorde,
But your benynge sufferaunce for my discharge
      I laid,
  For that I wolde not with you fall at discorde;
  But yet I beseche your grace that good recorde
May be brought forth, suche as can be founde,
With laureat tryumphe why Skelton sholde be
      crownde;

For elles it were to great a derogacyon
  Vnto your palas, our noble courte of Fame,
That any man vnder supportacyon   220
    Withoute deseruynge shulde haue the best
      game :
If he to the ample encrease of his name
Can lay any werkis that he hath compylyd,
I am contente that he be not exylide

Frome the laureat senate by force of proscrip-
      cyon ;
  Or elles, ye know well, I can do no lesse
But I must bannysshe hym frome my iury-
      diccyon,
  As he that aquentyth hym with ydilnes ;
  But if that he purpose to make a redresse,
What he hath done, let it be brought to syght; 230
Graunt my petycyon, I aske you but ryght.

Dame Pallas to the Quene of Fame.

To your request we be well condiscendid :
  Call forthe, let se where is your clarionar,
To blowe a blaste with his long breth extendid ;
  Eolus, your trumpet, that knowne is so farre,
  That bararag blowyth in euery mercyall warre,
Let hym blowe now, that we may take a vewe
What poetis we haue at our retenewe ;

To se if Skelton wyll put hymselfe in prease
  Amonge the thickeste of all the hole rowte ; 240

Make noyse enoughe, for claterars loue no peas;
  Let se, my syster, now spede you, go aboute;
  Anone, I sey, this trumpet were founde out,
And for no man hardely let hym spare
To blowe bararag tyll bothe his eyne stare.

Skelton Poeta.

Forthwith there rose amonge the thronge
  A wonderfull noyse, and on euery syde
They presid in faste; some thought they were to
    longe;
  Sume were to hasty, and wold no man byde;
  Some whispred, some rownyd, some spake, and
    some cryde,   250
With heuynge and shouynge, haue in and haue
    oute;
Some ranne the rexte way, sume ranne abowte.

There was suyng to the Quene of Fame;
  He plucked hym backe, and he went afore;
Nay, holde thy tunge, quod another, let me haue
    the name:
  Make rowme, sayd another, ye prese all to
    sore;
  Sume sayd, Holde thy peas, thou getest here
    no more;
A thowsande thowsande I sawe on a plumpe:
With that I harde the noyse of a trumpe,

That longe tyme blewe a full timorous blaste, 260
  Lyke to the boryall wyndes whan they blowe,

That towres and townes and trees downe caste,
   Droue clowdes together lyke dryftis of snowe;
   The dredefull dinne droue all the rowte on a
      rowe ;
Some tremblid, some girnid, some gaspid, some
      gasid,
As people halfe peuysshe, or men that were
      masyd.

Anone all was whyste, as it were for the nonys,
   And iche man stode gasyng and staryng vpon
      other :
With that there come in wonderly at ones
   A murmur of mynstrels, that suche another 270
   Had I neuer sene, some softer, some lowder;
Orpheus, the Traciane, herped meledyously
Weth Amphion, and other Musis of Archady :

Whos heuenly armony was so passynge sure,
   So truely proporsionyd, and so well did gree,
So duly entunyd with euery mesure,
   That in the forest was none so great a tre
   But that he daunced for ioye of that gle ;
The huge myghty okes them selfe dyd auaunce,
And lepe frome the hylles to lerne for to daunce:

In so moche the stumpe, whereto I me lente,   281
   Sterte all at ones an hundrethe fote backe :
With that I sprange vp towarde the tent
   Of noble Dame Pallas, wherof I spake ;
   Where I sawe come after, I wote, full lytell lake

Of a thousande poetes assembled togeder :
But Phebus was formest of all that cam theder ;

Of laurell leuis a cronell on his hede,
  With heris encrisped yalowe as the golde,
Lamentyng Daphnes, whome with the darte of
      lede   290
  Cupyde hath stryken so that she ne wolde
  Concente to Phebus to haue his herte in
      holde,
But, for to preserue her maidenhode clene,
Transformyd was she into the laurell grene.

Meddelyd with murnynge the moost parte of his
      muse,
  O thoughtfull herte, was euermore his songe !
Daphnes, my derlynge, why do you me refuse ?
  Yet loke on me, that louyd you haue so longe,
  Yet haue compassyon vpon my paynes
      stronge :   300
He sange also how, the tre as he did take
Betwene his armes, he felt her body quake.

Then he assurded into this exclamacyon
  Vnto Diana, the goddes inmortall ;
O mercyles madame, hard is your constellacyon,
  So close to kepe your cloyster virgynall,
  Enhardid adyment the sement of your wall !
Alas, what ayle you to be so ouerthwhart,
To bannysshe pyte out of a maydens harte ?

Why haue the goddes shewyd me this cruelte,
  Sith I contryuyd first princyples medycynable?
I helpe all other of there infirmite,   311
  But now to helpe myselfe I am not able;
  That profyteth all other is nothynge profytable
Vnto me; alas, that herbe nor gresse
The feruent axes of loue can not represse!

O fatall fortune, what haue I offendid?
  Odious disdayne, why raist thou me on this
    facyon?
But sith I haue lost now that I entended,
  And may not atteyne it by no medyacyon,
  Yet, in remembraunce of Daphnes transforma-
    cyon,   320
All famous poetis ensuynge after me
Shall were a garlande of the laurell tre.

This sayd, a grate nowmber folowyd by and by
  Of poetis laureat of many dyuerse nacyons;
Parte of there names I thynke to specefye:
  Fyrste, olde Quintiliane with his Declama-
    cyons;
  Theocritus with his bucolycall relacyons;
Esiodus, the iconomicar,
And Homerus, the fresshe historiar;

Prynce of eloquence, Tullius Cicero,   330
  With Salusty ageinst Lucius Catelyne,
That wrote the history of Iugurta also;

Ouyde, enshryned with the Musis nyne;
But blessed Bacchus, the pleasant god of wyne,
Of closters engrosyd with his ruddy flotis
These orators and poetes refresshed there throtis;

Lucan, with Stacius in Achilliedos;
Percius presed forth with problemes diffuse;
Virgill the Mantuan, with his Eneidos;   339
Iuuenall satirray, that men makythe to muse;
But blessed Bacchus, the pleasant god of
        wyne,
Of clusters engrosed with his ruddy flotes
These orators and poetes refreshed their throtes;

There Titus Lyuius hymselfe dyd auaunce
With decadis historious, whiche that he mengith
With maters that amount the Romayns in sub-
        staunce;
Enyus, that wrate of mercyall war at lengthe;
But blessyd Bachus, potenciall god of strengthe,
Of clusters engrosid with his ruddy flotis   349
Theis orators and poetis refresshed there throtis;

Aulus Gelius, that noble historiar;
Orace also with his new poetry;
Mayster Terence, the famous comicar,
With Plautus, that wrote full many a comody;
But blessyd Bachus was in there company,
Of clusters engrosyd with his ruddy flotis
Theis orators and poetis refresshed there throtis;

Senek full soberly with his tragediis ;
  Boyce, recounfortyd with his philosophy;
And Maxymyane, with his madde ditiis,   360
  How dotynge age wolde iape with yonge foly ;
  But blessyd Bachus most reuerent and holy,
Of clusters engrosid with his ruddy flotis
Theis orators and poetis refresshed there throtis ;

There came Johnn Bochas with his volumys
      grete ;
  Quintus Cursius, full craftely that wrate
Of Alexander ; and Macrobius that did trete
  Of Scipions dreme what was the treu probate ;
  But blessyd Bachus that neuer man forgate,
Of clusters engrosed with his ruddy flotis   370
These orators and poetis refresshid ther throtis ;

Poggeus also, that famous Florentine,
  Mustred ther amonge them with many a mad
      tale ;
With a frere of Fraunce men call sir Gagwyne,
  That frownyd on me full angerly and pale ;
  But blessyd Bachus, that bote is of all bale,
Of clusters engrosyd with his ruddy flotis
Theis orators and poetis refresshid there throtis ;

Plutarke and Petrarke, two famous clarkis ;
  Lucilius and Valerius Maximus by name ;   380
With Vincencius *in Speculo*, that wrote noble
      warkis ;

Propercius and Pisandros, poetis of noble fame ;
   But blissed Bachus, that mastris oft doth frame,
Of clusters engrosed with his ruddy flotis
Theis notable poetis refresshid there throtis.

And as I thus sad_y amonge them auysid,
   I saw Gower, that first garnisshed our Eng-
      lysshe rude,
And maister Chaucer, that nobly enterprysyd
   How that our Englysshe myght fresshely be
      ennewed ;
   The monke of Bury then after them ensuyd, 390
Dane Johnn Lydgate : theis Englysshe poetis
      thre,
As I ymagenyd, repayrid vnto me,

Togeder in armes, as brethern, enbrasid ;
   There apparell farre passynge beyonde that I
      can tell ;
With diamauntis and rubis there tabers were
      trasid,
   None so ryche stones in Turkey to sell ;
   Thei wantid nothynge but the laurell ;
And of there bounte they made me godely chere,
In maner and forme as ye shall after here.

Mayster Gower to Skelton.

Brother Skelton, your endeuorment   400
   So haue ye done, that meretoryously
Ye haue deseruyd to haue an enplement

In our collage aboue the sterry sky,
Bycause that ye encrese and amplyfy
The brutid Britons of Brutus Albion,
That 'welny was loste when that we were gone.

Poeta Skelton to Maister Gower.

Maister Gower, I haue nothyng deserued
    To haue so laudabyle a commendacion:
To yow thre this honor shalbe reserued,
    Arrectinge vnto your wyse examinacion   410
    How all that I do is vnder refformation,
For only the substance of that I entend,
Is glad to please, and loth to offend.

Mayster Chaucer to Skelton.

Counterwayng your besy delygence
    Of that we beganne in the supplement,
Enforcid ar we you to recompence,
    Of all our hooll collage by the agreament,
    That we shall brynge you personally present
Of noble Fame before the Quenes grace,
In whose court poynted is your place.   420

Poeta Skelton answeryth.

O noble Chaucer, whos pullisshyd eloquence
    Oure Englysshe rude so fresshely hath set out,
That bounde ar we with all deu reuerence,
    With all our strength that we can brynge about,
    To owe to yow our seruyce, and more if we
        mowte!

But what sholde I say? ye wote what I entende,
Whiche glad am to please, and loth to offende.

Mayster Lydgate to Skelton.

So am I preuentid of my brethern tweyne
In rendrynge to you thankkis meritory,
That welny nothynge there doth remayne   430
  Wherwith to geue you my regraciatory,
  But that I poynt you to be prothonatory
Of Fames court, by all our holl assent
Auaunced by Pallas to laurell preferment.

Poeta Skelton answeryth.

So haue ye me far passynge my meretis extollyd,
  Mayster Lidgate, of your accustomable
Bownte, and so gloryously ye haue enrollyd
  My name, I know well, beyonde that I am
    able,
  That but if my warkes therto be agreable,
I am elles rebukyd of that I intende,   440
Which glad am to please, and lothe to offende.

So finally, when they had shewyd there deuyse,
  Vnder the forme as I sayd tofore,
I made it straunge, and drew bak ones or twyse,
  And euer they presed on me more and more,
  Tyll at the last they forcyd me so sore,
That with them I went where they wolde me
    brynge,
Vnto the pauylyon where Pallas was syttyng.

Dame Pallas commaundid that they shold me
    conuay
  Into the ryche palace of the Quene of Fame; 450
There shal he here what she wyl to hym say
  When he is callid to answere to his name :
  A cry anone forthwith she made proclame,
All orators and poetis shulde thider go before,
With all the prese that there was, lesse and
  more.

Forthwith, I say, thus wandrynge in my thought,
  How it was, or elles within what howris,
I can not tell you, but that I was brought
  Into a palace with turrettis and towris,
  Engolerid goodly with hallis and bowris,   460
So curiously, so craftely, so connyngly wrowght,
That all the worlde, I trowe, and it were sought,

Suche an other there coude no man fynde ;
  Wherof partely I purpose to expounde,
Whyles it remanyth fresshe in my mynde.
  With turkis and grossolitis enpauyd was the
    grounde ;
  Of birrall enbosid wer the pyllers rownde ;
Of elephantis tethe were the palace gatis,
Enlosenged with many goodly platis

Of golde, entachid with many a precyous stone ; 470
  An hundred steppis mountyng to the halle,
One of iasper, another of whalis bone ;

Of dyamauntis pointed was the rokky wall;
The carpettis within and tappettis of pall;
The chambres hangid with clothes of arace;
Enuawtyd with rubies the vawte was of this
    place.

Thus passid we forth, walkynge vnto the pretory,
    Where the postis wer enbulyoned with saphiris
        indy blew,
Englasid glittering with many a clere story;
    Iacinctis and smaragdis out of the florthe they
        grew: 480
Vnto this place all poetis there did sue,
Wherin was set of Fame the noble Quene,
All other transcendynge, most rychely besene,

Vnder a gloryous cloth of astate,
    Fret all with orient perlys of Garnate,
Encrownyd as empresse of all this worldly fate,
    So ryally, so rychely, so passyngly ornate,
        It was excedyng byyonde the commowne rate:
This hous enuyrowne was a myle about;
If xii were let in, xii hundreth stode without.   490

Then to this lady and souerayne of this palace
    Of purseuantis ther presid in with many a
        dyuerse tale;
Some were of Poyle, and sum were of Trace,
    Of Lymerik, of Loreine, of Spayne, of Port-
        yngale,

Frome Napuls, from Nauern, and from Roun-
    ceuall,
Some from Flaunders, sum fro the se coste,
Some from the mayne lande, some fro the Frensche
    hoste:

With, How doth the north? what tydyngis in the
    sowth?
The west is wyndy, the est is metely wele;
It is harde to tell of euery mannes mouthe;   500
    A slipper holde the taile is of an ele,
    And he haltith often that hath a kyby hele;
Some shewid his salfecundight, some shewid his
    charter,
Some lokyd full smothely, and had a fals quarter;

With, Sir, I pray you, a lytyll tyne stande backe,
    And lette me come in to delyuer my lettre;
Another tolde how shyppes wente to wrak;
    There were many wordes smaller and gretter,
    With, I as good as thou, Ifayth and no better;
Some came to tell treuth, some came to lye,   510
Some came to flater, some came to spye:

There were, I say, of all maner of sortis,
    Of Dertmouth, of Plummouth, of Portismouth
        also;
The burgeis and the ballyuis of the v portis,
    With, Now let me come, and now let me go:
    And all tyme wandred I thus to and fro,

Tyll at the last theis noble poetis thre
Vnto me sayd, Lo, syr, now ye may se

Of this high courte the dayly besines ;
From you most we, but not longe to tary ;   520
Lo, hither commyth a goodly maystres,
Occupacyon, Famys regestary,
Whiche shall be to you a sufferayne accessary,
With syngular pleasurs to dryue away the
     tyme,
And we shall se you ageyne or it be pryme.

When they were past and wente forth on there
     way,
This gentilwoman, that callyd was by name
Occupacyon, in ryght goodly aray,
Came towarde me, and smylid halfe in game ;
I sawe hir smyle, and I then did the same ;   530
With that on me she kest her goodly loke ;
Vnder her arme, me thought, she hade a boke.

Occupacyoun to Skelton.

Lyke as the larke, vpon the somers day,
Whan Titan radiant burnisshith his bemis
     bryght,
Mountith on hy with her melodious lay,
Of the soneshyne engladid with the lyght,
So am I supprysed with pleasure and delyght
To se this howre now, that I may say,
How ye ar welcome to this court of aray.

Of your aqueintaunce I was in tymes past,   54**
  Of studyous doctryne when at the port salu
Ye fyrste aryuyd ; whan broken was your mast
  Of worldly trust, then did I you rescu ;
  Your storme dryuen shyppe I repared new,
So well entakeled, what wynde that euer blowe,
No stormy tempeste your barge shall ouerthrow.

Welcome to me as hertely as herte can thynke,
  Welcome to me with all my hole desyre !
And for my sake spare neyther pèn nor ynke ;
  Be well assurid I shall aquyte your hyre,   550
  Your name recountynge beyonde the lande of
    Tyre,
From Sydony to the mount Olympyan,
Frome Babill towre to the hillis Caspian.

Skelton Poeta answeryth.

I thanked her moche of her most noble offer,
  Affyaunsynge her myne hole assuraunce
For her pleasure to make a large profer,
  Enpryntyng her wordes in my remembraunce,
  To owe her my seruyce with true perseueraunce.
Come on with me, she sayd, let vs not stonde ;.
And with that worde she toke me by the honde.

                                              560
So passyd we forthe into the forsayd place,
  With suche communycacyon as came to our
    mynde ;
And then she sayd, Whylis we haue tyme and
  space

To walke where we lyst, let vs somwhat fynde
To pas the tyme with, but let vs wast no wynde,
For ydle iangelers haue but lytill braine ;
Wordes be swordes, and hard to call ageine.

Into a felde she brought me wyde and large,
    Enwallyd aboute with the stony flint,
Strongly enbateld, moche costious of charge :   570
    To walke on this walle she bed I sholde not
        stint;
    Go softly, she sayd, the stones be full glint.
She went before, and bad me take good holde :
I sawe a thowsande yatis new and olde,

Then questionyd I her what thos yatis ment ;
    Wherto she answeryd, and breuely me tolde,
How from the est vnto the occident,
    And from the sowth vnto the north so colde,
    Theis yatis, she sayd, which that ye beholde,
Be issuis and portis from all maner of nacyons ;   580
And seryously she shewyd me ther denominacyons.

They had wrytyng, sum Greke, sum Ebrew,
    Some Romaine letters, as I vnderstode ;
Some were olde wryten, sum were writen new,
    Some carectis of Caldy, sum Frensshe was full
        good ;
    But one gate specyally, where as I stode,
Had grauin in it of calcydony a capytall A ;
What yate call ye this ? and she sayd, Anglia.

The beldynge therof was passynge commendable;
  Wheron stode a lybbard, crownyd with golde
    and stones,   590
Terrible of countenaunce and passynge formyd-
    able,
  As quikly towchyd as it were flesshe and bones,
  As gastly that glaris, as grimly that gronis,
As fersly frownynge as he had ben fyghtyng,
And with his forme foote he shoke forthe this
    wrytyng:

Formidanda nimis Jovis ultima fulmina tollis : [a]
Unguibus ire parat loca singula livida curvis
Quam modo per Phœbes nummos raptura Celæno;
Arma, lues, luctus, fel, vis, fraus, barbara tellus;
Mille modis erras odium tibi quærere Martis: 600
Spreto spineto cedat saliunca roseto.

Then I me lent, and loked ouer the wall:
  Innumerable people presed to euery gate;
Shet were the gatis; thei might wel knock and
    cal,
  And turne home ageyne, for they cam al to late.
  I her demaunded of them and ther astate:
Forsothe, quod she, theys be haskardis and
    rebawdis,
Dysers, carders, tumblars with gambawdis,

---

a Cacosinthicon [1] ex industria. [*Side Note.*]
  [1] *Cacosinthicon*] Properly " *Cacosyntheton.*"

Furdrers of loue, with baudry aqueinted,
    Brainles blenkardis that blow at the cole,   610
Fals forgers of mony, for kownnage atteintid,
    Pope holy ypocrytis, as they were golde and
        hole,
Powle hatchettis, that prate wyll at euery ale
    pole,
Ryot, reueler, railer, brybery, theft,
With other condycyons that well myght be left:

Sume fayne themselfe folys, and wolde be callyd
    wyse,
    Sum medelynge spyes, by craft to grope thy
        mynde,
Sum dysdanous dawcokkis that all men dispyse,
    Fals flaterers that fawne thé, and kurris of
        kynde
    That speke fayre before thé and shrewdly
        behynde;   620
Hither they come crowdyng to get them a name,
But hailid they be homwarde with sorow and
    shame.

With that I herd gunnis russhe out at ones,
    Bowns, bowns, bowns! that all they out cryde;
It made sum lympe legged and broisid there
    bones;
    Sum were made peuysshe, porisshly pynk iyde,
    That euer more after by it they were aspyid;
And one ther was there, I wondred of his hap,
For a gun stone, I say, had all to-iaggid his cap,

Raggid, and daggid, and cunnyngly cut;   630
   The blaste of the brynston blew away his
      brayne;
Masid as a marche hare, he ran lyke a scut;
   And, sir, amonge all me thought I saw twaine,
   The one was a tumblar, that afterwarde againe
Of a dysour, a deuyl way, grew a ientilman,
Pers Prater, the secund, that quarillis beganne;

With a pellit of peuisshenes they had suche a
     stroke,
   That all the dayes of ther lyfe shall styck by
    ther rybbis:
Foo, foisty bawdias! sum smellid of the smoke;
   I saw dyuers that were cariid away thens in
     cribbis,   640
   Dasyng after dotrellis, lyke drunkardis that
    dribbis;
Theis titiuyllis with taumpinnis wer towchid and
    tappid;
Moche mischefe, I hyght you, amonge theem ther
   happid.

Sometyme, as it semyth, when the mone light
   By meanys of a grosely endarkyd clowde
Sodenly is eclipsid in the wynter night,
   In lyke maner of wyse a myst did vs shrowde;
   But wele may ye thynk I was no thyng prowde
Of that auenturis, whiche made me sore agast.
In derkenes thus dwelt we, tyll at the last   650

The clowdis gan to clere, the myst was rarifiid:
  In an herber I saw, brought where I was,
There birdis on the brere sange on euery syde ;
  With alys ensandid about in compas,
  The bankis enturfid with singular solas,
Enrailid with rosers, and vinis engrapid ;
It was a new comfort of sorowis escapid.

In the middis a coundight, that coryously was
    cast,
  With pypes of golde engusshing out stremes ;
Of cristall the clerenes theis waters far past,   660
  Enswymmyng with rochis, barbellis, and bremis,
  Whose skales ensilured again the son beames
Englisterd, that ioyous it was to beholde.
Then furthermore aboute me my syght I reuolde,

Where I saw growyng a goodly laurell tre,
  Enuerdurid with leuis contynually grene ;
Aboue in the top a byrde of Araby,
  Men call a phenix ; her wynges bytwene
  She bet vp a fyre with the sparkis full kene
*With braunches and bowghis of the swete olyue,
Whos flagraunt flower was chefe preseruatyue   671

*Ageynst all infeccyons with cancour enflamyd,
  Ageynst all baratows broisiours of olde,

---

a Oliva speciosa in campis. [*Side Note.*]
b Nota excellentiam virtutis in oliva. [*Side Note.*]

It passid all bawmys that euer were namyd,
  Or gummis of Saby so derely that be solde :
  There blew in that gardynge a soft piplyng
    colde
Enbrethyng of Zepherus with his pleasant wynde ;
All frutis and flowris grew there in there kynde.

Dryades there daunsid vpon that goodly soile,
  With the nyne Muses, Pierides by name ;   680
Phillis and Testalis, ther tressis with oyle
  Were newly enbybid ; and rownd about the
    same
  Grene tre of laurell moche solacyous game
They made, with chapellettes and garlandes
    grene ;
And formest of all dame Flora, the quene

Of somer, so formally she fotid the daunce ;
  There Cintheus sat twynklyng vpon his harpe
    stringis ;
And Iopas his instrument did auaunce,
  The poemis and storis auncient inbryngis
  Of Athlas astrology, and many noble thyngis, 690
Of wandryng of the mone, the course of the sun,
Of men and of bestis, and whereof they begone,

What thynge occasionyd the showris of rayne,
  Of fyre elementar in his supreme spere,
And of that pole artike whiche doth remayne
  Behynde the taile of Vrsa so clere ;

Of Pliades he prechid with ther drowsy chere,
Immoysturid with mislyng and ay droppyng dry,
And where the two Trions a man shold aspy,

And of the winter days that hy them so fast,   700
And of the wynter nyghtes that tary so longe,
And of the somer days so longe that doth last,
And of their shorte nyghtes; he browght in his
      songe
How wronge was no ryght, and ryght was no
      wronge :
There was counteryng of carollis in meter and
      verse
So many, that longe it were to reherse.

Occupacyon to Skelton.

How say ye? is this after your appetite?
May this contente you and your mirry mynde?
Here dwellith pleasure, with lust and delyte;
Contynuall comfort here ye may fynde,   710
Of welth and solace no thynge left behynde;
All thynge conuenable here is contryuyd,
Wherewith your spiritis may be reuyuid.

Poeta Skelton answeryth.

Questionles no dowte of that ye say;
Jupiter hymselfe this lyfe myght endure;
This ioy excedith all worldly sport and play,
Paradyce this place is of syngular pleasure:
O wele were hym that herof myght be sure,

And here to inhabite and ay for to dwell!
But, goodly maystres, one thynge ye me tell.   720

Occupacyon to Skelton.

Of your demawnd shew me the content,
  What it is, and where vpon it standis;
And if there be in it any thyng ment,
  Wherof the answere restyth in my handis,
  It shall be losyd ful sone out of the bandis
Of scrupulus dout; wherfore your mynde dis-
        charge,
And of your wyll the plainnes shew at large.

Poeta Skelton answeryth.

I thanke you, goodly maystres, to me most
        benynge,
  That of your bounte so well haue me assurid;
But my request is not so great a thynge,   730
  That I ne force what though it be discurid;
  I am not woundid but that I may be cured;
I am not ladyn of liddyrnes with lumpis,
As dasid doterdis that dreme in their dumpis.

Occupacyon to Skelton.

Nowe what ye mene, I trow I coniect;
  Gog gyue you good yere, ye make me to
        smyle;
Now, be your faith, is not this theffect
  Of your questyon ye make all this whyle,
  To vnderstande who dwellyth in yone pile,

And what blunderar is yonder that playth didil
    diddil?   740
He fyndith fals mesuris out of his fonde fiddill.

Interpolata, quæ industriosum postulat inter-
    pretem, satira in vatis adversarium.

Tressis agasonis species prior, altera Davi :
Aucupium culicis, limis dum torquet ocellum,
Concipit, aligeras rapit, appetit, aspice, muscas !
Maia quæque fovet, fovet aut quæ Jupiter, aut
    quæ ᵃ
Frigida Saturnus, Sol, Mars, Venus, algida Luna,
Si tibi contingat verbo aut committere scripto,
Quam sibi mox tacita sudant præcordia culpa !
Hinc ruit in flammas, stimulans hunc urget et
    illum,
Invocat ad rixas, vanos tamen excitat ignes,   750
Labra movens tacitus, rumpantur ut ilia Codro. ˎ

17. 4. 7. 2. 17. 5. 18.
18. 19. 1. 19. 8. 5. 12.

His name for to know if that ye lyst,
    Enuyous Rancour truely he hight :
Beware of hym, I warne you ; for and ye wist

ᵃ Nota Alchimiam et 7 metalla. [*Side Note.*]

How daungerous it were to stande in his lyght,
   Ye wolde not dele with hym, thowgh that ye
      myght,
For by his deuellysshe drift and graceles prouision
An hole reame he is able to set at deuysion:

For when he spekyth fayrest, then thynketh he
   moost yll;
Full gloryously can he glose, thy mynde for to
   fele ;   760
He wyll set men a feightynge and syt hymselfe
   styll,
   And smerke, lyke a smythy kur, at sperkes of
      steile ;
He can neuer leue warke whylis it is wele ;
To tell all his towchis it were to grete wonder ;
The deuyll of hell and he be seldome asonder.

Thus talkyng we went forth in at a postern gate ;
   Turnyng on the ryght hande, by a windyng
      stayre,
She brought me to a goodly chaumber of astate,
   Where the noble Cowntes of Surrey in a
      chayre
Sat honorably, to whome did repaire   770
Of ladys a beue with all dew reuerence :
Syt downe, fayre ladys, and do your diligence !

Come forth, ientylwomen, I pray you, she sayd ;
   I haue contryuyd for you a goodly warke,

And who can worke beste now shall be asayde;
  A cronell of lawrell with verduris light and
    darke
  I haue deuysed for Skelton, my clerke;
For to his seruyce I haue suche regarde,
That of our bownte we wyll hym rewarde:

For of all ladyes he hath the library,   780
  Ther names recountyng in the court of Fame;
Of all gentylwomen he hath the scruteny,
  In Fames court reportynge the same;
  For yet of women he neuer sayd shame,
But if they were counterfettes that women them
    call,
That list of there lewdnesse with hym for to brall.

With that the tappettis and carpettis were layd,
  Whereon theis ladys softly myght rest,
The saumpler to sow on, the lacis to enbraid;   789
  To weue in the stoule sume were full preste;
  With slaiis, with tauellis, with hedellis well
    drest,
The frame was browght forth with his weuyng
    pin:
God geue them good spede there warke to begin!

Sume to enbrowder put them in prese,
  Well gydyng ther glowtonn to kepe streit theyr
    sylk,
Sum pirlyng of goldde theyr worke to encrese

With fingers smale, and handis whyte as mylk ;
 With, Reche me that skane of tewly sylk ;
And, Wynde me that botowme of such an hew,
Grene, rede, tawny, whyte, blak, purpill, and
    blew.   800

Of broken warkis wrought many a goodly thyng,
 In castyng, in turnynge, in florisshyng of
    flowris,
With burris rowth and bottons surffillyng,
 In nedill wark raysyng byrdis in bowris,
 With vertu enbesid all tymes and howris ;
And truly of theyr bownte thus were they bent
To worke me this chapelet by goode aduysemente.

Occupacyon to Skelton.

Beholde and se in your aduertysement
 How theis ladys and gentylwomen all
For your pleasure do there endeuourment,   810
 And for your sake how fast to warke they fall :
 To your remembraunce wherfore ye must call
In goodly wordes plesauntly comprysid,
That for them some goodly conseyt be deuysid,

With proper captacyons of beneuolence,
 Ornatly pullysshid after your faculte,
Sith ye must nedis afforce it by pretence
 Of your professyoun vnto vmanyte,
 Commensyng your proces after there degre,   819
To iche of them rendryng thankis commendable,
With sentence fructuous and termes couenable.

Poeta Skelton.

Auaunsynge my selfe sum thanke to deserue,
  I me determynyd for to sharpe my pen,
Deuoutly arrectyng my prayer to Mynerue,
  She to vowchesafe me to informe and ken;
  To Mercury also hertely prayed I then,
Me to supporte, to helpe, and to assist,
To gyde and to gouerne my dredfull tremlyng
    fist.

As a mariner that amasid is in a stormy rage,
  Hardly bestad and driuen is to hope   830
Of that the tempestuows wynde wyll aswage,
  In trust whero? comforte his hart doth grope,
  From the anker he kuttyth the gabyll rope,
Committyth all to God, and lettyth his shyp ryde;
So I beseke Ihesu now to be my gyde.

To the ryght noble Countes of Surrey.

After all duly ordred obeisaunce,
  In humble wyse as lowly as I may,
Vnto you, madame, I make reconusaunce,
  My lyfe endurynge I shall both wryte and say,
  Recount, reporte, reherse without delay   840
The passynge bounte of your noble astate,
Of honour and worshyp which hath the formar
    date:

Lyke to Argyua by iust resemblaunce,
  The noble wyfe of Polimites kynge;

Prudent Rebecca, of whome remembraunce
    The Byble makith; with whos chast lyuynge
    Your noble demenour is counterwayng,
Whos passynge bounte, and ryght noble astate,
Of honour and worship it hath the formar date.

The noble Pamphila, quene of the Grekis londe,
    Habillimentis royall founde out industriously;
Thamer also wrought with her goodly honde   852
    Many diuisis passynge curyously;
    Whome ye represent and exemplify,
Whos passynge bounte, and ryght noble astate,
Of honour and worship it hath the formar date.

As dame Thamarys, whiche toke the kyng of
        Perce,
    Cirus by name, as wrytith the story;
Dame Agrippina also I may reherse
    Of ientyll corage the perfight memory;   860
    So shall your name endure perpetually,
Whos passyng bounte, and ryght noble astate,
Of honour and worship it hath the formar date.

To my lady Elisabeth Howarde.

To be your remembrauncer, madame, I am
        bounde,
    Lyke to Aryna, maydenly of porte,
Of ᵥertu and konnyng the well and perfight
        grounde;
    Whome dame Nature, as wele I may reporte,

Hath fresshely enbewtid with many a goodly
 sorte
Of womanly feturis, whos florysshyng tender age
Is lusty to loke on, plesaunte, demure, and sage:

Goodly Creisseid, fayrer than Polexene,   871
 For to enuyue Pandarus appetite ;
Troilus, I trowe, if that he had you sene,
 In you he wolde haue set his hole delight:
 Of all your bewte I suffyce not to wryght ;
But, as I sayd, your florisshinge tender age
Is lusty to loke on, plesaunt, demure, and sage.

To my lady Mirriell Howarde.

Mi litell lady I may not leue behinde,
 But do her seruyce nedis now I must ;
Beninge, curteyse, of ientyll harte and mynde, 880
 Whome fortune and fate playnly haue discust
 Longe to enioy plesure, delyght, and lust:
The enbuddid blossoms of roses rede of hew
With lillis whyte your bewte doth renewe.

Compare you I may to Cidippes, the mayd,
 That of Aconcyus whan she founde the byll
In her bosome, lorde, how she was afrayd !
 The ruddy shamefastnes in her vysage fyll,
 Whiche maner of abasshement became her not
  yll ;
Right so, madame, the roses redde of hew   890
With lillys whyte your bewte dothe renewe.

To my lady Anne Dakers of the Sowth.

Zeuxes, that enpicturid fare Elene the quene,
　　You to deuyse his crafte were to seke;
And if Apelles your countenaunce had sene,
　　Of porturature which was the famous Greke,
　　He coude not deuyse the lest poynt of your
　　　　cheke;
Princes of yowth, and flowre of goodly porte,
Vertu, conyng, solace, pleasure, comforte.

Paregall in honour vnto Penolepe,
　　That for her trowth is in remembraunce had;
Fayre Diianira surmountynge in bewte;　　　　901
　　Demure Diana womanly and sad,
　　Whos lusty lokis make heuy hartis glad;
Princes of youth, and flowre of goodly porte,
Vertu, connyng, solace, pleasure, comforte.

To mastres Margery Wentworthe.

　　With margerain ientyll,
　　　　The flowre of goodlyhede,
　　Enbrowdred the mantill
　　　　Is of your maydenhede.
　　Plainly I can not glose;　　　　910
　　　　Ye be, as I deuyne,
　　The praty primrose,
　　　　The goodly columbyne.
　　With margerain iantill,
　　　　The flowre of goodlyhede,

Enbrawderyd the mantyll
  Is of yowre maydenhede.
Benynge, corteise, and meke,
  With wordes well deuysid;
In you, who list to seke, 920
  Be vertus well comprysid.
With margerain iantill,
  The flowre of goodlyhede,
Enbrawderid the mantill
  Is of yowr maydenhede.

To mastres Margaret Tylney.

  I you assure,
  Ful wel I know
  My besy cure
  To yow I owe;
  Humbly and low 930
  Commendynge me
  To yowre bownte.
    As Machareus
  Fayre Canace,
  So I, iwus,
  Endeuoure me
  Your name to se
  It be enrolde,
  Writtin with golde.
    Phedra ye may 940
  Wele represent;
  Intentyfe ay
  And dylygent,

No tyme myspent;
Wherfore delyght
I haue to whryght
  Of Margarite,
Perle orient,
Lede sterre of lyght,
Moche relucent;   950
Madame regent
I may you call
Of vertues all.

To maystres Iane Blenner-Haiset.

  What though my penne wax faynt,
And hath smale lust to paint?
Yet shall there no restraynt
Cause me to cese,
Amonge this prese,
For to encrese
Yowre goodly name.   960
  I wyll my selfe applye,
Trust me, ententifly,
Yow for to stellyfye;
And so obserue
That ye ne swarue
For to deserue
Inmortall fame,
  Sith mistres Iane Haiset
Smale flowres helpt to sett
In my goodly chapelet,   970
Therfore I render of her the memory
Vnto the legend of fare Laodomi.

To maystres Isabell Pennell.

By saynt Mary, my lady,
Your mammy and your dady
Brought ferth a godely babi!
My mayden Isabell,
Reflaring rosabell,
The flagrant camamell;
The ruddy rosary,
The souerayne rosemary,   980
The praty strawbery;
The columbyne, the nepte,
The ieloffer well set,
The propre vyolet;
Enuwyd your colowre
Is lyke the dasy flowre
After the Aprill showre;
Sterre of the morow gray,
The blossom on the spray,   990
The fresshest flowre of May;
Maydenly demure,
Of womanhode the lure;
Wherfore I make you sure,
It were an heuenly helth,
It were an endeles welth,
A lyfe for God hymselfe,
To here this nightingale,
Amonge the byrdes smale,
Warbelynge in the vale,
Dug, dug,   1000
Iug, iug,

Good yere and good luk,
With chuk, chuk, chuk, chuk!

To maystres Margaret Hussey.

Mirry Margaret,
As mydsomer flowre,
Ientill as fawcoun
Or hawke of the towre;
  With solace and gladnes,
Moche mirthe and no madnes,
All good and no badnes,   1010
So ioyously,
So maydenly,
So womanly
Her demenyng
In euery thynge,
Far, far passynge
That I can endyght,
Or suffyce to wryght
Of mirry Margarete,
As mydsomer flowre,   1020
Ientyll as a fawcoun
Or hawke of the towre;
  As pacient and as styll,
And as full of good wyll,
As fayre Isaphill;
Colyaunder,
Swete pomaunder,
Good cassaunder;
Stedfast of thought,

Wele made, wele wrought;   1030
Far may be sought
Erst that ye can fynde
So corteise, so kynde
As mirry Margarete,
This midsomer flowre,
Ientyll as fawcoun
Or hawke of the towre.

To mastres Geretrude Statham.

Though ye wer hard hertyd,
And I with you thwartid
With wordes that smartid,   1040
Yet nowe doutles ye geue me cause
To wryte of you this goodli clause,
Maistres Geretrude,
With womanhode endude,
With virtu well renwde.

  I wyll that ye shall be
In all benyngnyte
Lyke to dame Pasiphe;
For nowe dowtles ye geue me cause
To wryte of yow this goodly clause,   1050
Maistres Geretrude,
With womanhode endude,
With vertu well renude.

  Partly by your councell,
Garnisshed with lawrell
Was my fresshe coronell;
Wherfore doutles ye geue me cause

To wryte of you this goodly clause,
Maistres Geretrude,
With womanhode endude,   1060
With vertu well renude.

To maystres Isabell Knyght.

But if I sholde aquyte your kyndnes,
Els saye ye myght
That in me were grete blyndnes,
I for to be so myndles,
And cowde not wryght
Of Isabell Knyght.

It is not my custome nor my gyse
To leue behynde
Her that is bothe womanly and wyse,   1070
And specyally which glad was to deuyse
The menes to fynde
To please my mynde,

In helpyng to warke my laurell grene
With sylke and golde :
Galathea, the made well besene,
Was neuer halfe so fayre, as I wene,
Whiche was extolde
A thowsande folde

By Maro, the Mantuan prudent,   1080
Who list to rede ;
But, and I had leyser competent,
I coude shew you suche a presedent
In very dede
Howe ye excede.

Occupacyon to Skelton.

Withdrawe your hande, the tyme passis fast;
  Set on your hede this laurell whiche is wrought;
Here you not Eolus for you blowyth a blaste?
  I dare wele saye that ye and I be sought:
  Make no delay, for now ye must be brought 1090
Before my ladys grace, the Quene of Fame,
Where ye must breuely answere to your name.

Skelton Poeta.

Castyng my syght the chambre aboute,
  To se how duly ich thyng in ordre was,
Towarde the dore, as we were comyng oute,
  I sawe maister Newton sit with his compas,
  His plummet, his pensell, his spectacles of glas,
Dyuysynge in pycture, by his industrious wit,
Of my laurell the proces euery whitte.

Forthwith vpon this, as it were in a thought,   1100
  Gower, Chawcer, Lydgate, theis thre
Before remembred, me curteisly brought
  Into that place where as they left me,
  Where all the sayd poetis sat in there degre.
But when they sawe my lawrell rychely wrought,
All other besyde were counterfete they thought

In comparyson of that whiche I ware:
  Sume praysed the perle, some the stones
    bryght;

Wele was hym that therevpon myght stare;
 Of this warke they had so great delyght, 1110
 The silke, the golde, the flowris fresshe to
  syght,
They seyd my lawrell was the goodlyest
That euer they saw, and wrought it was the best.

In her astate there sat the noble Quene
 Of Fame: perceyuynge how that I was cum,
She wonderyd me thought at my laurell grene;
 She loked hawtly, and gaue on me a glum:
 Thhere was amonge them no worde then but
  mum,
For eche man herkynde what she wolde to me
 say;
Wherof in substaunce I brought this away. 1120

The Quene of Fame to Skelton.

My frende, sith ye ar before vs here present
 To answere vnto this noble audyence,
Of that shalbe resonde you ye must be content;
 And for as moche as, by the hy pretence
 That ye haue now thorow preemynence
Of laureat triumphe, your place is here reseruyd,
We wyll vnderstande how ye haue it deseruyd.

Skelton Poeta to the Quene of Fame.

Ryght high and myghty princes of astate,
 In famous glory all other transcendyng,
Of your bounte the accustomable rate 1130

Hath bene full often and yet is entendyng
To all that to reason is condiscendyng,
But if hastyue credence by mayntenance of myght
Fortune to stande betwene you and the lyght:

But suche euydence I thynke for to enduce,
And so largely to lay for myne indempnite,
That I trust to make myne excuse
Of what charge soeuer ye lay ageinst me ;
For of my bokis parte ye shall se,
Whiche in ycur recordes, I knowe well, be
     enrolde,   1140
And so Occupacyon, your regester, me tolde.

Forthwith she commaundid I shulde take my
     place ;
Caliope poynted me where I shulde sit :
With that, Occupacioun presid in a pace ;
Be mirry, she sayd, be not aferde a whit,
Your discharge here vnder myne arme is it.
So then commaundid she was vpon this
To shew her boke ; and she sayd, Here it is.

The Quene of Fame to Occupacioun.

Yowre boke of remembrauns we will now that
     ye rede ;
If ony recordis in noumbyr can be founde,   1150
What Skelton hath compilid and wryton in dede

Rehersyng by ordre, and what is the grownde,
Let se now for hym how ye can expounde;
For in owr courte, ye wote wele, his name can
  not ryse
But if he wryte oftenner than ones or twyse.

Skelton Poeta.

With that of the boke losende were the claspis:
  The margent was illumynid all with golden
    railles
And byse, enpicturid with gressoppes and waspis,
  With butterfllyis and fresshe pecoke taylis,
  Enflorid with flowris and slymy snaylis;   1160
Enuyuid picturis well towchid and quikly;
It wolde haue made a man hole that had be ryght
  sekely,

To beholde how it was garnysshyd and bounde,
  Encouerde ouer with golde of tissew fyne;
The claspis and bullyons were worth a thousande
    pounde;
  With balassis and charbuncles the borders did
    shyne;
  With *aurum musicum* euery other lyne
Was wrytin: and so she did her spede,
Occupacyoun, inmediatly to rede.

*Occupacyoun redith and expoundyth sum parte
of Skeltons bokes and baladis with ditis of
plesure, in as moche as it were to longe a proces
to reherse all by name that he hath compylyd,
&c.*

Of your oratour and poete laureate^a   1170
Of Englande, his workis here they begynne:
In primis the Boke of Honorous Astate;
    Item the Boke how men shulde fle synne;
    Item Royall Demenaunce worshyp to wynne;
Item the Boke to speke well or be styll;
Item to lerne you to dye when ye wyll;

Of Vertu also the souerayne enterlude;^b
    The Boke of the Rosiar; Prince Arturis Crea-
        cyoun;
The False Fayth that now goth, which dayly is
        renude;
    Item his Diologgis of Ymagynacyoun;   1180
    Item Antomedon¹ of Loues Meditacyoun;

---

a Honor est benefactivæ operationis signum: Aristotiles.
Diverte a malo, et fac bonum: Pso. Nobilis est ille quem
nobilitat sua virtus: Cassianus. Proximus ille Deo qui scit
ratione tacere: Cato. Mors ultima linea rerum: Horat.
[*Side Note.*]
    b Virtuti omnia parent: Salust. Nusquam tuta fides: Vir-
gilius. Res est soliciti plena timoris amor: Ovid. Si volet
usus, quem penes, &c.: Horace. [*Side Note.*]
    ¹ *Antomedon*] Qy. " Automedon?"

Item New Gramer in Englysshe compylyd ;
Item Bowche of Courte, where Drede was be-
gyled ;

His commedy, Achademios callyd by name ;
Of Tullis Familiars the translacyoun ;
Item Good Aduysement, that brainles doth blame ;
The Recule ageinst Gaguyne of the Frenshe
nacyoun ;
Item the Popingay, that hath in commenda-
cyoun
Ladyes and gentylwomen suche as deseruyd,
And suche as be counterfettis they be reseruyd ;

[b] And of Soueraynte a noble pamphelet ;   1191
And of Magnyfycence a notable mater,
How Cownterfet Cowntenaunce of the new get
With Crafty Conueyaunce dothe smater and
flater,
And Cloked Collucyoun is brought in to clater
With Courtely Abusyoun ; who pryntith it wele
in mynde
Moche dowblenes of the worlde therin he may
fynde ;

[a] Non est timor Dei ante oculos eorum: Psalmo.   Concedat
laurea linguæ: Tullius.   Fac cum consilio, et in æternum
non peccabis: Salamon.   [*Side Note.*]
[b] Non mihi sit modulo rustica papilio: Vates.   Dominare
in virtute tua: Pso.   Magnificavit eum in conspectu regum:
Sapient.   Fugere pudor, verumque, fidesque: In quorum
subiere locum fraudesque, dolique, Insidiæque, et vis, et amor
sceleratus habendi: Ovid.   Filia Babylonis misera: Psalmo.
[*Side Note.*]

Of manerly maistres Margery Mylke and Ale ;
    To her he wrote many maters of myrthe ;
Yet, thoughe I say it, therby lyith a tale,   1200
    For Margery wynshed, and breke her hinder
        girth ;
    Lor, how she made moche of her gentyll birth !
With, Gingirly, go gingerly ! her tayle was made
    of hay ;
Go she neuer so gingirly, her honesty is gone
    away ;

Harde to make ought of that is nakid nought ;*
    This fustiane maistres and this giggisse gase,
Wonder is to wryte what wrenchis she wrowght,
    To face out her foly with a midsomer mase ;
    With pitche she patchid her pitcher shuld not
        crase ;
It may wele ryme, but shroudly it doth accorde,
To pyke out honesty of suche a potshorde :   1211

         Patet per versus.
Hinc puer hic natus ; vir conjugis hinc spoliatus [b]
Jure thori ; est foetus Deli de sanguine cretus ;
Hinc magis extollo, quod erit puer alter Apollo ;
Si quæris qualis ? meretrix castissima talis ;
        Et relis, et ralis, et reliqualis.

a De nihilo nihil fit: Aristotiles.   Le plus displeysant
pleiser puent. [*Side Note.*]
b Nota. [*Side Note.*]

A good herynge of thes olde talis;
Fynde no mo suche fro Wanflete to Walis.
Et reliqua omelia de diversis tractatibus.

ᵃ Of my ladys grace at the contemplacyoun,
 Owt of Frenshe into Englysshe prose, 1220
Of Mannes Lyfe the Peregrynacioun,
 He did translate, enterprete, and disclose;
 The Tratyse of Triumphis of the Rede Rose,
Wherein many storis ar breuely contayned
That vnremembred longe tyme remayned;

The Duke of Yorkis creauncer whan Skelton was,
 Now Henry the viij. Kyng of Englonde,
A tratyse he deuysid and browght it to pas,
 ᵇ Callid *Speculum Principis*, to bere in his honde,
 Therin to rede, and to vnderstande 1230
All the demenour of princely astate,
To be our Kyng, of God preordinate;

ᶜAlso the Tunnynge of Elinour Rummyng,
 With Colyn Clowt, Iohnn Iue, with Ioforth
 Iack;

a Apostolus: Non habemus hic civitatem manentem, sed
futuram perquærimus. Notat bellum Cornubiense, quod in
campestribus et in patentioribus vastisque solitudinibus prope
Grenewiche gestum est. [*Side Note.*]

b Erudimini qui judicatis terram: Pso. [*Side Note.*]

c Quis stabit mecum adversus operantes iniquitatem? Pso.
Arrident melius seria picta jocis: In fabulis Æsopi. [*Side
Note.*]

To make suche trifels it asketh sum konnyng,
    In honest myrth parde requyreth no lack ;
    The whyte apperyth the better for the black,
And after conueyauns as the world goos,
It is no foly to vse the Walshemannys hoos ;

The vmblis of venyson, the botell of wyne,[a]   1240
    To fayre maistres Anne that shuld haue be sent,
He wrate therof many a praty lyne,
    Where it became, and whether it went,
    And how that it was wantonly spent ;
The Balade also of the Mustarde Tarte
Suche problemis to paynt it longyth to his arte ;

Of one Adame all a knaue, late dede and gone,—[b]
    Dormiat in paee, lyke a dormows !—
He wrate an Epitaph for his graue stone,   1249
    With wordes deuoute and sentence agerdows,
    For he was euer ageynst Goddis hows,
All his delight was to braule and to barke
Ageynst holy chyrche, the preste, and the clarke ;

Of Phillip Sparow the lamentable fate,
    The dolefull desteny, and the carefull chaunce,

a Implentur veteris Bacchi pinguisque ferinæ: Virgilius.
Aut prodesse volunt aut delectare poetæ: Horace. | Side
Note.]
    b Adam, Adam, ubi es? Genesis. Resp. Ubi nulla re-
quies, ubi nullus ordc, sed sempiternus horror inhabitat: Job.
| Side Note.]

Dyuysed by Skelton after the funerall rate;
  Yet sum there be therewith that take greuaunce,
  And grudge therat with frownyng counte-
      naunce;
ᵃ But what of that? hard it is to please all men;
Who list amende it, let hym set to his penne; 1260
    For the gyse now adays
    Of sum iangelyng iays
    Is to discommende
    That they can not amende,
    Though they wolde spende
    All the wittis they haue.
     What ayle them to depraue
    Phillippe Sparows graue?
    His *Dirige*, her Commendacioun
    Can be no derogacyoun,   1270
    But myrth and consolacyoun,
    Made by protestacyoun,
    No man to myscontent
    With Phillippis enteremente.
     Alas, that goodly mayd,
    Why shulde she be afrayd?
    Why shulde she take shame
    That her goodly name,
    Honorably reportid,
    Shulde be set and sortyd,   1280
    To be matriculate
    With ladyes of astate?

a Etenim passer invenit sibi domum: Psalmo. [*Side Note.*]

I coniure thé, Phillip Sparow,
By Hercules that hell did harow,
And with a venomows arow
Slew of the Epidawris
One of the Centawris,
Or Onocentauris,
Or Hippocentauris ;
By whos myght and maine   1290
An hart was slayne
With hornnis twayne
Of glitteryng golde ;
And the apples of golde
Of Hesperides withholde,
And with a dragon kepte
That neuer more slepte,
By merciall strength
He wan at length ;
And slew Gerione   1300
With thre bodys in one ;
With myghty corrage
Adauntid the rage
Of a lyon sauage ;
Of Diomedis stabyll
He brought out a rabyll
Of coursers and rounsis
With lepes and bounsis ;
And with myghty luggyng,
Wrastelynge and tuggyng,   1310
He pluckid the bull
By the hornid scull,

And offred to Cornucopia ;
And so forthe *per cetera :*
    Also by Hectates bowre
In Plutos gastly towre ;
    By the vgly Eumenides,
That neuer haue rest nor ease ;
    By the venemows serpent
That in hell is neuer brente,   1320
In Lerna the Grekis fen
That was engendred then ;
    By Chemeras flamys,
And all the dedely namys
Of infernall posty,
Where soulis fry and rosty ;
    By the Stigiall flode,
And the stremes wode
Of Cochitos bottumles well ;
    By the feryman of hell,   1330
Caron with his berde hore,
That rowyth with a rude ore,
And with his frownsid fortop
Gydith his bote with a prop :
    I coniure [1] Phillippe, and call,
In the name of Kyng Saull ;
Primo Regum expres,
He bad the Phitones
To witche craft her to dres,
And by her abusiouns,   1340

---

[1] *coniure*] Qy. " *coniure* thé ? " as before and after.

And damnable illusiouns
Of meruelous conclusiouns,
And by her supersticiouns
Of wonderfull condiciouns,
She raysed vp in that stede
Samuell that was dede ;
But whether it were so,
He were *idem in numero,*
The selfe same Samuell,
How be it to Saull he did tell   1350
The Philistinis shulde hym askry,
And the next day he shulde dye,
I wyll my selfe discharge
To letterd men at large :
But, Phillip, I coniure thé
Now by theys names thre,
Diana in the woddis grene,
Luna that so bryght doth shene,
Proserpina in hell,
That thou shortely tell,   1360
And shew now vnto me
What the cause may be
Of this perplexyte !

Inferias, Philippe, tuas Scroupe pulchra Joanna [a]
Instanter petiit : cur nostri carminis illam
Nunc pudet ? est sero ; minor est infamia vero.

a Phillyppe answeryth. [*Side Note.*]

Then such that haue disdaynyd
And of this worke complaynyd,
I pray God they be paynyd
No wors than is contaynyd   1370
In verses two or thre
That folowe as ye may se:
Luride, cur, livor, volucris pia funera damnas?
Talia te rapiant rapiunt quæ fata volucrem!
Est tamen invidia mors tibi continua:

The Gruptyng and the groynninge of the gron-
    nyng swyne; *
Also the Murnyng of the mapely rote;
How the grene couerlet sufferd grete pine,
    Whan the flye net was set for to catche a cote,
    Strake one with a birdbolt to the hart rote; 1380
Also a deuoute Prayer to Moyses hornis,
Metrifyde merely, medelyd with scornis;

b Of paiauntis that were played in Ioyows Garde;
    He wrate of a muse throw a mud wall;
How a do cam trippyng in at the rere warde,
    But, lorde, how the parker was wroth with all!
    And of Castell Aungell the fenestrall,

a Porcus se ingurgitat cæno, et luto se immergit: Guarinus
Veronens. Et sicut opertorium mutabis eos, et mutabuntur:
Pso. c. Exaltabuntur cornua justi: Psalmo. [*Side Note.*]
    b Tanquam parieti inclinato et maceriæ depulsæ: Psalmo.
Militat omnis amans, et habet sua castra Cupido: Ovid.
[*Side Note.*]

Glittryng and glistryng and gloryously glasid,
It made sum mens eyn dasild and dasid;   1389

The Repete of the recule of Rosamundis bowre,[a]
  Of his pleasaunt paine there and his glad
    distres
In plantynge and pluckynge a propre ieloffer
    flowre;
But how it was, sum were to recheles,
Not withstandynge it is remedeles;
What myght she say? what myght he do therto?
Though Iak sayd nay, yet Mok there loste her
    sho;

How than lyke a man he wan the barbican [b]
  With a sawte of solace at the longe last;
The colour dedely, swarte, blo, and wan
  Of Exione, her lambis [1] dede and past,   1400
    The cheke and the nek but a shorte cast;
In fortunis fauour euer to endure,
No man lyuyng, he sayth, can be sure;

  a Introduxit me in cubiculum suum: Cant.   Os fatuæ [2]
ebullit stultitiam.   Cant.   [Side Note.]
  b Audaces fortuna juvat: Virgilius.   Nescia mens hominum
sortis [3] fatique futuri: Virgilius.   [Side Note.]
  [1] lambis] Marshe's ed. "lambe is," — which may be the
right reading.   MS. defective here.
  [2] fatuæ] Altered purposely by Skelton from "fatuorum"
of the Vulgate, Prov. xv. 2. (not Cant.)
  [3] sortis, &c.] "fati sortisque futuræ."   Æn. x. 501.

*How dame Minerua[1] first found the olyue tre,
    she red
And plantid it there where neuer before was
    none ; *vnshred*
An hynde vnhurt hit by casuelte, *not bled*
    Recouerd whan the forster was gone ; *and sped*
The hertis of the herd began for to grone, *and
    fled*
The howndes began to yerne and to quest ; *and
    dred*   1409
With litell besynes standith moche rest ; *in bed*

*His Epitomis of the myller and his ioly make ;
    How her ble was bryght as blossom on the
    spray,
A wanton wenche and wele coude bake a cake ;
    The myllar was loth to be out of the way,
    But yet for all that, be as be may,
Whether he rode to Swaffhamm or to Some,
The millar durst not leue his wyfe at home ;

a Oleæque Minerva inventrix: Georgicorum.   Atque ag-
mina cervi pulverulenta [fuga] glomerant: Æneid. iv.   [*Side
Note.*]
    b Duæ molentes in pistrino, una assumetur, altera relinque-
tur: Isaias.[2]   Foris vastabit eum timor, et intus pavor: Pso.[3]
| *Side Note.*]

    [1] *How dame Minerua, &c.*]   The words which I have printed
in Italics destroy both sense and metre.   But they are found
in both eds.   MS. defective here.
    [2] *Isaias*]   *Matt.* xxiv. 41.
    [3] *Pso.*]   *Deut.* xxxii. 25, where "Foris vastabit *eos gladius,*
et, &c."

With, Wofully arayd,[1] and Shamefully betrayd,[a]
  Of his makyng deuoute medytacyons;
Vexilla regis he deuysid to be displayd;   1420
  With Sacris solemniis, and other contempla-
      cyouns,
  That in them comprisid consyderacyons;
Thus passyth he the tyme both nyght and day,
Sumtyme with sadnes, sumtyme with play;

Though Galiene and Dioscorides,[b]
  With Ipocras, and mayster Auycen,
By there phesik doth many a man ease,
  And though Albumasar can thé enforme and
      ken
  What constellacions ar good or bad for men,   1429
Yet whan the rayne rayneth and the gose wynkith,
Lytill wotith the goslyng what the gose thynkith;

He is not wyse ageyne the streme that stryuith;[c]
  Dun is in the myre, dame, reche me my spur;

a Opera quæ ego facio ipsa perhibent testimonium de me:
In Evang. &c.   [Side Note.]
  b Honora medicum; propter necessitatem creavit eum al-
tissimus, &c.   Superiores constellationes influunt in corpora
subjecta et disposita, &c.   Nota.   [Side Note.]
  c Spectatum admisse,[2] risus teneatur amor? Horace. Nota.
[Side Note.]
  1 Wofully arayd] See vol. i. p. 165.
  2 Spectatum admisse, &c.] "Spectatum admissi risum teneatis,
amici?" A. P. 5.   Qy. Is the barbarous alteration of this
line only a mistake of the printer?

Nedes must he rin that the deuyll dryuith;
  When the stede is stolyn, spar the stable dur;
  A ientyll hownde shulde neuer play the kur;
It is sone aspyed where the thorne prikkith;
And wele wotith the cat whos berde she likkith;

^a With Marione clarione, sol, lucerne,
  Graund juir, of this Frenshe prouerbe olde, 1440
How men were wonte for to discerne
  By candelmes day what wedder shuld holde;
  But Marione clarione was caught with a colde
      colde,   (*anglice* a cokwolde,
And all ouercast with cloudis vnkynde,
This goodly flowre with stormis was vntwynde;

^b This ieloffer ientyll, this rose, this lylly flowre,
  This primerose pereles, this propre vyolet,
This columbyne clere and fresshest of coloure,
  This delycate dasy, this strawbery pretely set,
  With frowarde frostis, alas, was all to-fret! 1450
But who may haue a more vngracyous lyfe
Than a chyldis birde and a knauis wyfe?

          ^c Thynke what ye wyll
          Of this wanton byll;

----

a Lumen ad revelationem gentium: Pso. clxxv. [*Side Note.*] [Luc. ii. 32.]
  b Velut rosa vel lilium, O pulcherrima mulierum, &c.: Cantat ecclesia. [*Side Note.*]
  c Notate verba, signata mysteria: Gregori. [*Side Note.*]

By Mary Gipcy,
Quod scripsi, scripsi :
Uxor tua, sicut vitis,
Habetis in custodiam,
Custodite sicut scitis,
Secundum Lucam, &c.   1460

Of the Bonehoms of Ashrige besyde Barkamstede,
    That goodly place to Skelton moost kynde,
Where the sank royall is, Crystes blode so rede,
    Wherevpon he metrefyde after his mynde ;
A pleasaunter place than Ashrige is, harde
    were to fynde,
As Skelton rehersith, with wordes few and playne,
In his distichon made on verses twaine ;

Fraxinus in clivo frondetque viret sine rivo, [a]
Non est sub divo similis sine flumine vivo ;

The Nacyoun of Folys he left not behynde ; [b]   1470
    Item Apollo that whirllid vp his chare,
That made sum to snurre and snuf in the wynde ;
    It made them to skip, to stampe, and to stare,
    Whiche, if they be happy, haue cause to beware
In ryming and raylyng with hym for to mell,
For drede that he lerne them there A, B, C, to
    spell.

a Nota penuriam aquæ, nam canes ibi hauriunt ex puteo
altissimo. [*Side Note.*]
b Stultorum infinitus est numerus, &c. : Ecclesia. Factum
est cum Apollo esset Corinthi : Actus Apostolorum. Stimu-
los sub pectore vertit Apollo : Virgilius. [*Side Note.*]

Poeta Skelton.

With that I stode vp, halfe sodenly afrayd ;
　Suppleyng to Fame, I besought her grace,
And that it wolde please her, full tenderly I
　　prayd, .
　Owt of her bokis Apollo to rase.　　　　1480
Nay, sir, she sayd, what so in this place
ᵃ Of our noble courte is ones spoken owte,
It must nedes after rin all the worlde aboute.

God wote, theis wordes made me full sad ;
　And when that I sawe it wolde no better be,
But that my peticyon wolde not be had,
　What shulde I do but take it in gre ?
ᵇ For, by Juppiter and his high mageste,
I did what I cowde to scrape out the scrollis,
Apollo to rase out of her ragman rollis.　　　1490

ᶜ Now hereof it erkith me lenger to wryte ;
　To Occupacyon I wyll agayne resorte,
Whiche redde on still, as it cam to her syght,
　Rendrynge my deuisis I made in disporte
　Of the Mayden of Kent callid Counforte,
Of Louers testamentis and of there wanton wyllis,
And how Iollas louyd goodly Phillis ;

---

a Fama repleta malis pernicibus evolat alis, &c. [*Side Note.*]
　b Ego quidem sum Pauli, ego Apollo: Corᵐ. [*Side Note.*]
　c Malo me Galatea petit, lasciva puella: Virgilius.　Nec, si muneribus certes, concedet Iollas: 2. Bucol. [*Side Note.*]

Diodorus Siculus of my translacyon
  Out of fresshe Latine into owre Englysshe
    playne,
Recountyng commoditis of many a straunge
    nacyon ; *a*   1500
  Who redyth it ones wolde rede it agayne ;
Sex volumis engrosid together it doth containe :
But when of the laurell she made rehersall,
All orators and poetis, with other grete and
    smale,

A thowsande thowsande, I trow, to my dome,*b*
Triumpha, triumpha! they cryid all aboute ;
Of trumpettis and clariouns the noyse went to
    Rome ;
  The starry heuyn, me thought, shoke with the
    showte ;
  The grownde gronid and tremblid, the noyse
    was so stowte :
The Quene of Fame commaundid shett fast the
    boke ;   1510
And therwith sodenly out of my dreme I woke.

---

a Mille hominum species, et rerum discolor usus: Horace.[1]
[*Side Note.*]
  b Millia millium et decies millies centena millia, &c.:
Apocalipsis. Virtute [2] senatum laureati possident: Eccle-
siastica. Cauit'. [*Side Note.*]

  [1] *Horace*] Persius, V. 52.
  [2] *Virtute*] Faukes's ed. (which alone has these marginal
notes) " *Vite.*" The reference " Cauit'" I do not understand.

My mynde of the grete din was somdele amasid,
 I wypid myne eyne for to make them clere;
Then to the heuyn sperycall vpwarde I gasid,
 Where I saw Ianus, with his double chere,
 Makynge his almanak for the new yere;
He turnyd his tirikkis, his voluell ran fast:
Good luk this new yere! the olde yere is past.

  a Mens tibi sit consulta, petis? sic consule menti;
  Æmula sit Jani, retro speculetur et ante.   1520

   Skeltonis alloquitur librum suum.
Ite, Britannorum lux O radiosa, Britannum
Carmina nostra pium vestrum celebrate Catullum!
 Dicite, Skeltonis vester Adonis erat;
 Dicite, Skeltonis vester Homerus erat.
Barbara cum Latio pariter jam currite versu;
Et licet est verbo pars maxima texta Britanno,
 Non magis incompta nostra Thalia patet,
 Est magis inculta nec mea Calliope.
Nec vos pœniteat livoris tela subire,
Nec vos pœniteat rabiem tolerare caninam,   1530
Nam Maro dissimiles non tulit ille minas,
 Immunis nec enim Musa Nasonis erat.

   Lenuoy.
  Go, litill quaire,
  Demene you faire;

   a Vates. [*Side Note.*]

Take no dispare,
Though I you wrate
After this rate
In Englysshe letter;
So moche the better
Welcome shall ye   1540
To sum men be:
For Latin warkis
Be good for clerkis;
Yet now and then
Sum Latin men
May happely loke
Vpon your boke,
And so procede
In you to rede,
That so indede
Your fame may sprede   1550
In length and brede.
But then I drede
Ye shall haue nede
You for to spede
To harnnes bryght,
By force of myght,
Ageyne enuy
And obloquy:
And wote ye why?   1560
Not for to fyght
Ageyne dispyght,
Nor to derayne
Batayle agayne

Scornfull disdayne,
Nor for to chyde,
Nor for to hyde
You cowardly;
But curteisly
That I haue pende   1570
For to deffend,
Vnder the banner
Of all good manner,
Vnder proteccyon
Of sad correccyon,
With toleracyon
And supportacyon
Of reformacyon,
If they can spy
Circumspectly   1580
Any worde defacid
That myght be rasid,
Els ye shall pray
Them that ye may
Contynew still
With there good wyll.

Ad serenissimam Majestatem Regiam, pariter cum
      Domino
Cardinali, Legato a latere honorificatissimo, &c.

Lautre Enuoy.
Perge, liber, celebrem pronus regem venerare
Henricum octavum, resonans sua præmia laudis.

Cardineum dominum pariter venerando salutes,
Legatum a latere, et fiat memor ipse precare 1590
Prebendæ, quam promisit mihi credere quondam,
Meque suum referas pignus sperare salutis
Inter spemque metum.

> Twene hope and drede
> My lyfe I lede,
> But of my spede
> Small sekernes':
> Howe be it I rede
> Both worde and dede
> Should be agrede 1600
> In noblenes :
> Or.els, &c.

ADMONET SKELTONIS OMNES ARBORES DARE LOCUM VIRIDI
LAURO JUXTA GENUS SUUM.

Fraxinus in silvis, altis in montibus ornus,
Populus in fluviis, abies, patulissima fagus,
Lenta salix, platanus, pinguis ficulnea ficus,
Glandifera et quercus, pirus, esculus, ardua pinus,
Balsamus exudans, oleaster, oliva Minervæ,
Juniperus, buxus, lentiscus cuspide lenta,
Botrigera et domino vitis gratissima Baccho,
Ilex et sterilis labrusca perosa colonis,
Mollibus exudans fragrantia thura Sabæis
Thus, redolens Arabis pariter notissima myrrha, 10
Et vos, O coryli fragiles, humilesque myricæ,
Et vos, O cedri redolentes, vos quoque myrti,
Arboris omne genus viridi concedite lauro!
  Prennees en gre   *The Laurelle.*

---

* These Latin lines, with the copy of French verses which
follow them, and the translations of it into Latin and English,
are from Faukes's ed.—where, though they have really no
connexion with *The Garlande of Laurell*, they are considered
as a portion of that poem, see the colophon, p. 244 ; collated
with Marshe's ed. of Skelton's *Workes*, 1568,—where they
occur towards the end of the vol., the last three placed to-
gether, and the first a few pages after.—Marshe's ed. " Ad-
monitio *Skeltonis* ut *omnes Arbores viridi Laureo* concedant. `

EN PARLAMENT A PARIS.

Iustice est morte,
Et Veryte sommielle ;
Droit et Raison
Sont alez aux pardons :
Lez deux premiers
Nul ne les resuelle ;
Et lez derniers
Sount corrumpus par dons.

OUT OF FRENSHE INTO LATYN.

Abstulit atra dies Astræam ; cana Fides sed
   Somno pressa jacet ; Jus iter arripuit,
Et secum Ratio proficiscens limite longo :
   Nemo duas primas evigilare parat ;
Atque duo postrema absunt, et munera tantum
   Impediunt nequeunt quod remeare domum.

OWT OF LATYNE INTO ENGLYSSHE.

Justyce now is dede ;
Trowth with a drowsy hede,
As heuy as the lede,
Is layd down to slepe,
And takith no kepe ;
And Ryght is ouer the fallows
Gone to seke hallows,
With Reason together,
No man can tell whether :

No man wyll vndertake   10
The first twayne to wake;
And the twayne last
Be withholde so fast
With mony, as men sayne,
They can not come agayne.

A grant tort,
Foy dort.

Here endith a ryght delectable tratyse vpon a goodly Garlonde or Chapelet of Laurell, dyuysed by mayster Skelton, Poete Laureat.

SPEKE, PARROT.*

THE BOKE COMPILED BY MAISTER SKELTON, POET LAUREAT,
CALLED SPEAKE, PARROT.

[Lectoribus auctor recipit¹ opusculi hujus auxesim.

Crescet in immensum me vivo pagina præsens ;
Hinc mea dicetur Skeltonidis aurea fama.

Parot.]

My name is Parrot, a byrd of paradyse,
  By nature deuysed of a wonderous kynde,
Dyentely dyeted with dyuers dylycate spyce,
  Tyl Euphrates, that flode, dryueth me into
    Inde ;ᵃ

---

a Lucanus.² Tigris et Euphrates uno se fonte resolvunt.
[*Side Note.*]

* From the ed. by Lant of *Certayne bokes compyled by mays-
ter Skelton,* &c., n. d., collated with the same work ed. Kynge
and Marche, n. d., and ed. Day, n. d.; with Marshe's ed. of
Skelton's *Workes,* 1568; and with a MS. in the Harleian Col-
lection, 2252. fol. 133, which has supplied much not given in
the printed copies, and placed between brackets in the present
edition. The margiral notes are found only in MS.

¹ *recipit*] MS. "*recepit.*" The next two lines are given
very inaccurately here in MS., but are repeated (with a slight
variation) more correctly at the end of the poem. The Latin
portions of the MS. are generally of ludicrous incorrectness,
the transcriber evidently not having understood that lan-
guage.

² *Lucanus*] See *Phar.* iii. 256. But the line here quoted is
from Boethii *Consol. Phil.* lib. v. met. 1.

Where men of that countrey by fortune me
    fynd,
And send me to greate ladyes of estate ;
Then Parot must haue an almon or a date :

[a] A cage curyously caruen, with syluer pyn,   10
    Properly paynted, to be my couertowre ;
A myrrour of glasse, that I may toote therin ;
    These maidens ful mekely with many a diuers
        flowre
    Freshly they dresse, and make swete my
        bowre,
With, Speke, Parrot, I pray you, full curtesly
    they say ;
Parrot is a goodly byrd, a prety popagey :

[b] With my becke bent my lyttyl wanton eye,
    My fedders freshe as is the emrawde grene,
About my neck a cyrculet lyke the ryche rubye,
    My lyttyll leggys, my feet both fete and clene,20
    I am a mynyon to wayt vppon a quene ;
My proper Parrot, my lyttyl prety foole ;
With ladyes I lerne, and go with them to scole.

Hagh, ha, ha, Parrot, ye can laugh pretyly !
    Parrot hath not dyned of al this long day :

a Topographia, quam habet hæc avicula in deliciis. [*Side Note.*]

b Delectatur in factura sua, tamen res est forma fugax.
[*Side Note.*]

Lyke your pus cate, Parrot can mute and cry
  *In Lattyn, in Ebrew, Araby, and Caldey;
  In Greke tong Parrot can bothe speke and say,
  As Percyus, that poet, doth reporte of me,
  Quis expedivit psittaco suum chaire?   30

Dowse French of Parryse Parrot can lerne,[b]
  Pronounsynge my purpose after my properte,
With, *Perliez byen*, Parrot, *ou perlez rien ;*
  With Douch, with Spanysh, my tong can agre ;
  In Englysh to God Parrot can supple,
Cryst saue Kyng Henry the viii., our royall kyng,
The red rose in honour to florysh and sprynge!

With Kateryne incomparable, our ryall quene also,[c]
  That pereles pomegarnet, Chryst saue her noble
    grace !
Parrot, *saves* [1] *habler Castiliano*,   40

a Psittacus a vob:s aliorum nomina disco: Hoc per me
didici dicere,[2] Cæsar, ave. [*Side Note.*]
  b Docibilem se pandit in omni idiomate. Polichronitudo
Basileos. [*Side Note.*]
  c Katerina universalis vitii ruina, Græcum est. Fidasso
de cosso, i. habeto fidem in temet ipso. Auctoritate[m] in-
consultam taxat hic. Lege Flaccum, et observa plantatum
diabolum. [*Side Note.*]
  1 *saves*] So MS. Eds. "*sauies :*"—"*habler*" ought to be
"*hablar ;*" but throughout this work I have not altered the
spelling of quotations in *modern* languages, because probably
Skelton wrote them inaccurately.
  2 *dicere*] In Martial thus:
        " *Psittacus a vobis aliorum nomina discam :*
          Hoc didici per me dicere, Cæsar, ave."   xiv. 73.

With *fidasso de cosso* in Turkey and in Trace ;
Vis consilii expers, as techith me Horace,
Mole ruit sua, whose dictes ar pregnaunte,
Souentez foys, Parrot, *en souenaunte*.

^a^My lady maystres, dame Philology,
    Gaue me a gyfte in my nest whan I laye,
To lerne all language, and it to spake aptely :
Now *pandez mory*, wax frantycke, some men saye,
    Phroneses for Freneses may not holde her way.
An almon now for Parrot, dilycatly drest ;   50
In *Salve festa dies*, *toto* theyr doth best.

^b^*Moderata juvant*, but *toto* doth excede ;
    Dyscressyon is moder of noble vertues all ;
Myden agan in Greke tonge we rede ;
    But reason and wyt wantyth theyr prouyncyall
    When wylfulnes is vycar generall.
Hæc res acu tangitur, Parrot, *par ma foy :*
Ticez vous, Parrot, *tenez vous coye.*

Besy, besy, besy, and besynes agayne !
    Que pensez voz, Parrot? what meneth this be-
      synes ?   60

---

a Sæpenumero hæc pensitans psittacus ego pronuntio.[1]
Aphorismo, quia paronomasia certe incomprehensibilis. [*Side Note.*]

    b Aptius hic loquitur animus quam lingua. Notum adagium et exasperans. [*Side Note.*]

    [1] *pronuntio*] Probably not the right reading. The MS. seems to have either " pō sio " or " pō fio."

Vitulus in Oreb troubled Arons brayne,
  Melchisedeck mercyfull made Moloc mercyles ;
To wyse is no vertue, to medlyng, to restles ;
In mesure is tresure, *cum sensu maturato ;*
Ne tropo sanno, ne tropo mato.

Aram was fyred with Caldies fyer called Ur ;
  Iobab was brought vp in the lande of Hus ;
The lynage of Lot toke supporte of Assur ;
  Iereboseth is Ebrue, who lyst the cause dyscus.
Peace, Parrot, ye prate, as ye were *ebrius :*   70
Howst thé, *lyuer god van hemrik, ic seg ;*
In Popering grew peres, whan Parrot was an eg.

What is this to purpose? Ouer in a whynny meg !
  Hop Lobyn of Lowdeon wald haue e byt of
    bred ;
The iebet of Baldock was made for Jack Leg ;
  An arrow vnfethered and without an hed,
  A bagpype without blowynge standeth in no
    sted :
Some run to far before, some run to far behynde,
Some be to churlysshe, and some be to kynde.

Ic dien serueth for the erstrych fether,   80
  Ic dien is the language of the land of Beme ;
In Affryc tongue *byrsa* is a thonge of lether ;
  In Palestina there is Ierusalem.
  Colostrum now for Parot, whyte bred and
    swete creme !

Our Thomasen she doth trip, our Ienet she doth
    shayle :
Parrot hath a blacke beard and a fayre grene
    tayle.

Moryshe myne owne shelfe, the costermonger
    sayth ;
    Fate, fate, fate, ye Irysh water lag ;
In flattryng fables men fynde but lyttyl fayth :
    But *moveatur terra*, let the world wag ;   90
    Let syr Wrigwrag wrastell with syr Delarag ;
Euery man after his maner of wayes,
Pawbe une aruer, so the Welche man sayes.

Suche shredis of sentence, strowed in the shop
    Of auncyent Aristippus and such other mo,
I gader togyther and close in my crop,
    Of my wanton conseyt, *unde depromo*
    Dilemmata docta in pædagogio
Sacro vatum, whereof to you I breke :
I pray you, let Parot haue lyberte to speke.   100

But ware the cat, Parot, ware the fals cat !
    With, Who is there? a mayd? nay, nay, I
        trow :
Ware ryat, Parrot, ware ryot, ware that !
    Mete, mete for Parrot, mete, I say, how !
    Thus dyuers of language by lernyng I grow :
With, Bas me, swete Parrot, bas me, swete swete ;
To dwell amonge ladyes Parrot is mete.

Parrot, Parrot, Parrot, praty popigay!
   With my beke I can pyke my lyttel praty too.
My delyght is solas, pleasure, dysporte, and pley;
   Lyke a wanton, whan I wyll, I rele to and
       froo: 111
Parot can say, *Cæsar, ave*, also;
But Parrot hath no fauour to Esebon:
Aboue all other byrdis, set Parrot alone.

Ulula, Esebon, for Ieromy doth wepe!
   Sion is in sadnes, Rachell ruly doth loke;
Madionita Ietro, our Moyses kepyth his shepe;
   Gedeon is gon, that Zalmane vndertoke,
   Oreb *et* Zeb, of *Judicum* rede the boke;
Now Geball, Amon, and Amaloch, — harke,
       harke!   120
Parrot pretendith to be a bybyll clarke.

O Esebon, Esebon! to thé is cum agayne
   Seon, the regent *Amorræorum*,
And Og, that fat hog of Basan, doth retayne,
   The crafty *coistronus Cananæorum;*
   And *asylum*, whilom *refugium miserorum*,
Non fanum, sed profanum, standyth in lyttyll
       sted:
Ulula, Esebon, for Iepte is starke ded!

Esebon, Marybon, Wheston next Barnet;
   A trym tram for an horse myll it were a nyse
       thyng;   130

Deyntes for dammoysels, chaffer far fet:
    Bo ho doth bark wel, but Hough ho he rulyth
       the ring;
    From Scarpary to Tartary renoun therin doth
       spryng,
With, He sayd, and we said, ich wot now what
       ich wot,
Quod magnus est dominus Judas Scarioth.

Tholomye and Haly were cunnyng and wyse
    In the volvell, in the quadrant, and in the
       astroloby,
To pronostycate truly the chaunce of fortunys
       dyse;
    Som trete of theyr tirykis, som of astrology,
    Som *pseudo-propheta* with chiromancy: 140
Yf fortune be frendly, and grace be the guyde,
Honowre with renowne wyll ren on that syde.

           Monon calon agaton,
           Quod Parato
           In Græco.

Let Parrot, I pray you, haue lyberte to prate,
    For *aurea lingua Græca* ought to be magny-
       fyed,
Yf it were cond perfytely, and after the rate,
    As *lingua Latina,* in scole matter occupyed;
    But our Grekis theyr Greke so well haue ap-
       plyed,   150

That they cannot say in Greke, rydynge by the
    way,
How, hosteler, fetche my hors a botell of hay!

Neyther frame a silogisme in *phrisesomorum*,
    Formaliter et Græce, cum medio termino :
Our Grekys ye walow in the washbol *Argoli-*
    corum ;
    For though ye can tell in Greke what is
    phormio,
    Yet ye seke out your Greke in *Capricornio ;*
For they [1] scrape out good scrypture, and set in
    a gall,
Ye go about to amende, and ye mare all.

Some argue *secundum quid ad simpliciter,*   160
    And yet he wolde be rekenyd *pro Areopagita ;*
And some make distinctions *multipliciter,*
    Whether *ita* were before *non,* or *non* before *ita,*
    Nether wise ncr wel lernid, but like *herma-*
    phrodita :
Set *sophia* asyde, for euery·Jack Raker
And euery mad medler must now be a maker.

In Academia Parrot dare no probleme kepe ;
    For *Græce fari* so occupyeth the chayre,
That *Latinum fari* may fall to rest and slepe,

---

[1] *they*] Qy. " ye " here—or " they " in the three preceding
lines ?

And *syllogisari* was drowned at Sturbrydge
    fayre;   170
Tryuyals and quatryuyals so sore now they
    appayre,
That Parrot the popágay hath pytye to beholde
How the rest of good lernyng is roufled vp and
    trold.

Albertus de modo significandi,
    And *Donatus* be dryuen out of scole;
Prisians hed broken now handy dandy,
    And *Inter didascolos* is rekened for a fole;
    Alexander, a gander of Menanders pole,
With *Da Cansales*, is cast out of the gate,
And *Da Racionales* dare not shew his pate.   180

Plauti in his comedies a chyld shall now reherse,
    And medyll with Quintylyan in his Declama-
    cyons,
That Pety Caton can scantly construe a verse,
    With *Aveto in Græco,* and such solempne salu-
    tacyons,
Can skantly the tensis of his coniugacyons;
Settynge theyr myndys so moche of eloquens,
That of theyr scole maters lost is the hole
    sentens.

Now a nutmeg, a nutmeg, *cum gariopholo,*
    For Parrot to pyke vpon, his brayne for to
    stable,   189

Swete synamum styckis and *pleris cum musco!* [1]
    In Paradyce, that place of pleasure perdurable,
    The progeny of Parrottis were fayre and fauor-
        able ;
    Nowe *in valle* Ebron Parrot is fayne to fede :
    Cristecrosse and saynt Nycholas, Parrot, be your
        good spede !

The myrrour that I tote in, *quasi diaphanum,*
    Vel quasi speculum, in ænigmate,
Elencticum, or ells *enthymematicum,*
    For logicions to loke on, somwhat *sophistice :*
    Retoricyons and oratours in freshe humanyte,
    Support Parrot, I pray you, with your suffrage
        ornate,   200
Of *confuse tantum* auoydynge the chekmate.

But of that supposicyon that callyd is arte
    Confuse distributive, as Parrot hath deuysed,
Let euery man after his merit take his parte,
    For in this processe Parrot nothing hath sur-
        mysed,
    No matter pretendyd, nor nothyng enterprysed,
But that *metaphora, allegoria* with all,
Shall be his protectyon, his pauys, and his wall.

---

[1] *pleris cum musco*] Ed. of Kynge and Marche, "*pleris* com musco." Eds. of Day, and Marshe, "*pleris* commusco." Instead of "*pleris*," the Rev. J. Mitford proposes "flarnis" (*species placentæ*).

For Parot is no churlish chowgh, nor no flekyd
    pye,
  Parrot is no pendugum, that men call a
    carlyng,
Parrot is no woodecocke, nor no butterfly,   210
  Parrot is no stameryng stare, that men call a
    starlyng;
  But Parot is my owne dere harte and my dere
    derling;
Melpomene, that fayre mayde, she burneshed his
    beke:
I pray you, let Parrot haue lyberte to speke.

Parrot is a fayre byrd for a lady;
God of his goodnes him framed and wrought;
When Parrot is ded, she dothe not putrefy:
  Ye, all thyng mortall shall torne vnto nought,
  Except mannes soule, that Chryst so dere
    bought;   220
That neuer may dye, nor neuer dye shall:
Make moche of Parrot, the popegay ryall.

For that pereles prynce that Parrot dyd
    create,
  He made you of nothynge by his magistye:
Poynt well this probleme that Parrot doth prate,
  And remembre amonge how Parrot and ye
  Shall lepe from this lyfe, as mery as we be;
Pompe, pryde, honour, ryches, and worldly lust,
Parrot sayth playnly, shall tourne all to dust.

Thus Parrot dothe pray you   230
    With hert most tender,
To rekyn with this recule now,
    And it to remember.

Psittacus, ecce, cano, nec sunt mea carmina Phœbo
    Digna scio, tamen est plena camena deo.

Secundum Skeltonida famigeratum,
    In Piersorum catalogo numeratum.
Itaque consolamini invicem in verbis istis, &c.
Candidi lectores, callide callete ; vestrum fovete
    Psittacum, &c.

[*Galathea.*[a]

Speke, Parrotte, I pray yow, for Maryes saake,
Whate mone he made when Pamphylus loste hys
    make.

Parrotte.

My propire Besse,   240
My praty Besse,
    Turne ones agayne to me : [b]
For slepyste thou, Besse,

---

a Hic occurrat memoriæ Pamphilus de amore Galatheæ.
[*Side Note.*]

b In ista cantilena[1] ore stilla plena abjectis frangibulis
et aperit. [*Side Note.*]

1 *In ista cantilena, &c.*] Grossly corrupted. The Rev. J.
Mitford proposes " *ore stillanti.*" MS. has " *eperit.*"

Or wakeste thow, Besse,
    Myne herte hyt ys with thé.

My deysy delectabyll,
My prymerose commendabyll,
ᵃ My vyolet amyabyll,
My ioye inexplicabill,
Now torne agayne to me.   250

I wylbe ferme and stabyll,
And to yow seruyceabyll,
And also prophytabyll,
Yf ye be agreabyll
To turne agayne to me,
        My propyr Besse.

ᵇ Alas, I am dysdayned,
And as a man halfe maymed,
My harte is so sore payned!
I pray thé, Besse, vnfayned,   260
    Yet com agayne to me!

Be loue I am constreyned
To be with yow retayned,
Hyt wyll not be refrayned:

---

a Quid quæritis tot capita, tot census?   [*Side Note.*]
    b Maro: Malo me Galatea petit, lasciva puella, Et fugit ad
salices, &c.   [*Side Note.*]

I pray yow, be reclaymed,
And torne agayne to me,
　　My propyr Besse.
Quod Parot, the popagay royall.

Martialis cecinit carmen fit mihi scutum :—
Est mihi lasciva pagina, vita proba.] [1]

Galethea.

Now kus me, Parrot, kus me, kus, kus, kus :
Goddys blessyng lyght on thy swete lyttyll
　　mus ! [a]   270
　　　　Vita et anima,
　　　　Zoe kai psyche.

Concumbunt Grœce. Non est hic sermo pudicus. [b]

Ergo　　　　*Attica dictamina* [c]
　　　　Sunt plumbi lamina,

---

a Zoe kai psyche.   Non omnes capiunt verbum istud, sed
quibus datum est desuper.   [*Side Note.*]
　b Aquinates.[2]   [*Side Note.*]
　c Sua consequentia magni æstimatur momenti Attica sane
eloquentia.   [*Side Note.*]

　[1] *Est mihi lasciva pagina, vita proba*] "*Lasciva est nobis*
pagina, vita proba est."   *Ep.* i. 5.
　[2] *Aquinates*] Has crept into the text in eds., and is not
clearly distinguished from the text in MS.   But it is cer-
tainly a marginal note—meaning Juvenal, from whom " *Con-*
cumbunt Grœce," &c. is quoted : see *Sat.* vi. 191.

Vel spuria vitulamina:
Avertat hæc Urania!
[*Amen.*]

Amen, Amen,
And set to a D,
And then it is, Amend
Our new found A, B, C.

Cum cæteris paribus.

[*Lenuoy primere*
Go, litell quayre, namyd the Popagay,   280
Home to resorte Jerobesethe perswade;
For the cliffes of Scaloppe they rore wellaway,
And the sandes of Cefas begyn to waste and
fade,
For replicacion restles that he of late ther
made;
Now Neptune and Eolus ar agreed of lyclyhode,
For Tytus at Dover abydythe in the rode;

Lucina she wadythe among the watry floddes,
And the cokkes begyn to crowe agayne the
day;
Le tonsan de Jason is lodgid among the shrowdes,
Of Argus revengyd, recover when he may; 290
Lyacon of Libyk and Lydy hathe cawghte hys
pray:
Goe, lytyll quayre, pray them that yow beholde,
In there remembraunce ye may be inrolde.

Yet some folys say that ye arre ffurnysshyd with
    knakkes,
That hang togedyr as fethyrs in the wynde;
But lewdlye ar they lettyrd that your lernyng
    lackys,
Barkyng and whyning, lyke churlysshe currys
    of kynde, ·
For whoo lokythe wyselye in your warkys may
    fynde
Muche frutefull mater : but now, for your defence
Agayne all remordes arme yow with paciens.   300

Monostichon.
Ipse sagax æqui ceu verax nuntius ito.
Morda puros mal desires.   Portugues.
Penultimo die Octobris,   33°.

Secunde Lenuoy.

Passe forthe, Parotte, towardes some passengere,
    Require hym to convey yow ovyr the salte fome;
Addressyng your selfe, lyke a sadde messengere,
    To ower soleyne seigneour Sadoke, desire hym
        to cum home,
Makyng hys pylgrimage by *nostre dame de
    Crome ;*
For Jerico and Jerssey shall mete togethyr assone
As he to exployte the man owte of the mone.

With porpose and graundepose he may fede hym
    fatte,

Thowghe he pampyr not hys paunche with the
grete seall :   310
We haue longyd and lokyd long tyme for that,
Whyche cawsythe pore suters haue many a
hongry mele :
As presydent and regente he rulythe every
deall.
Now pas furthe, good Parott, ower Lorde be your
stede,
In this your journey to prospere and spede !

And thowe sum dysdayne yow, and sey how ye
prate,
And howe your poemys arre barayne of pol-
yshed eloquens,
There is none that your name woll abbrogate
Then nodypollys and gramatolys of smalle in-
tellygens ;
To rude ys there reason to reche to your
sentence :   320
Suche malyncoly mastyvys and mangye curre
dogges
Ar mete for a swyneherde to hunte after hogges.

Monostichon.

Psittace, perge volans, fatuorum tela retundas.
Morda puros mall desers.   Portugues.
In diebus Novembris,
34.

Le dereyn Lenveoy.

Prepayre yow, Parrot, breuely your passage to
    take,
Of Mercury vndyr the trynall aspecte,
And sadlye salute ower solen syre Sydrake,
    And shewe hym that all the world dothe con-
      iecte,
    How the maters he mellis in com to small
      effecte;
For he wantythe of hys wyttes that all wold rule
    alone ;   329
Hyt is no lytyll bordon to bere a grete mylle stone :

To bryng all the see into a cheryston pytte,
    To nombyr all the sterrys in the fyrmament,
To rule ix realmes by one mannes wytte,
    To suche thynges ympossybyll reason cannot
      consente :
    Muche money, men sey, there madly he hathe
      spente :
Parrot, ye may prate thys vndyr protestacion,
Was neuyr suche a senatour syn Crystes incarna-
    cion.

Wherfor he may now come agayne as he wente,
    Non sine postica sanna, as I trowe,   339
From Calys to Dovyr, to Caunterbury in Kente,
    To make reconyng in the resseyte how Robyn
      loste hys bowe,

To sowe corne in the see sande, ther wyll no
  crope growe.
Thow ye be tauntyd, Parotte, with tonges attayntyd,
Yet your problemes ar preignaunte, and with
  loyalte acquayntyd.

Monostichon.

I, properans, Parrot[e],[1] malas sic corripe linguas.
Morda puros mall desires.   *Portigues.*
    15 *kalendis Decembris,*
      34.

Distichon miserabile.

Altior, heu, cedro, crudelior, heu, leopardo!
Heu, vitulus bubali fit dominus Priami!

Tetrastichon,—Unde species Priami est digna
    imperio.

Non annis licet et Priamus sed honore voceris:
  Dum foveas vitulum, rex, regeris, Britonum;
Rex, regeris, non ipse regis: rex inclyte, calle;
Subde tibi vitulum, ne fatuet nimium.   351

    God amend all,
    That all amend may!
    Amen, quod Parott,

---

[1] *Parrot[e]* Must be considered here as a Latin word, and a
trisyllable ¯¯˘.

The royall popagay.

Kalendis Decembris,
34.

Lenvoy royall.

Go, propyr Parotte, my popagay,
　That lordes and ladies thys pamflett may behold,
With notable clerkes : supply to them, I pray,
　Your rudenes to pardon, and also that they wolde
Vouchesafe to defend yow agayne the brawlyng
　　scolde,　　　　　　　　　　　　　　360
Callyd Detraxion, encankryd with envye,
Whose tong ys attayntyd with slaundrys obliqui.

For trowthe in parabyll ye wantonlye pronounce,
　Langagys diuers, yet vndyr that dothe reste
Maters more precious then the ryche jacounce,
　Diamounde, or rubye, or balas of the beste,
　Or eyndye sapher with oryente perlys dreste :
Wherfor your remorde[r]s ar madde, or else
　　starke blynde,
Yow to remorde erste or they know your mynde.

Distichon.

I, volitans,[1] *Parrote, tuam moderare Minervam :*
Vix tua percipient, qui tua teque legent.　　371

[1] *volitans*] MS. "*vtilans*"—not, I think, a mistake for "*ru-tilans :*" compare *ante*, "Psittace, perge, *volans*," p. 262 and "I, properans, Parrot," p. 264.

Hyperbato[n].

Psittacus hi notus seu Persius est puto notus,
Nec reor est nec erit licet est erit.[1]
Maledite soyte bouche malheurewse !
34.

Laucture de Parott.

O my Parrot, *O unice dilecte, votorum meorum*
omnis lapis, lapis pretiosus operimentum
tuum !

Parrott.

Sicut Aaron populumque, sic bubali vitulus, sic
bubali vitulus, sic bubali vitulus.

Thus myche Parott hathe opynlye expreste :
Let se who dare make vp the reste.

Le Popagay sen va complayndre.

Helas ! I lamente the dull abusyd brayne,
The enfatuate fantasies, the wytles wylfulnes
Of on and hothyr at me that haue dysdayne :
Som sey, they cannot my parables expresse ;
Som sey, I rayle att ryott recheles ;   380

---

[1] Thus corrected by a reviewer in *Gent. Mag.*
Pittacus hic *notus seu Persius est puto notus,*
Nec reor est, nec erit, nec *licet est,* nec *erit.*

Some say but lityll, and thynke more in there
    thowghte,
How thys prosses I prate of, hyt ys not all for
    nowghte.

O causeles cowardes, O hartles hardynes !
    O manles manhod, enfayntyd all with fere !
O connyng clergye, where ys your redynes
    To practise or postyll thys prosses here and
    there ?
For drede ye darre not medyll with suche gere,
Or elles ye pynche curtesy, trulye as I trowe,
Whyche of yow fyrste dare boldlye plucke the
    crowe.

The skye is clowdy, the coste is nothyng clere; 390
    Tytan hathe truste vp hys tressys of fyne
    golde ;
Iupyter for Saturne darre make no royall chere ;
    Lyacon· lawghyth there att, and berythe hym
    more bolde ;
Racell, rulye ragged, she is like to cache colde ;
Moloc, that mawmett, there darre no man withsay ;
The reste of suche reconyng may make a fowle
    fraye.

Dixit, quod Parrott, the royall popagay.

    Cest chose maleheure[u]se,
    Que mall bouche.

Parrotte.

Jupiter ut nitido deus est veneratus Olympo ;
   Hic coliturque deus.   400
Sunt data thura Jovi, rutilo solio residenti ;
   Cum Jove thura capit.
Jupiter astrorum rector dominusque polorum ;
   Anglica sceptra regit.

Galathea.

I compas the conveyaunce vnto the capitall
   Of ower clerke Cleros, whythyr, thydyr, and
      why not hethyr ?
For passe a pase apase ys gon to cache a molle,
   Over Scarpary *mala vi*, Monsyre cy and
      sliddyr:
   Whate sequele shall folow when pendugims
      mete togethyr ?
Speke, Parotte, my swete byrde, and ye shall
   haue a date,   410
Of frantycknes and folysshnes whyche ys the
   grett state ?

Parotte.

Difficille hit ys to answere thys demaunde ;
   Yet, aftyr the sagacite of a popagay, —
Frantiknes dothe rule and all thyng commaunde ;
   Wylfulnes and braynles no[w] rule all the
      raye ;
   Agayne ffrentike frenesy there dar no man sey
      nay,

For ffrantiknes, and wylfulnes, and braynles en-
sembyll,
The nebbis of a lyon they make to trete and
trembyll;

To jumbyll, to stombyll, to tumbyll down lyke
folys,
To lowre,[1] to droupe, to knele, to stowpe, and
to play cowche quale,   420
To fysshe afore the nette, and to drawe polys;
He make[th] them to bere babylles, and to
bere a lowe sayle;
He caryeth a kyng in hys sleve, yf all the
worlde fayle;
He facithe owte at a fflusshe, with, shewe, take
all!
Of Pope Julius cardys he ys chefe cardynall.

He tryhumfythe, he trumpythe, he turnythe all
vp and downe,
With, skyregalyard, prowde palyard, vaunte-
perler, ye prate!
Hys woluys hede, wanne, bloo as lede, gapythe
ouer the crowne:
Hyt ys to fere leste he wolde were the garland
on hys pate,
Peregall with all prynces farre passyng his
estate;   430

----

1 *lowre*] Qy. "lowte?"

For of ower regente the regiment he hathe, *ex
    qua vi*,
Patet per versus, quod *ex vi bolte harvi*.

Now, Galathea, lett Parrot, I pray yow, haue hys
    date;
    Yett dates now ar deynte, and wax verye
        scante,
For grocers were grugyd at and groynyd at but
    late;
    Grete reysons with resons be now reprobitante,
    For reysons ar no resons, but resons currant:
Ryn God, rynne Devyll! yet the date of ower
    Lord
And the date of the Devyll dothe shrewlye accord.
    Dixit, quod Parrott, the popagay royall.

Galathea.

Nowe, Parott, my swete byrde, speke owte yet
    ons agayne,   440
Sette asyde all sophyms, and speke now trew
    and playne.

Parotte.

So many morall maters, and so lytell vsyd;
    So myche newe makyng, and so madd tyme
        spente;
So myche translacion in to Englyshe confused;
    So myche nobyll prechyng, and so lytell amend-
        ment;

So myche consultacion, almoste to none entente;
So myche provision, and so lytell wytte at nede ;—
Syns Dewcalyons flodde there can no clerkes rede.

So lytyll dyscressyon, and so myche reasonyng;
  So myche hardy dardy, and so lytell manly-
    nes ;   450
So prodigall expence, and so shamfull reconyng ;
  So gorgyous garmentes, and so myche wrechyd-
    nese ;
  So myche portlye pride, with pursys penyles ;
So myche spente before, and so myche vnpayd
    behynde ; —
Syns Dewcalyons flodde there can no clerkes
    fynde.

So myche forcastyng, and so farre an after dele ;
  So myche poietyke pratyng, and so lytell
    stondythe in stede ;
So lytell secretnese, and so myche grete councell ;
  So manye bolde barons, there hertes as dull as
    lede ;
  So many nobyll bodyes vndyr on dawys hedd ;
So royall a kyng as reynythe vppon vs all ; — 461
Syns Dewcalions flodde was nevyr sene nor shall.

So many complayntes, and so smalle redresse ;
  So myche callyng on, and so smalle takyng
    hede ;
So myche losse of merchaundyse, and so remedy-
    les ;

So lytell care for the comyn weall, and so
    myche nede ;
So myche dowȝtfull daunger, and so lytell
    drede ;
So myche pride of prelattes, so cruell and so
    kene ; —
Syns Dewcalyons flodde, I trowe, was nevyr
    sene.

So many thevys hangyd, and thevys never the
    lesse ;   470
  So myche prisonment ffor matyrs not worthe
    an hawe ;
So myche papers weryng for ryghte a smalle
    exesse ;
  So myche pelory pajauntes vndyr colower of
    good lawe ;
  So myche towrnyng on the cooke stole for
    euery guy gaw ;
So myche mokkyshe makyng of statutes of
    array ; —
Syns Dewcalyons flodde was nevyr, I dar sey.

So braynles caluys hedes, so many shepis
    taylys ;
  So bolde a braggyng bocher, and flesshe sold
    so dere ;
So many plucte partryches, and so fatte quaylles ;
  So mangye a mastyfe curre, the grete grey
    houndes pere ;   480

So bygge a bulke of brow auntlers cabagyd
    that yere;
So many swannes dede, and so small revell; —
Syns Dewcalyons flodde, I trow, no man can
    tell.

So many trusys takyn, and so lytyll perfyte
    trowthe;
So myche bely joye, and so wastefull banket-
    yng;
So pynchyng and sparyng, and so lytell profyte
    growthe;
So many howgye howsys byldyng, and so small
    howseholding;
Suche statutes apon diettes, suche pyllyng and
    pollyng;
So ys all thyng wrowghte wylfully withowte reson
    and skylle; —
Syns Dewcalyons flodde the world was never so
    yll.   490

So many vacabondes, so many beggers bolde;
So myche decay of monesteries and of relygious
    places;
So hote hatered agaynste the Chyrche, and
    cheryte so colde;
So myche of my lordes grace, and in hym no
    grace ys;
So many holow hartes, and so dowbyll faces;
VOL. II.   18

So myche sayntuary brekyng, and preuylegidde
    barrydd ; —
Syns Dewcalyons flodde was nevyr sene nor
    lyerd.

So myche raggyd ryghte of a rammes horne ;
    So rygorous revelyng[1] in a prelate specially ;
So bold and so braggyng, and was so baselye
    borne ;   500
So lordlye of hys lokes and so dysdayneslye ;
    So fatte a magott, bred of a flesshe flye ;
Was nevyr suche a ffylty gorgon, nor suche an
    epycure,
Syn[s] Dewcalyons flodde, I make thé faste and
    sure.

So myche preuye wachyng in cold wynters
    nyghtes ;
So myche serchyng of loselles, and ys hymselfe
    so lewde ;
So myche coniuracions for elvyshe myday sprettes ;
    So many bullys of pardon puplysshyd and
    . shewyd ;
So myche crossyng and blyssyng, and hym all
    beshrewde ;
Suche pollaxis and pyllers, suche mvlys trapte
    with gold ;—   510
Sens Dewcalyons flodde in no cronycle ys told.

---

[1] *revelyng*] So MS. *literatim*,—meant for " ruelyng " (ruling).

Dixit, quod Parrot.

Crescet in immensum me vivo Psittacus iste ;
Hinc mea dicetur Skeltonidis inclyta fama.

Quod Skelton Lawryat,
Orator Regius.
34.]

HERE AFTER FOLOWETH A LYTELL BOKE, WHICHE
HATH TO NAME

WHY COME YE NAT TO COURTE?[*]

COMPYLED BY MAYSTER SKELTON, POETE LAUREATE.

The relucent mirror for all Prelats and Presidents,
as well spirituall as temporall, sadly to loke
vpon, deuised in English by Skelton.

> All noble men,[1] of this take hede,
> And beleue it as your Crede.

> To hasty of sentence,
> To ferce for none offence,
> To scarce of your expence,
> To large in neglygence,
> To slacke in recompence,
> To haute in excellence,

---

[*] From the ed. by Kele, n. d., collated with that by Wyght,
n. d., with that by Kytson, n. d., and with Marshe's ed. of
Skelton's *Workes*, 1568.

[1] *All noble men, &c.*] These twenty-eight introductory lines,
which are found in all the eds. of this poem, are also printed,
as a distinct piece, in the various editions of *Certaine bokes
compyled by Mayster Skelton*, &c., n. d., and in Marshe's ed.
of Skelton's *Workes*, 1568.

To lyght [in] intellegence,
And to lyght in credence ;   10
Where these kepe resydence,
Reson is banysshed thence,
And also dame Prudence,
With sober Sapyence.
All noble men, of this take hede,
And beleue it as your Crede.

Than without collusyon,
Marke well this conclusyon,
Thorow suche abusyon,
And by suche illusyon,   20
Vnto great confusyon
A noble man may fall,
And his honour appall ;
And yf ye thynke this shall
Not rubbe you on the gall,
Than the deuyll take all !
All noble men, of this take hede,
And beleue it as your Crede.

Hæc vates ille,
De quo loquuntur mille.   30

WHY COME YE NAT TO COURT?

For age is a page
For the courte full vnmete,
For age cannat rage,
Nor basse her swete swete :

But whan age seeth that rage
Dothe aswage and refrayne,
Than wyll age haue a corage
To come to court agayne.
  But
Helas, sage ouerage
So madly decayes,   40
That age for dottage
Is reconed now adayes :
  Thus age (a graunt domage)
Is nothynge set by,
And rage in arerage
Dothe rynne lamentably.
  So
  That rage must make pyllage,
To catche that catche may,
And with suche forage
Hunte the boskage,   50
That hartes wyll ronne away ;
Bothe hartes and hyndes,
With all good myndes :
Fare well, than, haue good day !
  Than, haue good daye, adewe !
For defaute of rescew,
Some men may happely rew,
And some theyr hedes mew ;
The tyme dothe fast ensew,
That bales begynne to brew : 60
I drede, by swete Iesu,
This tale wyll be to trew ;

In faythe, dycken, thou krew,
In fayth, dicken, thou krew, &c.
Dicken, thou krew doutlesse;
For, trewly to expresse,
There hath ben moche excesse,
With banketynge braynlesse,
With ryotynge rechelesse,
With gambaudynge thryftlesse,   70
With spende and wast witlesse,
Treatinge of trewse restlesse,
Pratynge for peace peaslesse.
The countrynge at Cales
Wrang vs on the males:
Chefe counselour was carlesse,
Gronynge, grouchyng, gracelesse;
And to none entente
Our talwod is all brent,
Our fagottes are all spent,   80
We may blowe at the cole:
Our mare hath cast her fole,
And Mocke hath lost her sho;
What may she do therto?
An ende of an olde song,
Do ryght and do no wronge,
As ryght as a rammes horne;
For thrifte is threde bare worne,
Our shepe are shrewdly shorne,
And trouthe is all to-torne;   90
Wysdom is laught to skorne,
Fauell is false forsworne,

Iauell is nobly borne,
Hauell and Haruy Hafter,
Iack Trauell and Cole Crafter,
We shall here more herafter ;
With pollynge and shauynge,
With borowynge and crauynge,
With reuynge and rauynge,
With swerynge and starynge,   100
Ther vayleth no resonynge,
For wyll dothe rule all thynge,
Wyll, wyll, wyll, wyll, wyll,
He ruleth alway styll.
Good reason and good skyll,
They may garlycke pyll,
Cary sackes to the myll,
Or pescoddes they may shyll,
Or elles go rost a stone :
There is no man but one   110
That hathe the strokes alone ;
Be it blacke or whight,
All that he dothe is ryght,
As right as a cammocke croked.
This byll well ouer loked,
Clerely perceuye we may
There went the hare away,
The hare, the fox, the gray,
The harte, the hynde, the buck :
God sende vs better luck !   120
God sende vs better lucke, &c.
  Twit, Andrewe, twit, Scot,
Ge heme, ge scour thy pot ;

For we haue spente our shot :
We shall haue a *tot quot*
From the Pope of Rome,
To weue all in one lome
A webbe of lylse wulse,
Opus male dulce:
The deuyll kysse his cule !   130
For, whyles he doth rule,
All is warse and warse ;
The deuyll kysse his arse !
For whether he blesse or curse,
It can not be moche worse.
From Baumberow to Bothombar
We haue cast vp our war,
And made a worthy trewse,
With, gup, leuell suse !
Our mony madly lent,   140
And mor madly spent :
From Croydon to Kent,
Wote ye whyther they went?
From Wynchelsey to Rye,
And all nat worth a flye ;
From Wentbridge to Hull ;
Our armye waxeth dull,
With, tourne all home agayne,
And neuer a Scot slayne.
Yet the good Erle of Surray,   150
The Frenche men he doth fray,
And vexeth them day by day
With all the power he may ;

The French men he hath faynted,
And made theyr hertes attaynted:
Of cheualry he is the floure;
Our Lorde be his soccoure!
The French men he hathe so mated,
And theyr courage abated,
That they are but halfe men;   160
Lyke foxes in theyr denne,
Lyke cankerd cowardes all,
Lyke vrcheons in a stone wall,
They kepe them in theyr holdes,
Lyke henherted cokoldes.
    But yet they ouer shote vs
Wyth crownes and wyth scutus;
With scutis and crownes of gold
I drede we are bought and solde;
It is a wonders warke: 170
They shote all at one marke,
At the Cardynals hat,
They shote all at that;
Oute of theyr stronge townes
They shote at him with crownes;
With crownes of golde enblased
They make him so amased,
And his eyen so dased,
That he ne se can
To know God nor man.   180
He is set so hye
In his ierarchy
Of frantycke frenesy

And folysshe fantasy,
That in the Chambre of Starres
All maters there he marres;
Clappyng his rod on the borde,
No man dare speke a worde,
For he hathe all the sayenge,
Without any renayenge;   190
He rolleth in his recordes,
He sayth, How saye ye, my lordes?
Is nat my reason good?
Good euyn, good Robyn Hood!
Some say yes, and some
Syt styll as they were dom:
Thus thwartyng ouer thom,
He ruleth all the roste
With braggynge and with bost;
Borne vp on euery syde   200
With pompe and with pryde,
With, trompe vp, alleluya!
For dame Philargerya
Hathe so his herte in holde,
He loueth nothyng but golde;
And Asmodeus of hell
Maketh his membres swell
With Dalyda to mell,
That wanton damosell.
Adew, Philosophia,   210
Adew, Theologia!
Welcome, dame Simonia,
With dame Castrimergia,

To drynke and for to eate
Swete ypocras and swete meate!
To kepe his flesshe chast,
In Lent for a repast
He eateth capons stewed,
Fesaunt and partriche mewed,
Hennes, checkynges, and pygges;   220
He foynes and he frygges,
Spareth neither mayde ne wyfe:
This is a postels lyfe!

Helas! my herte is sory
To tell of vayne glory:
But now vpon this story
I wyll no further ryme
Tyll another tyme,
Tyll another tyme, &c.

What newes, what newes?   230
Small newes the true is,
That be worth ii. kues;
But at the naked stewes,
I vnderstande how that
The sygne of the Cardynall Hat,
That inne is now shyt vp,
With, gup, hore, gup, now gup,
Gup, Guilliam Trauillian,
With, iast you, I say, Jullian!
Wyll ye bere no coles?   240
A mayny of marefoles,
That occupy theyr holys,
Full of pocky molys.

What here ye of Lancashyre?
They were nat payde their hyre;
They are fel as any fyre.
  What here ye of Chesshyre?
They haue layde all in the myre;
They grugyd, and sayde
Theyr wages were nat payde;   250
Some sayde they were afrayde
Of the Scottysshe hoste,
For all theyr crack and bost,
Wylde fyre and thonder;
For all this worldly wonder,
A hundred myle asonder
They were whan they were next;
That is a trew text.
  What here ye of the Scottes?
They make vs all sottes,   260
Poppynge folysshe dawes;
They make vs to pyll strawes;
They play their olde pranckes,
After Huntley bankes:
At the streme of Banockes burne
They dyd vs a shrewde turne,
Whan Edwarde of Karnaruan
Lost all that his father wan.
  What here ye of the Lorde Dakers?
He maketh vs Jacke Rakers;   270
He sayes we ar but crakers;
He calleth vs England men
Stronge herted lyke an hen;

For the Scottes and he
To well they do agre,
With, do thou for me,
And I shall do for thé.
Whyles the red hat doth endure,
He maketh himselfe cock sure;
The red hat with his lure   280
Bryngeth all thynges vnder cure.

    But, as the worlde now gose,
What here ye of the Lorde Rose?
Nothynge to purpose,
Nat worth a cockly fose:
Their hertes be in thyr hose.
The Erle of Northumberlande
Dare take nothynge on hande:
Our barons be so bolde,
Into a mouse hole they wolde   290
Rynne away and crepe;
Lyke a mayny of shepe,
Dare nat loke out at dur
For drede of the mastyue cur,
For drede of the bochers dogge
Wold wyrry them lyke an hogge.

    For and this curre do gnar,
They must stande all a far,
To holde vp their hande at the bar.
For all their noble blode   300
He pluckes them by the hode,
And shakes them by the eare,
And brynge[s] them in suche feare;

He bayteth them lyke a bere,
Lyke an oxe or a bull:
Theyr wyttes, he saith, are dull;
He sayth they haue no brayne
Theyr astate to mayntayne;
And maketh them to bow theyr kne
Before his maieste.   310
Juges of the kynges lawes,
He countys them foles and dawes;
Sergyantes of the coyfe eke,
He sayth they are to seke
In pletynge of theyr case
At the Commune Place,
Or at the Kynges Benche;
He wryngeth them suche a wrenche,
That all our lerned men
Dare nat set theyr penne   320
To plete a trew tryall
Within Westmynster hall;
In the Chauncery where he syttes,
But suche as he admyttes
None so hardy to speke;
He sayth, thou huddypeke,
Thy lernynge is to lewde,
Thy tonge is nat well thewde,
To seke before our grace;
And openly in that place   330
He rages and he raues,
And cals them cankerd knaues;
Thus royally he dothe deale

Vnder the kynges brode seale ;
And in the Checker he them cheks ;
In the Ster Chambre he noddis and beks,
And bereth him there so stowte,
That no man dare rowte,
Duke, erle, baron, nor lorde,
But to his sentence must accorde ;   340
Whether he be knyght or squyre,
All men must folow his desyre.

What say ye of the Scottysh kynge?
That is anothẻr thyng.
He is but an yonglyng,
A stalworthy stryplyng :
There is a whyspring and a whipling,
He shulde be hyder brought ;
But, and it were well sought,
I trow all wyll be nought,   350
Nat worth a shyttel cocke,
Nor worth a sowre calstocke.
There goth many a lye
Of the Duke of Albany,
That of shulde go his hede,
And brought in quycke or dede,
And all Scotlande owers
The mountenaunce of two houres.
But, as some men sayne,
I drede of some false trayne   360
Subtelly wrought shall be
Vnder a fayned treatee ;
But within monethes thre

Men may happely se
The trechery and the prankes
Of the Scottysshe bankes.
   What here ye of Burgonyons,
And the Spainyardes onyons?
They haue slain our Englisshmen
Aboue threscore and ten: 370
For all your amyte,
No better they agre.
   God saue my lorde admyrell!
What here ye of Mutrell?
There with I dare nat mell.
   Yet what here ye tell
Of our graunde counsell?
I coulde say some what,
But speke ye no more of that,
For drede of the red hat   380
Take peper in the nose;
For than thyne heed of gose,
Of by the harde arse.
   But there is some trauarse
Bytwene some and some,
That makys our syre to glum;
It is some what wronge,
That his berde is so longe;
He morneth in blacke clothynge.
I pray God saue the kynge!   390
Where euer he go or ryde,
I pray God be his gyde!

Thus wyll I conclude my style,
And fall to rest a whyle,
And so to rest a whyle, &c.
   Ones yet agayne
Of you I wolde frayne,
Why come ye nat to court?—
To whyche court?
To the kynges courte,   400
Or to Hampton Court?—
Nay, to the kynges court:
The kynges courte
Shulde haue the excellence;
But Hampton Court
Hath the preemynence,
And Yorkes Place,
With my lordes grace,
To whose magnifycence
Is all the conflewence,   410
Sutys and supplycacyons,
Embassades of all nacyons.
Strawe for lawe canon,
Or for the lawe common,
Or for lawe cyuyll!
It shall be as he wyll:
Stop at law tancrete,
An obstract or a concrete;
Be it soure, be it swete,
His wysdome is so dyscrete,   420
That in a fume or an hete,
Wardeyn of the Flete,
Set hym fast by the fete!

And of his royall powre
Whan him lyst to lowre,
Than, haue him to the Towre,
Saunz aulter remedy,
Haue hym forthe by and by
To the Marshalsy,
Or to the Kynges Benche !   430
He dyggeth so in the trenche
Of the court royall,
That he ruleth them all.
So he dothe vndermynde,
And suche sleyghtes dothe fynde,
That the kynges mynde
By hym is subuerted,
And so streatly coarted
In credensynge his tales,
That all is but nutshales   440
That any other sayth ;
He hath in him suche fayth.

Now, yet all this myght be
Suffred and taken in gre,
If that that he wrought
To any good ende were brought ;
But all he bringeth to nought,
By God, that me dere bought !
He bereth the kyng on hand,
That he must pyll his lande,   450
To make his cofers ryche ;
But he laythe all in the dyche,
And vseth suche abusyoun,

That in the conclusyoun
All commeth to confusyon.
Perceyue the cause why,
To tell the trouth playnly,
He is so ambicyous,
So shamles, and so vicyous,
And so supersticyous,   460
And so moche obliuyous
From whens that he came,
That he falleth into a *cæciam*, [1]
Whiche, truly to expresse,
Is a forgetfulnesse,
Or wylfull blyndnesse,
Wherwith the Sodomites
Lost theyr inward syghtes,
The Gommoryans also
Were brought to deedly wo,   470
As Scrypture recordis:
A cæcitate cordis,
In the Latyne synge we,
Libera nos, Domine !
But this madde Amalecke,
Lyke to a Mamelek,
He regardeth lordes
No more than potshordes ;
He is in suche elacyon
Of his exaltacyon,   480
And the supportacyon
Of our souerayne lorde,
That, God to recorde,

─────────────

[1] *a cæciam*] Eds. " *Acisiam.* " Compare v. 472.

He ruleth all at wyll,
Without reason or skyll:
How be it the primordyall
Of his wretched originall,
And his base progeny,
And his gresy genealogy,
He came of the sank royall, 490
That was cast out of a bochers stall.
But how euer he was borne,
Men wolde haue the lesse scorne,
If he coulde consyder
His byrth and rowme togeder,
And call to his mynde
How noble and how kynde
To him he hathe founde
Our souereyne lorde, chyfe grounde
Of all this prelacy, 500
And set hym nobly
In great auctoryte,
Out from a low degre,
Whiche he can nat se:
For he was parde
No doctor of deuinyte,
Nor doctor of the law,
Nor of none other saw;
But a poore maister of arte,
God wot, had lytell parte 510
Of the quatriuials,
Nor yet of triuialis,
Nor of philosophy,

Nor of philology,
Nor of good pollycy,
Nor of astronomy,
Nor acquaynted worth a fly
With honorable Haly,
Nor with royall Ptholomy,
Nor with Albumasar,   520
To treate of any star
Fyxt or els mobyll;
His Latyne tonge dothe hobbyll,
He doth but cloute and cobbill
In Tullis faculte,
Called humanyte;
Yet proudly he dare pretende
How no man can him amende:
But haue ye nat harde this,
How an one eyed man is   530
Well syghted when.
He is amonge blynde men?
   Than, our processe for to stable,
This man was full vnable
To reche to suche degre,
Had nat our prynce be
Royall Henry the eyght,
Take him in suche conceyght,
That he set him on heyght,
In exemplyfyenge   540
Great Alexander the kynge,
In writynge as we fynde;
Whiche of his royall mynde,

And of his noble pleasure,
Transcendynge out of mesure,
Thought to do a thynge
That perteyneth to a kynge,
To make vp one of nought,
And made to him be brought
A wretched poore man,   550
Whiche his lyuenge wan
With plantyng of lekes
By the dayes and by the wekes,
And of this poore vassall
He made a kynge royall,
And gaue him a realme to rule,
That occupyed a showell,
A mattoke, and a spade,
Before that he was made
A kynge, as I haue tolde,   560
And ruled as he wolde.
Suche is a kynges power,
To make within an hower,
And worke suche a myracle,
That shall be a spectacle
Of renowme and worldly fame :
In lykewyse now the same
Cardynall is promoted,
Yet with lewde condicyons cotyd,
As herafter ben notyd,   570
Presumcyon and vayne glory,
Enuy, wrath, and lechery,
Couetys and glotony,

Slouthfull to do good,
Now frantick, now starke wode.
　Shulde this man of suche mode
Rule the swerde of myght,
How can he do ryght?
For he wyll as sone smyght
His frende as his fo;　　　　　　　　530
A prouerbe longe ago.
　Set vp a wretche on hye
In a trone triumphantlye,
Make him a great astate,
And he wyll play checke mate
With ryall maieste,
Counte him selfe as good as he;
A prelate potencyall,
To rule vnder Bellyall,
As ferce and as cruell　　　　　　　590
As the fynd of hell.
His seruauntes menyall
He dothe reuyle, and brall,
Lyke Mahounde in a play;
No man dare him withsay:
He hath dispyght and scorne
At them that be well borne;
He rebukes them and rayles,
Ye horsons, ye vassayles,
Ye knaues, ye churles sonnys,　　　　600
Ye rebads, nat worth two plummis,
Ye raynbetyn beggers reiagged,
Ye recrayed ruffyns all ragged!

With, stowpe, thou hauell,
Rynne, thou iauell!
Thou peuysshe pye pecked,
Thou losell longe necked!
Thus dayly they be decked,
Taunted and checked,
That they ar so wo,   610
That wot not whether to go.
No man dare come to the speche
Of this gentell Iacke breche,
Of what estate he be,
Of spirituall dygnyte,
Nor duke of hye degre,
Nor marques, erle, nor lorde;
Whiche shrewdly doth accorde,
Thus he borne so base
All noble men shulde out face,   620
His countynaunce lyke a kayser.
My lorde is nat at layser;
Syr, ye must tary a stounde,
Tyll better layser be founde;
And, syr, ye must daunce attendaunce,
And take pacient sufferaunce,
For my lordes grace
Hath nowe no tyme nor space
To speke with you as yet.
And thus they shall syt,   630
Chuse them syt or flyt,
Stande, walke, or ryde,
And his layser abyde

Parchaunce halfe a yere,
And yet neuer the nere.
   This daungerous dowsypere,
Lyke a kynges pere;
And within this xvi. yere
He wolde haue ben ryght fayne
To haue ben a chapleyne,   640
And haue taken ryght gret payne
With a poore knyght,
What soeuer he hyght.
The chefe of his owne counsell,
They can nat well tell
Whan they with hym shulde mell,
He is so fyers and fell;
He rayles and he ratis,
He calleth them doddypatis;
He grynnes and he gapis,   650
As it were iack napis.
Suche a madde bedleme
For to rewle this reame,
It is a wonders case:
That the kynges grace
Is toward him so mynded,
And so farre blynded,
That he can nat parceyue
How he doth hym disceyue,
I dought, lest by sorsery,   660
Or suche other loselry,
As wychecraft, or charmyng;
For he is the kynges derlyng,

And his swete hart rote,
And is gouerned by this mad kote:
For what is a man the better
For the kynges letter?
For he wyll tere it asonder;
Wherat moche I wonder,
Howe suche a hoddypoule   670
So boldely dare controule,
And so malapertly withstande
The kynges owne hande,
And settys nat by it a myte;
He sayth the kynge doth wryte
And writeth he wottith nat what;
And yet for all that,
The kynge his clemency
Despensyth with his demensy.
   But what his grace doth thinke,   680
I haue no pen nor inke
That therwith can mell;
But wele I can tell
How Frauncis Petrarke,
That moche noble clerke,
Wryteth how Charlemayn
Coude nat him selfe refrayne,
But was rauysht with a rage
Of a lyke dotage:
But how that came aboute,   690
Rede ye the story oute,
And ye shall fynde surely
It was by nycromansy,

By carectes and coniuracyon,
Vnder a certeyne constellacion,
And a certayne fumygacion,
Vnder a stone on a golde ryng,
Wrought to Charlemayn the king,
Whiche constrayned him forcebly
For to loue a certayne body   700
Aboue all other inordinatly.
This is no fable nor no lye ;
At Acon it was brought to pas,
As by myne auctor tried it was.
But let mi masters mathematical
Tell you the rest, for me they shal ;
They haue the full intellygence,
And dare vse the experyens,
In there obsolute consciens
To practyue suche abolete sciens ;   710
For I abhore to smatter
Of one so deuyllysshe a matter.
  But I wyll make further relacion
Of this isagogicall colation,
How maister Gaguine, the crownycler
Of the feytis of war
That were done in Fraunce,
Maketh remembraunce,
How Kynge Lewes of late
Made vp a great astate   720
Of a poore wretchid man,
Wherof moche care began.
Iohannes Balua was his name,

Myne auctor writeth the same ;
Promoted was he
To a cardynalles dygnyte
By Lewes the kyng aforesayd,
With hym so wele apayd,
That he made him his chauncelar
To make all or to mar, 730
And to rule as him lyst,
Tyll he cheked at the fyst,
And agayne all reason
Commyted open trayson
And [1] against his lorde souerayn ;
Wherfore he suffred payn,
Was hedyd, drawen, and quarterd,
And dyed stynkingly marterd.
Lo, yet for all that
He ware a cardynals hat, 740
In hym was small fayth,
As myne auctor sayth :
Nat for that I mene
Suche a casuelte shulde be sene,
Or suche chaunce shulde fall
Vnto our cardynall.
　Allmyghty God, I trust,
Hath for him dyscust
That of force he must
Be faythfull, trew, and iust 750
To our most royall kynge,

---

[1] *And*] Perhaps ought to be thrown out. Compare v. 1062.

Chefe rote of his makynge;
Yet it is a wyly mouse
That can bylde his dwellinge house
Within the cattes eare
Withouten drede or feare.
It is a nyce reconynge,
To put all the gouernynge,
All the rule of this lande
Into one mannys hande :   760
One wyse mannys hede
May stande somwhat in stede;
But the wyttys of many wyse
Moche better can deuyse,
By theyr cyrcumspection,
And theyr sad dyrrection,
To cause the commune weale
Longe to endure in heale.
Christ kepe King Henry the eyght
From trechery and dysceyght,   770
And graunt him grace to know
The faucon from the crow,
The wolfe from the lam,
From whens that mastyfe cam!
Let him neuer confounde
The gentyll greyhownde:
Of this matter the grownde
Is easy to expounde,
And soone may be perceyued,
How the worlde is conueyed.   780
    But harke, my frende, one worde
In ernest or in borde :

Tell me nowe in this stede
Is maister Mewtas dede,
The kynges Frenche secretary,
And his vntrew aduersary?
For he sent in writynge
To Fraunces the French kyng
Of our maisters counsel in eueri thing:
That was a peryllous rekenyng!— 790
Nay, nay, he is nat dede;
But he was so payned in the hede,
That he shall neuer ete more bred.
Now he is góne to another stede,
With a bull vnder lead,
By way of commissyon,
To a straunge iurisdictyon,
Called Dymingis Dale,
Farre byyonde Portyngale,
And hathe his pasport to pas 800
Ultra Sauromatas,
To the deuyll, syr Sathanas,
To Pluto, and syr Bellyall,
The deuyls vycare generall,
And to his college conuentuall,
As well calodemonyall
As to cacodemonyall,
To puruey for our cardynall
A palace pontifycall,
To kepe his court prouyncyall, 810
Vpon artycles iudicyall,
To contende and to stryue

For his prerogatyue,
Within that consystory
To make sommons peremtory
Before some prothonotory
Imperyall or papall.
Vpon this matter mistycall
I haue tolde you part, but nat all:
Herafter perchaunce I shall 820
Make a larger memoryall,
And a further rehersall,
And more paper I thinke to blot,
To the court why I cam not;
Desyring you aboue all thynge
To kepe you from laughynge
Whan ye fall to redynge
Of this wanton scrowle,
And pray for Mewtas sowle,
For he is well past and gone; 830
That wolde God euerychone
Of his affynyte
Were gone as well as he!
Amen, amen, say ye,
Of your inward charyte;
        Amen,
Of your inward charyte.
    It were great rewth,
For wrytynge of trewth
Any man shulde be 840
In perplexyte
Of dyspleasure ;

For I make you sure,
Where trouth is abhorde,
It is a playne recorde
That there wantys grace;
In whose place
Dothe occupy,
Full vngracyously,
Fals flatery,   850
Fals trechery,
Fals brybery,
Subtyle Sym Sly,
With madde foly;
For who can best lye,
He is best set by.
Than farewell to thé,
Welthfull felycite!
For prosperyte
Away than wyll fle.   860
Than must we agre
With pouerte;
For mysery,
With penury,
Myserably
And wretchydly
Hath made askrye
And outcry,
Folowynge the chase
To dryue away grace.   870
Yet sayst thou percase,
We can lacke no grace,

For my lordes grace,
And my ladies grace,
With trey duse ase,
And ase in the face,
Some haute and some base,
Some daunce the trace
Euer in one case :
Marke me that chase   880
In the tennys play,
For synke quater trey
Is a tall man :
He rod, but we ran,
Hay, the gye and the gan!
The gray gose is no swan ;
The waters wax wan,
And beggers they ban,
And they cursed Datan,
De tribu Dan,   890
That this warke began,
Palam et clam,
With Balak and Balam,
The golden ram
Of Flemmyng dam,
Sem, Iapheth, or Cam.
  But howe comme to pas,
Your cupboard that was
Is tourned to glasse,
From syluer to brasse,   900
From golde to pewter,
Or els to a newter,

To copper, to tyn,
To lede, or alcumyn ?
A goldsmyth your mayre ;
But the chefe of your fayre
Myght stande nowe by potters,
And suche as sell trotters :
Pytchars, potshordis,
This shrewdly accordis   910
To be a cupborde for lordys.
  My lorde now and syr knyght,
Good euyn and good nyght !
For now, syr Trestram,
Ye must weare bukram,
Or canues of Cane,
For sylkes are wane.
Our royals that shone,
Our nobles are gone
Amonge the Burgonyons,   920
And Spanyardes onyons,
And the Flanderkyns.
Gyll swetis, and Cate spynnys,
They are happy that wynnys ;
But Englande may well say,
Fye on this wynnyng all way !
Now nothynge but pay, pay,
With, laughe and lay downe,
Borowgh, cyte, and towne.
  Good Sprynge of Lanam   930
Must counte what became
Of his clothe makynge :

He is at suche takynge,
Though his purse wax dull,
He must tax for his wull
By nature of a newe writ;
My lordys grace nameth it
A *quia non satisfacit:*
In the spyght of his tethe
He must pay agayne   940
A thousande or twayne
Of his golde in store;
And yet he payde before
An hunderd pounde and more,
Whiche pyncheth him sore.
My lordis grace wyll brynge
Downe this hye sprynge,
And brynge it so lowe,
It shall nat euer flowe.

Suche a prelate, I trowe,   950
Were worthy to rowe
Thorow the streytes of Marock
To the gybbet of Baldock :
He wolde dry vp the stremys
Of ix. kinges realmys,
All ryuers and wellys,
All waters that swellys ;
For with vs he so mellys
That within Englande dwellys,
I wolde he were somwhere ellys ;   960
For els by and by
He wyll drynke vs so drye,

And suck vs so nye,
That men shall scantly
Haue peny or halpeny.
God saue his noble grace,
And graunt him a place
Endlesse to dwell
With the deuyll of hell!
For, and he were there,   970
We nede neuer feere
Of the fendys blake :
For I vndertake
He wolde so brag and crake,
That he wolde than make
The deuyls to quake,
To shudder and to shake,
Lyke a fyer drake,
And with a cole rake
Brose them on a brake,   980
And bynde them to a stake,
And set hell on fyer,
At his owne desyer.
He is suche a grym syer,
And suche a potestolate,
And suche a potestate,
That he wolde breke the braynes
Of Lucyfer in his chaynes,
And rule them echone
In Lucyfers trone.   990
I wolde he were gone ;
For amonge vs is none

That ruleth but he alone,
Without all good reason,
And all out of season :
For Folam peason
With him be nat geson ;
They growwe very ranke
Vpon euery banke
Of his herbers grene,   1000
With my lady bryght and shene ;
On theyr game it is sene
They play nat all clene,
And it be as I wene.

But as touchynge dyscrecyon,
With sober dyrectyon,
He kepeth them in subiectyon :
They can haue no protectyon
To rule nor to guyde,
But all must be tryde,   1010
And abyde the correctyon
Of his wylfull affectyon.
For as for wytte,
The deuyll spede whitte !
But braynsyk and braynlesse,
Wytles and rechelesse,
Careles and shamlesse,
Thriftles and gracelesse,
Together are bended
And so condyscended,   1020
That the commune welth
Shall neuer haue good helth,

But tatterd and tuggyd,
Raggyd and ruggyd,
Shauyn and shorne,
And all threde bare worne.
Suche gredynesse
Suche nedynesse,
Myserablenesse,
With wretchydnesse,   1030
Hath brought in dystresse
And moche heuynesse
And great dolowre
Englande, the flowre
Of relucent honowre,
In olde commemoracion
Most royall Englyssh nacion.
Now all is out of facion,
Almost in desolation;
I speke by protestacion: 1040
God of his miseracyon
Send better reformacyon!
    Lo, for to do shamfully
He iugeth it no foly!
But to wryte of his shame,
He sayth we ar to blame.
What a frensy is this,
No shame to do amys,
And yet he is ashamed
To be shamfully named!   1050
And ofte prechours be blamed,
Bycause they haue proclamed

His madnesse by writynge,
His symplenesse resytynge,
Remordynge and bytynge,
With chydyng and with flytynge,
Shewynge him Goddis lawis :
He calleth the prechours dawis,
And of holy scriptures sawis
He counteth them for gygawis,   1060
And putteth them to sylence
And ¹ with wordis of vyolence,
Lyke Pharao, voyde of grace,
Dyd Moyses sore manase,
And Aron sore he thret,
The worde of God to let;
This maumet in lyke wyse
Against the churche doth ryse;
The prechour he dothe dyspyse,
With crakynge in suche wyse,   1070
So braggynge all with bost,
That no prechour almost
Dare speke for his lyfe
Of my lordis grace nor his wyfe,
For he hath suche a bull,
He may take whom he wull,
And as many as him lykys;
May ete pigges in Lent for pikys,
After the sectes of heretykis,
For in Lent he wyll ete   1080
All maner of flesshe mete

¹ *Ana*] Perhaps ought to be thrown out.   Compare v. 735.

That he can ony where gete;
With other abusyons grete,
Wherof for to trete
It wolde make the deuyll to swete,
For all priuileged places
He brekes and defaces,
All placis of relygion
He hathe them in derisyon,
And makith suche prouisyon   1090
To dryue them at diuisyon,
And fynally in conclusyon
To bringe them to confusyon;
Saint Albons to recorde
Wherof this vngracyous lorde
Hathe made him selfe abbot,
Against their wylles, God wot.
All this he dothe deale
Vnder strength of the great seale,
And by his legacy,   1100
Whiche madly he dothe apply
Vnto an extrauagancy
Pyked out of all good lawe,
With reasons that ben rawe.
Yet, whan he toke first his hat,
He said he knew what was what;
All iustyce he pretended,
All thynges sholde be amended,
All wronges he wolde redresse,
All iniuris he wolde represse,   1110
All periuris he wolde oppresse;

And yet this gracelesse elfe,
He is periured himselfe,
As playnly it dothe appere,
Who lyst to enquere
In the regestry
Of my Lorde of Cantorbury,
To whom he was professed
In thre poyntes expressed;
The fyrst to do him reuerence,   1120
The seconde to owe hym obedyence,
The thirde with hole affectyon
To be vnder his subiectyon :
But now he maketh obiectyon,
Vnder the protectyon
Of the kynges great seale,
That he setteth neuer a deale
By his former othe,
Whether God be pleased or wroth.
He makith so proude pretens,   1130
That in his equipolens
He iugyth him equiualent
With God omnipotent :
But yet beware the rod,
And the stroke of God !
  The Apostyll Peter
Had a pore myter
And a poore cope
Whan he was creat Pope,
First in Antioche ;   1140
He dyd neuer approche

Of Rome to the see
Weth suche dygnyte.
    Saynt Dunstane, what was he?
Nothynge, he sayth, lyke to me:
There is a dyuersyte
Bytwene him and me;
We passe hym in degre,
As *legatus a latere.*
    Ecce, sacerdos magnus,   1150
That wyll hed vs-and hange vs,
And streitly strangle vs
And he may fange vs!
Decre and decretall,
Constytucyon prouincyall,
Nor no lawe canonicall,
Shall let the preest pontyficall
To syt *in causa sanguinis.*
Nowe God amende that is amys!
For I suppose that he is   1160
Of Ieremy the whyskynge rod,
The flayle, the scourge of almighty God.
    This Naman Sirus,
So fell and so irous,
So full of malencoly,
With a flap afore his eye,
Men wene that he is pocky,
Or els his surgions they lye,
For, as far as they can spy
By the craft of surgery,   1170
It is *manus Domini.*

And yet this proude Antiochus,
He is so ambicious,
So elate, and so vicious,
And so cruell hertyd,
That he wyll nat be conuertyd;
For he setteth God apart,
He is nowe so ouerthwart,.
And so payned with pangis,
That all his trust hangis   1180
In Balthasor, whiche heled
Domingos nose that was wheled;
That Lumberdes nose meane I,
That standeth yet awrye;
It was nat heled alderbest,
It standeth somwhat on the west;
I meane Domyngo Lomelyn,
That was wont to wyn
Moche money of the kynge
At the cardys and haserdynge: 1190
Balthasor, that helyd Domingos nose
From the puskylde pocky pose,
Now with his gummys of Araby
Hath promised to hele our cardinals eye;
Yet sum surgions put a dout,
Lest he wyll put it clene out,
And make him lame of his neder limmes:
God sende him sorowe for his sinnes!
   Some men myght aske a question,
By whose suggestyon   1200
I toke on hand this warke,
Thus boldly for to barke?

And men lyst to harke,
And my wordes marke,
I wyll answere lyke a clerke ;
For trewly and vnfayned,
I am forcebly constrayned,
At Iuuynals request,
To wryght of this glorious gest,
Of this vayne gloryous best,   1210
His fame to be encrest
At euery solempne feest ;
Quia difficile est
Satiram non scribere.
Now, mayster doctor, howe say ye,
What soeuer your name be ?
What though ye be namelesse,
Ye shall not escape blamelesse,
Nor yet shall scape shamlesse :
Mayster doctor in your degre,   1220
Yourselfe madly ye ouerse ;
Blame Iuuinall, and blame nat me :
Maister doctor Diricum,
Omne animi vitium, &c.
As Iuuinall dothe recorde,
A small defaute in a great lorde,
A lytell cryme in a great astate,
Is moche more inordinate,
And more horyble to beholde,
Than any other a thousand folde.   1230
Ye put to blame ye wot nere whom ;
Ye may weare a cockes come ;

Your fonde hed in your furred hood,
Holde ye your tong, ye can no goode:
And at more conuenyent tyme
I may fortune for to ryme
Somwhat of your madnesse;
For small is your sadnesse
To put any man in lack,
And say yll behynde his back: 1240
And my wordes marke truly,
That ye can nat byde thereby,
For *smegma non est cinnamomum,*
But *de absentibus nil nisi bonum.*
Complayne, or do what ye wyll,
Of your complaynt it shall nat skyl:
This is the tenor of my byl,
A daucock ye be, and so shalbe styll.

Sequitur Epitoma
De morbilloso Thoma,
Necnon obscœno
De Polyphemo, &c.

Porro perbelle dissimulatum
Illum Pandulphum, tantum legatum,
Tam formidatum nuper prælatum,
Ceu Naman Syrum nunc elongatum,
In solitudine jam commoratum,
Neapolitano morbo gravatum,
Malagmate, cataplasmate stratum,
Pharmacopolæ ferro foratum,

Nihilo magis alleviatum,
Nihilo melius aut medicatum, 10
Relictis famulis ad famulatum,
Quo tollatur infamia,
Sed major patet insania ;
A modo ergo ganea
Abhorreat ille ganeus,
Dominus male creticus,
Aptius dictus tetricus,
Fanaticus, phreneticus,
Graphicus sicut metricus
    Autumat. 20
Hoc genus dictaminis
Non eget examinis
In centiloquio
Nec centimetro
Honorati
Grammatici
Mauri.

DECASTICHON VIRJLENTUM IN GALERATUM LYCAONTA
MARINUM, &c.

Proh dolor, ecce, maris lupus, et nequissimus ursus,
Carnificis vitulus, Britonumque bubulcus iniquus,
Conflatus vitulus vel Oreb, vel Salmane vel Zeb,
Carduus, et crudelis Asaphque Datan reprobatus,
Blandus et Achitophel regis, scelus omne Britan-
    num,
Ecclesias qui namque Thomas confundit ubique,
Non sacer iste Thomas, sed duro corde Goleas,

Quem gestat mulus,—Sathane, cacet, obsecro, culus
Fundens asphaltum, precor! Hunc versum lege
        cautum ;
Asperius nihil est misero quum surget in altum. 10

APOSTROPHA AD LONDINI CIVES (CITANTE MULUM ASINO
    AUREO GALERATO) IN OCCURSUM ASELLI, &c.

Excitat, en, asinus mulum, mirabile visu,
Calcibus! O vestro cives occurrite asello,
Qui regnum regemque regit, qui vestra gubernat
Prædia, divitias, nummos, gazas, spoliando!

Dixit alludens, immo illudens, paradoxam de
        asino aureo galerato.
            xxxiiii.

        Hæc vates ille,
        De quo loquuntur mille.

SKELTON, LAUREATE, &c

HOWE THE DOUTY DUKE OF ALBANY,* LYKE A COWARDE
KNYGHT, RAN AWAYE SHAMFULLY, WITH AN HUNDRED
THOUSANDE TRATLANDE SCOTTES AND FAINT HARTED
FRENCHEMEN, BESIDE THE WATER OF TWEDE, &c.

REIOYSE, Englande,
And vnderstande
These tidinges newe,
Whiche be as trewe
As the gospell :
This duke so fell
Of Albany,
So cowardly,
With all his hoost
Of the Scottyshe coost,   10
For all theyr boost,
Fledde lyke a beest ;
Wherfore to ieste
Is my delyght
Of this cowarde knyght,
And for to wright
In the dispyght
Of the Scottes ranke
Of Huntley banke,

* From Marshe's ed. of Skelton's *Workes*, 1568.

Of Lowdyan,   20
Of Locryan,
And the ragged ray
Of Galaway.
   Dunbar, Dunde,
Ye shall trowe me,
False Scottes are ye :
Your hartes sore faynted,
And so[1] attaynted,
Lyke cowardes starke,
At the castell of Warke,   30
By the water of Twede,
Ye had euill spede ;
Lyke cankerd curres,
Ye loste your spurres,
For in that fraye
Ye ranne awaye,
With, hey, dogge, hay !
For Sir William Lyle
Within shorte whyle,
That valiaunt knyght,   40
Putte you to flyght ;
By his valyaunce
Two thousande of Fraunce
There he putte backe,
To your great lacke,
And vtter shame
Of your Scottysshe name.

            [1] *so*; Qy. " sore ? "

Your chefe cheftayne,
Voyde of all brayne,
Duke of all Albany,   50
Than shamefuly
He reculed backe,
To his great lacke,
Whan he herde tell
That my lorde amrell
Was comyng downe,
To make hym frowne
And to make hym lowre,
With the noble powre
Of my lorde cardynall,   60
As an hoost royall,
After the auncient manner,
With sainct Cutberdes banner,
And sainct Williams also;
Your capitayne ranne to go,
To go, to go, to go,
And brake vp all his hoost
For all his crake and bost,
Lyke a cowarde knyght,
He fledde, and durst nat fyght,   70
He ranne awaye by night.
　　But now must I
Your Duke ascry
Of Albany
With a worde or twayne
In sentence playne.
　　Ye duke so doutty,
So sterne, so stoutty,

In shorte sentens,   80
Of your pretens
What is the grounde,
Breuely and rounde
To me expounde,
Or els wyll I
Euydently
Shewe as it is;
For the cause is this,
Howe ye pretende
For to defende
The yonge Scottyshe kyng,   90
But ye meane a thyng,
And ye coude bryng
The matter about,
To putte his eyes out
And put hym downe,
And set hys crowne
On your owne heed
Whan he were deed.
Such trechery
And traytory   .00
Is all your cast;
Thus ye haue compast
With the Frenche kyng
A fals rekenyng
To enuade Englande,
As I vnderstande:
But our kyng royall,
Whose name ouer all,
Noble Henry the eyght,

Shall cast a beyght,   110
And sette suche a snare,
That shall cast you in care,
Bothe Kyng Fraunces and thé,
That knowen ye shall be
For the moost recrayd
Cowardes afrayd,
And falsest forsworne,
That euer were borne.
  O ye wretched Scottes,
Ye puaunt pyspottes,   120
It shalbe your lottes
To be knytte vp with knottes
Of halters and ropes
About your traytours throtes!
O Scottes pariured,
Vnhaply vred,
Ye may be assured
Your falshod discured
It is and shal. be.
From the Scottish se   130
Vnto Gabione!
For ye be false echone,
False and false agayne,
Neuer true nor playne,
But flery, flatter, and fayne,
And euer to remayne
In wretched beggary
And maungy misery,
In lousy lothsumnesse

And scabbed scorffynesse,   140
And in abhominacion
Of all maner of nacion,
Nacion moost in hate,
Proude and poore of state.
Twyt, Scot, go kepe thy den,
Mell nat with Englyshe men;
Thou dyd nothyng but barke
At the castell of Warke.
Twyt, Scot, yet agayne ones,
We shall breke thy bones,   150
And hang you vpon polles,
And byrne you all to colles;
With, twyt, Scot, twyt, Scot, twyt,
Walke, Scot, go begge a byt
Of brede at ylke mannes hecke:
The fynde, Scot, breke thy necke!
Twyt, Scot, agayne I saye,
Twyt, Scot of Galaway,
Twyt, Scot, shake thy dogge,[1] hay!
Twyt, Scot, thou ran away.   160
   We set nat a flye
By your Duke of Albany;
We set nat a prane
By suche a dronken drane;
We set nat a myght
By suche a cowarde knyght,
Suche a proude palyarde,

---

[1] *thy dogge*] Qy. "thé, dogge?" but see notes.

Suche a skyrgaliarde,
Suche a starke cowarde,
Suche a proude pultrowne,   170
Suche a foule coystrowne,
Suche a doutty dagswayne;
Sende him to F[r]aunce agayne,
To bring with hym more brayne
From Kynge Fraunces of Frauns:
God sende them bothe myschauns!
Ye Scottes all the rable,
Ye shall neuer be hable
With vs for to compare;
What though ye stampe and stare?   180
God sende you sorow and care!
With vs whan euer ye mell,
Yet we bear away the bell,
Whan ye cankerd knaues
Must crepe into your caues
Your heedes for to hyde,
For ye dare nat abyde.
Sir Duke of Albany,
Right inconuenyently
Ye rage and ye raue,   190
And your worshyp depraue:
Nat lyke Duke Hamylcar,
With the Romayns that made war,
Nor lyke his sonne Hanyball,
Nor lyke Duke Hasdruball
Of Cartage in Aphrike;
Yet somwhat ye be lyke

In some of their condicions,
And their false sedycions,
And their dealyng double,   200
And their weywarde trouble:
But yet they were bolde,
And manly manyfolde,
Their enemyes to assayle
In playn felde and battayle;
But ye and your hoost,
Full of bragge and boost,
And full of waste wynde,
Howe ye wyll beres bynde,
And the deuill downe dynge,   210
Yet ye dare do nothynge,
But lepe away lyke frogges,
And hyde you vnder logges,
Lyke pygges and lyke hogges,
And lyke maungy dogges.
What an army were ye?
Or what actyuyte
Is in you, beggers braules,
Full of scabbes and scaules,
Of vermyne and of lyce,   220
And of all maner vyce?
  Syr duke, nay, syr ducke,
Syr drake of the lake, sir ducke
Of the donghyll, for small lucke
Ye haue in feates of warre;
Ye make nought, but ye marre;
Ye are a fals entrusar,

And a fals abusar,
And an vntrewe knyght;
Thou hast to lytell myght   230
Agaynst Englande to fyght;
Thou art a graceles wyght
To put thy selfe to flyght:
A vengeaunce and dispight
On thé must nedes lyght,
That durst nat byde the sight
Of my lorde amrell,
Of chiualry the well,
Of knighthode the floure
In euery marciall shoure,   240
The noble Erle of Surrey,
That put thé in suche fray;
Thou durst no felde derayne,
Nor no batayle mayntayne
Against our st[r]onge captaine,
But thou ran home agayne,
For feare thou shoulde be slayne,
Lyke a Scottyshe keteryng,
That durst abyde no reknyng;
Thy hert wolde nat serue thé: 250
The fynde of hell mot sterue thé!
   No man hath harde
Of suche a cowarde,
And such a mad ymage
Caried in a cage,
As it were a cotage;
Or of suche a mawment

Caryed in a tent;
In a tent! nay, nay,
But in a mountayne gay,   260
Lyke a great hill
For a wyndmil,
Therin to couche styll,
That no man hym kyll;
As it were a gote
In a shepe cote,
About hym a parke
Of a madde warke,
Men call it a toyle;
Therin, lyke a royle,   270
Sir Dunkan, ye dared,
And thus ye prepared
Youre carkas to kepe,
Lyke a sely shepe,
A shepe of Cottyswolde,
From rayne and from colde,
And from raynning of rappes,
And suche after clappes;
Thus in your cowardly castell
Ye decte you to dwell: 280
Suche a captayne of hors,
It made no great fors
If that ye had tane
Your last deedly bane
With a gon stone,
To make you to grone.
But hyde thé, sir Topias,

Nowe into the castell of Bas,
And lurke there, lyke an as,
With some Scotyshe [l]as,   290
With dugges, dugges, dugges :
I shrewe thy Scottishe lugges,
Thy munpynnys, and thy crag,
For thou can not but brag,
Lyke a Scottyshe hag :
Adue nowe, sir Wrig wrag,
Adue, sir Dalyrag !
Thy mellyng is but mockyng ;
Thou mayst giue vp thy cocking,
Gyue it vp, and cry creke,   300
Lyke an huddypeke.
  Wherto shuld I more speke
Of suche a farly freke,
Of suche an horne keke,
Of suche an bolde captayne,
That dare nat turne agayne,
Nor durst nat crak a worde,
Nor durst nat drawe his swerde
Agaynst the Lyon White,
But ran away quyte ?   310
He ran away by nyght,
In the owle flyght,
Lyke a cowarde knyght.
Adue, cowarde, adue,
Fals knight, and mooste vntrue !
I render thé, fals rebelle,
To the flingande fende of helle.

Harke yet, sir duke, a worde,
In ernest or in borde :
What, haue ye, villayn, forged,   320
And virulently dysgorged,
As though ye wolde parbrake,
Your auauns to make,
With wordes enbosed,
Vngraciously engrosed,
Howe ye wyll vndertake
Our royall kyng to make
His owne realme to forsake ?
Suche lewde langage ye spake.
Sir Dunkan, in the deuill waye,   330
Be well ware what ye say :
Ye saye that he and ye,—
Whyche he and ye ? let se ;
Ye meane Fraunces, French kyng,
Shulde bring about that thing.
I say, thou lewde lurdayne,
That neyther of you twayne
So hardy nor so bolde
His countenaunce to beholde :
If our moost royall Harry   340
Lyst with you to varry,
Full soone ye should miscary,
For ye durst nat tarry
With hym to stryue a stownde ;
If he on you but frounde,
Nat for a thousande pounde
Ye durst byde on the grounde,

Ye wolde ryn away rounde,
And cowardly tourne your backes,
For all your comly crackes,   350
And, for feare par case
To loke hym in the face,
Ye wolde defoyle the place,
And ryn your way apace.
Thoughe I trym you thys trace
With Englyshe somwhat base,
Yet, *saue voster grace*,
Therby I shall purchace
No displesaunt rewarde,
If ye wele can regarde   360
Your cankarde cowardnesse
And your shamfull doublenesse.

Are ye nat frantyke madde,
And wretchedly bestadde,
To rayle agaynst his grace,
That shall bring you full bace,
And set you in suche case,
That bytwene you twayne
There shalbe drawen a trayne
That shalbe to your payne?   370
To flye ye shalbe fayne.
And neuer tourne agayne.

What, wold Fraunces, our friar,
Be suche a false lyar,
So madde a cordylar,
So madde a murmurar?
Ye muse somwhat to far;

All out of ioynt ye iar :
God let you neuer thriue !
Wene ye, daucockes, to driue   380
Our kyng out of his reme ?
Ge heme, ranke Scot, ge heme,
With fonde Fraunces, French kyng :
Our mayster shall you brynge
I trust, to lowe estate,
And mate you with chekmate.

Your braynes arr ydell ;
It is time for you to brydell,
And pype in a quibyble ;
For it is impossible   390
For you to bring about,
Our kyng for to dryue out
Of this his realme royall
And lande imperiall ;
So noble a prince as he
In all actyuite
Of hardy merciall actes,
Fortunate in all his faytes.[1]

And nowe I wyll me dresse
His valiaunce to expresse,   400
Though insufficient am I
His grace to magnify
And laude equiualently ;
Howe be it, loyally,
After myne allegyaunce,
My pen I wyll auaunce

    [1] *faytes*] Qy. "factes?"

To extoll his noble grace,
In spyght of thy cowardes face,
In spyght of Kyng Fraunces,
Deuoyde of all nobles,   410
Deuoyde of good corage,
Deuoyde of wysdome sage,
Mad, frantyke, and sauage ;
Thus he dothe disparage
His bloce with fonde dotage.
A prince to play the page
It is a rechelesse rage,
And a lunatyke ouerage.
What though my stile be rude ?
With trouthe it is ennewde :   420
Trouth ought to be rescude,
Trouthe should nat be subdude.
    But nowe will I expounde
What noblenesse dothe abounde,
And what honour is founde,
And what vertues be resydent
In our royall regent,
Our perelesse president,
Our kyng most excellent :
    In merciall prowes   430
Lyke vnto Hercules ;
In prudence and wysdom
Lyke vnto Salamon ;
In his goodly person ,
Lyke vnto Absolon ;
In loyalte and foy

Lyke to Ector of Troy ;
And his glory to incres,
Lyke to Scipiades ;
In royal mageste   440
Lyke vnto Ptholome,
Lyke to Duke Iosue,
And the valiaunt Machube ;
That if I wolde reporte
All the roiall sorte
Of his nobilyte,
His magnanymyte,
His animosite,
His frugalite,
His lyberalite,   450
His affabilite,
His humanyte,
His stabilite,
His humilite,
His benignite,
His royall dignyte,
My lernyng is to small
For to recount them all.

What losels than are ye,
Lyke cowardes as ye be,   460
To rayle on his astate,
With wordes inordinate !

He rules his cominalte
With all benignite ;
His noble baronage,
He putteth them in corage

To exployte dedes of armys,
To the domage and harmys
Of suche as be his foos ;
Where euer he rydes or goos,   470
His subiectes he dothe supporte,
Maintayne them with comforte
Of his moste princely porte,
As all men can reporte.
  Than ye be a knappishe sorte,
Et faitez a luy grant torte,
With your enbosed iawes
To rayle on hym lyke dawes ;
The fende scrache out your mawes!
  All his subiectes and he   480
Moost louyngly agre
With hole hart and true mynde,
They fynde his grace so kynde ;
Wherwith he dothe them bynde
At all houres to be redy
With hym to lyue and dye,
And to spende their hart blode,
Their bodyes and their gode,
With hym in all dystresse,
Alway in redynesse   490
To assyst his noble grace ;
In spyght of thy cowardes face,
Moost false attaynted traytour,
And false forsworne faytour.
  Auaunte, cowarde recrayed!
Thy pride shalbe alayd ;

With sir Fraunces of Fraunce
We shall pype you a daunce,
Shall tourne you to myschauns.
  I rede you, loke about;   500
For ye shalbe driuen out
Of your lande in shorte space :
We will so folowe in the chace,
That ye shall haue no grace
For to tourne your face ;
And thus, Sainct George to borowe,
Ye shall haue shame and sorowe.

Lenuoy.

Go, lytell quayre, quickly ;
  Shew them that shall you rede,
How that ye are lykely   510
  Ouer all the worlde to sprede.
The fals Scottes for dred,
  With the Duke of Albany,
Beside the water of Twede
  They fledde full cowardly.
Though your Englishe be rude,
  Barreyne of eloquence,
Yet, breuely to conclude,
  Grounded is your sentence
On trouthe, vnder defence   520
  Of all trewe Englyshemen,
This mater to credence
  That I wrate with my pen.

SKELTON LAUREAT, OBSEQUIOUS ET LOYALL.[1]
TO MY LORDE CARDYNALS RIGHT NOBLE GRACE, ETC.

Lenuoy.

Go, lytell quayre, apace,
    In moost humble wyse,
Before his noble grace,
    That caused you to deuise
    This lytel enterprise ;
And hym moost lowly pray,
    In his mynde to comprise
Those wordes his grace dyd saye
Of an ammas gray.

Ie foy enterment en sa bone grace.

---

[1] *Skelton Laureat, obsequious et loyall*] Perhaps these words
are a portion of the superscription to the *Lenuoy* which fol-
lows. The *Lenuoy* itself does not, I apprehend, belong to the
poem on the Duke of Albany. See *Account of Skelton, &c.*

A LAWDE AND PRAYSE MADE FOR OUR SOUEREIGNE
LORD THE KYNG.[1]

Candida, pu- THE Rose both White and Rede
nica, &c.
    In one Rose now dothe grow;
Thus thorow every stede
    Thereof the fame dothe blow:
    Grace the sede did sow:
England, now gaddir flowris,
Exclude now all dolowrs.

Nobilis Hen- Noble Henry the eight,
ricus, &c.
    Thy loving souereine lorde,
Of kingis line moost streight,
    His titille dothe recorde:
    In whome dothe wele acorde
Alexis yonge of age,
Adrastus wise and sage.

1 *A lawde and prayse made for our souereigne lord the kyng*]
Such (in a different handwriting from that of the poem) is
the endorsement of the MS., which consists of two leaves,
bound up in the volume marked *B*. 2. 8, (pp. 67-69,) among
the Records of the Treasury of the Receipt of the Exchequer,
now at the Rolls House. [Printed for the first time by Dyce,
from a manuscript discovered by Mr. W. H. Black.]   Qy. is
this poem the piece which, in the catalogue of his own writ-
ings, Skelton calls " The Boke of the Rosiar," *Garlande of
Laurell*, v. 1178, vol. ii. 221?

Astrea, Justice hight,
   That from the starry sky
Shall now com and do right,
   This hunderd yere scantly
   A man kowd not aspy
That Right dwelt vs among,
And that was the more wrong :

Sedibus æ-theriis, &c.

Right shall the foxis chare,
   The wolvis, the beris also,
That wrowght have moche care,
   And browght Englond in wo :
   They shall wirry no mo,
Nor wrote the Rosary
By extort trechery :

Arcebit vul-pes, &c.

Of this our noble king
   The law they shall not breke ;
They shall com to rekening ;
   No man for them wil speke :
   The pepil durst not creke
Theire grevis to complaine,
They browght them in soche paine :

Ne tanti re-gis, &c.

Therfor no more they shall
   The commouns ouerbace,
That wont wer ouer all
   Both lorde and knight to face ;
   For now the yeris of grace
And welthe ar com agayne,
That maketh England faine.

Ecce Plato-nis secla, &c.

Rediit jam pulcher Adonis, &c. Adonis of freshe colour,
    Of yowthe the godely flour,
  Our prince of high honour,
    Our paves, our succour,
    Our king, our emperour,
  Our Priamus of Troy,
  Our welth, our worldly joy;

Anglorum radians, &c. Vpon vs he doth reigne,
    That makith our hartis glad,
  As king moost soueraine
    That ever Englond had;
    Demure, sober, and sad,
  And Martis lusty knight;
  God save him in his right!
                Amen.

Bien men souient.[1]

*Per me laurigerum Britonum Skeltonida
vatem.*

[1] *Bien men souient*] These words are followed in the MS.
by a sort of flourished device, which might perhaps be read—

" *Deo* (2i̊) *gratias.*"

POEMS ATTRIBUTED TO SKELTON.

POEMS

ATTRIBUTED TO SKELTON.

VERSES PRESENTED TO KING HENRY THE SEVENTH AT THE
FEAST OF ST. GEORGE CELEBRATED AT WINDSOR IN THE
THIRD YEAR OF HIS REIGN.*

O MOSTE famous noble king! thy fame doth spring and
    spreade,
Henry the Seventh, our soverain, in eiche regeon;
All England hath cause thy grace to love and dread,
    Seing embassadores seche fore protectyon,
    For ayd, helpe, and succore, which lyeth in thie electyone.
England, now rejoyce, for joyous mayest thou bee,
To see thy kyng so floreshe in dignetye.

This realme a seasone stoode in greate jupardie,
    When that noble prince deceased, King Edward,
Which in his dayes gate honore full nobly;

---

   * Ashmole, who first printed these lines from " *MS. penes
Arth. Com. Anglesey, fol.* 169," thinks that they were proba-
bly by Skelton: see *Order of the Garter*, p. 594.

After his decesse nighe hand all was marr'd;
Eich regione this land dispised, mischefe when they hard:
Wherefore rejoyse, for joyous mayst thou be,
To see thy kynge so floresh in high dignetye.

Fraunce, Spayne, Scoteland, and Britanny, Flanders also,
   Three of them present keepinge thy noble feaste
Of St. George in Windsor, ambassadors comying more,[1]
   Iche of them in honore, bothe the more and the lesse,[2]
   Seeking thie grace to have thie noble begeste:
Wherefore now rejoise, and joyous maiste thou be,
To see thy kynge so florishing in dignetye.

O knightly ordere, clothed in robes with gartere!
   The queen's grace and thy mother clothed in the same;
The nobles of thie realme riche in araye, aftere,
   Lords, knights, and ladyes, unto thy greate fame:
   Now shall all embassadors know thie noble name,
By thy feaste royal; nowe joyeous mayest thou be,
To see thie king so florishinge in dignety.

Here this day St. George, patron of this place,
   Honored with the gartere cheefe of chevalrye;
Chaplenes synging processyon, keeping the same,
   With archbushopes and bushopes beseene nobly;
   Much people presente to see the King Henrye:
Wherefore now, St. George, all we pray to thee
To keepe our soveraine in his dignetye.

---

[1] *more*] The rhyme requires "mo."
[2] *lesse*] The rhyme requires "leste."

THE EPITAFFE OF THE MOSTE NOBLE AND VALYAUNT
JASPAR LATE DUKE OF BEDDEFORDE.*

BYDYNGE al alone, with sorowe sore encombred,
In a frosty fornone, faste by Seuernes syde,
The wordil beholdynge, wherat moch I wondred
To se the see and sonne to kepe both tyme and tyde,

---

* The old ed. is a quarto, n. d. Above these words, on the
title-page, is a woodcut, exhibiting the author (with a falcon
on his hand) kneeling and presenting his work to the king.
On the reverse of the last leaf is Pynson's device.

If not really written by Smert, (or Smart,) the duke's fal-
coner, (see stanza 3, and the subscription at the conclusion,
" *Smerte, maister de ses ouzeaus,*") this curious poem was not,
at all events, as the style decidedly proves, the composition
of Skelton, to whom it was first attributed by Bishop Tanner.

I now print it from a transcript of the (probably unique)
copy in the Pepysian library,—a transcript which appears to
have been made with the greatest care and exactness; but I
think right to add, that I have not had an opportunity of
seeing the original myself.

Jasper Tudor, second son of Owen Tudor by Katherine
widow of King Henry the Fifth, was created Earl of Pem-
broke, in 1452, by his half-brother, King Henry the Sixth.
After that monarch had been driven from the throne by Ed-
ward, Jasper was attainted, and his earldom conferred on
another. He was again restored to it, when Henry had re-
covered the crown; but being taken prisoner at the battle of
Barnet, he lost it a second time. After the battle of Bos-
worth, Henry the Seventh not only reinstated Jasper (his
uncle) in the earldom of Pembroke, but also created him
Duke of Bedford, in 1485; subsequently appointed him Lieu-
tenant of Ireland for one year, and granted to him and his

The ayre ouer my hede so wonderfully to glyde,
ᶜ And howe Saturne by circumference borne is aboute;
Whiche thynges to beholde, clerely me notyfyde,
One verray God to be therin to haue no dowte.

And as my fantasy flamyd in that occupacyon,
Fruteles, deuoyde of all maner gladnes,
Of one was I ware into greate desolacyon,
To the erthe prostrate, rauynge for madnes;
By menys so immoderate encreased was his sadnes,
That by me can not be compyled
His dedly sorowe and dolorous dystres,
Lyfe in hym by deth so ny was exiled.

Hym better to beholde, so ferre oute of frame,
Nerre I nyghed, farsyd with fragyllyte;
Wherwith Smert I perceyued he called was by name,
Which ouer haukes and houndes had auctoryte;
Though the roume vnmete were for his pouer degre,
Yet fortune so hym farthered to his lorde;
Wherfore him to lye in soch perplexite,
What it myghte mene I gan to mysylfe recorde.

I shogged him, I shaked him, I ofte aboute him went,
And al to knowe why so care his carayn hyued;

___

heirs male the office of Earl Marshal of England with an
nuity of twenty pounds. The duke married Kathe
daughter of Richard Wydevile Earl Rivers, and widow of
Henry Stafford Duke of Buckingham. He died 21st Dec.
1495, and, according to his own desire, expressed in his will,
was buried in the abbey of Keynsham, where he founded a
chantry for four priests to sing mass for the souls of his father,
his mother, and his elder brother Edmond Earl of Richmond.
He left no children except a natural daughter. See Sand-
ford's *Geneal. Hist.* p. 292. ed. 1707.

ᶜ Color Ficcio. [*Side Note.*]

His temples I rubbyd, and by the nose him hente;
Al as in vayne was, he coude nat be reuyued;
He waltered, he wende, and with himsilfe stryued,
Such countenaunce contynuyng; but or I parte the place,
Vp his hede he caste; whan his woful goste aryued,
Those wordes saynge with righte a pytous face:

O sorowe, sorowe beyonde al sorowes sure!
All sorowes sure surmountynge, lo! *a*
Lo, which payne no pure may endure,
Endure may none such dedely wo!
Wo, alas, ye inwrapped, for he is go!
Go is he, whose valyaunce to recounte,
To recounte, all other it dyd surmounte.

Gone is he, alas, that redy was to do
Eche thynge that to nobles required! *b*
Gone is he, alas, that redy was to do
Eche thynge that curtesye of him desyred!
Whose frowarde fate falsely was conspyred
By Antraphos vnasured and her vngracyous charmys;
Jaspar I mene is gone, Mars son in armys.

He that of late regnyd in glory,
With grete glosse buttylly glased,*c*
Nowe lowe vnder fote doth he ly,.
With wormys ruly rente and rasyd.
His carayne stynkyrge, his fetures fasyd;
Brother and vncle to kynges yesterday,
Nowe is he gone and lafte vs as mased;
Closed here lyeth he in a clote of clay:
Shall he come agayne? a, nay, nay!
Where is he become, I can nat discusse:
Than with the prophet may we say,
Non inuentus est locus eius.

---

a Metricus primus. Color. repeticio. [*Side Note.*]
b Metricus secundus. C. recitacio simplex. [*Side Note.*]
c M. iii. C. narracio. [*Side Note.*]

Restynge in him was honoure with sadnesse.
Curtesy, kyndenesse, with great assuraunce,
a Dispysynge vice, louynge alway gladnesse,
Knyghtly condicyons, feythful alegeaunce,
Kyndely demenoure, gracyous vtteraunce;
Was none semelyer, feture ne face;
Frendely him fostered quatriuial aliaunce;
Alas, yet dede nowe arte thou, Jaspar, alas!

Wherfore sorowe to oure sorowe none can be founde,
Ne cause agayne care to mollyfy oure monys:
b Alas, the payne!
For his body and goste,
That we loued moste,
In a graue in the grounde
Deth depe hath drounde
Among robel and stonys:
Wherfore complayne.

Complayne, complayne, who can complayne;
For I, alas, past am compleynte!
To compleyne wyt can not sustayne,
c Deth me with doloure so hath bespraynte;
For in my syghte,
Oure lorde and knyghte,
Contrary to righte,
Deth hath ateynte.
As the vylest of a nacyon,
Deuoyde of consolacyon,
By cruel crucyacyon,
He hath combryd hym sore;
He hath him combryd sore,

---

a Metricus quartus et retrogradiens.   **Color. discripcio.**
[*Side Note.*]
b Metricus quintus.   [*Side Note.*]
c M. vi.   M. vii.   C. iteracio.   [*Side Note.*]

That Fraunce and Englonde bere byfore
Armys of both quarteryd,
And with *hony soyte* was garteryd,
Se howe he is nowe marteryd!
Alas for sorowe therfore,
Alas for sorowe therfore!
Oute and weleaway,
For people many a score
For him that yel and rore,
Alas that we were bore
To se this dolorous day!

With asshy hue compleyne also, I cry,
Ladyes, damosels, mynyonat and gorgayse;
Knyghtes aunterus of the myghty monarchy,
Complayne also; for he that in his dayes
To enhaunce wonte was your honoure, youre prayse,
Now is he gone, of erthly blysse ryfyld;
For dredeful Deth withouten delayse
Ful dolorously his breth hath stifild.

Terys degoutynge, also complayne, complayne,
Houndes peerles, haukes withoute pereialyte,
Sacris, faucons, heroners hautayne; *a*
For nowe darked is youre pompe, your prodogalyte,
Youre plesures been past vnto penalyte;
Of with your rich caperons, put on your mourning hodes;
For Iaspar, your prynce by proporcyon of qualyte,
Paste is by Deth thcse daungerous flodys.

He that manhode meyntened and magnamynite,
His blasynge blys nowe is with balys blechyd; *b*
Through Dethes croked and crabbed cruelte,
In doloure depe nowe is he drowned and drechyd;

---

a C. transsumpcio. [*Side Note.*]
b M. viii. [*Side Note.*]

His starynge standerde, that in stoures strechyd
With a sable serpent, nowe set is on a wall,
His helme heedles, cote corseles, woful and wrechyd,
With a swerde handeles, there hange they all.

Gewellys of late poysyd at grete valoyre,
He ded, they desolate of every membre,
Stykynge on stakes as thynges of none shaloyre;
For the corse that they couched cast is in sendre
ᵃ By cruel compulsyon caused to surrendre
Lyfe vp to Deth that al ouerspurneth:
O, se howe this worlde tourneth!
Some laugheth, some mourneth:
Yet, ye prynces precyous and tendre,
Whyle that ye here in glory soiourneth,
The deth of our mayster rue to remembre.

O turmentoure, traytoure, torterous tyraunte,
ᵇ So vnwarely oure duke haste thou slayne,
That wyt and mynde are vnsuffycyaunte
Agayne thy myschyf malyce to mayntayne!
We that in blysse wonte were to bayne,
With fortune flotynge moste fauourably,
Nowe thorow thrylled and persyd with payne,
Langoure we in feruente exstasy.

O murtherer vnmesurable, withouten remors,
Monstruus of entrayle, aborryd in kynde,
ᶜ Thou haste his corse dystressed by force,
Whos parayle alyue thou can not fynde!
Howe durst thou his flessh and spyryte vntynde,
Dissendynge fro Cyzyle, Jerusalem, and Fraunce?
O bazalyke bryboure, with iyes blynde,
Sore may thou rue thy vtterquidaunce!

---

a M. ix. [*Side Note.*]
b C. exclamacio. [*Side Note.*]
c C. reprobacio. [*Side Note.*]

Thou haste berafte, I say, the erthly ioye
Of one, broder and vncle to kynges in degre,
Lynyally descendynge fro Eneas of Troye,
Grete vncle and vncle to prynces thre,
Brother to a saynte by way of natyuyte,
Vncle to another whom men seketh blyue,
Blynde, croked, lame, for remedyes hourly;
Thus God that bromecod had gyuen a prerogatyue.

And yet thou, dolorous Deth, to the herte hast him stynged:
Wenest thou, felon, such murther to escape?
I say, the brewstors of Wales on the wyl be reuenged *a*
For thy false conspyracy and frowarde fate:
We his seruantes also sole disconsolate
Haste thou lafte; so that creatures more maddyr
In erthe none wandreth atwene senit and naddyr.

Wherfore, to the felde, to the felde, on with plate and **male,**
Beest, byrde, foule, eche body terrestryal! *b*
Seke we this murtherer him to assayle;
Vnafrayde ioyne in ayde, ye bodyes celestyal;
Herry saynt, with iyes faynte to the also I cal,
For thy brothers sake, help Deth to take, that al may on him
      wonder;
For and he reyne, by drift sodeyne he wil ech kynd encumbre.

Dethe.

Fouccner, thou arte to blame,
And oughte take shame
To make suche pretense; *c*
For I Deth hourly
May stande truly
At ful lawful defence:

---

a C. newgacio. [*Side Note.*]
b M. x. [*Side Note.*]
c M. xi. C. prosopopeya. [*Side Note.*]

Deth hath no myghte,
Do wronge no righte,
Fauoure frende ne fo,
But as an instrumente
At commaundemente
Whether to byde or go.

I am the instromente
Of one omnipotente,
That knowest thou fyrme and playne;
Wherfore fro Dethe
Thy wo and wreth
I wolde thou shulde reteyne,
And agayne God
For thy bromecod
Batayle to darayne.

Than, if it be ryghte, most of myght, thy godhed I acuse,
a For thy myght contrary to right thou doste gretly abuse;
Katyffes vnkind thou leuest behind, paynis, Turkes, and
     Iewis,
And our maister gret thou gaue wormes to ete; wheron gretly
     I muse:
Is this wel done? answer me sone; make, Lorde, thyn
     excuse.

Dyd thou disdayne that he shuld rayne? was that els the
     cause?
In his rayne he was moste fayne to mynester thy lawes;
Than certayn, and thou be playn and stedfaste in thy sawes,
b Euery knyght that doth right, ferynge drede ne awes,
Of thy face bryghte shall haue syghte,
After this worldly wawes:

---

a M. xii. C. Introductio. [*Side Note.*]
b M. xiii. C. onomotopeya. [*Side Note.*]

Than, gode Lorde, scripture doth record, verefieng that
    cause,
That our bromcod with the, gode God, in heuen shal rest and
    pause.

For first of nought thou him wroght of thy special grace,
And wers than noght him also boght in Caluery in that
    place;
Thou by thoght oft he were broght with Satanas to trace,*a*
Yet, Lorde, to haue pyte thou oght on the pycture of thy
    face.

We neyther he dampned to be, willyngly thou wilt noght; *b*
Yet dampned shal he and we be, if thy mercy helpe nought:
Discrecion hast thou gyuen, yde [Lorde?]; what wold we
    more ought?
After deth to lyue with the, if we offende nought.

There is a cause yet of oure care, thou creatoure alofte,
That thy gospel doth declare, whiche I forgete noughte;
Howe vnwarly our welfare fro vs shal be broughte
By Deth that none wyl spare, Lorde, that knowe we
    noughte: *c*
In syn drowned if we dare, and so sodenly be coughte,
Than of blysse ar we bare; that fylleth me ful of thoughte.

Thou knowest, Lorde, beste thysylfe,
Man is but duste, stercorye, and fylthe,
Of himsylfe vnable,
Saue only of thy specyal grace,
A soule thou made to occupye place,
To make man ferme and stable; *d*

---

    a M. xiiii. C. probacio. [*Side Note.*]
    b M. xv. [*Side Note.*]
    c M. xvi. [*Side Note.*]
    d C. degressio. M. xvii. [*Side Note.*]

Which man to do as thou ordeyned,
With fendes foule shal neuer be payned,
But in blysse be perdurable;
And if he do the contrarye,
After this lyfe than shal he dye,
Fendes to fede vnsaciable;
For which fendys foule thou made a centre,
In which centre thou made an entre,
That such that to breke thy commaundementes wolde auenter
Theder downe shulde dessende;
But oure maister, whan Deth hym trapte,
In pure perseueraunce so was wrapte,
That thou inuisyble his speryte thyder rapte
Where thy sheltrons him shal defende.

If we nat offende,	To se his face
He wyl purcháce	*a* We shal assende,
A gloryous place	By his grete grace,
At oure laste ende;	If we nat offende.

Thou haste enuapored, I say, alofte
The soule of Jaspar, that thou wroughte,
Seruyce to do latrial:
And why, Lorde, I dyd the reproue,
Was for perfyte zele and loue,
To the nat preiudicyal;
For, Lorde, this I knowe expresse,
This worldly frute is bytternesse,
Farcyd with wo and payne,
Lyfe ledynge dolorously in distresse,
Shadowed with Dethes lykenesse,
As in none certayne.

Yet, me semeth so, thou art non of tho that vs so shuld begyle:
He is nat yet ded; I lay my hed, thou hast him hid for a while;

---

a M. quatrinalis.   C. transuersio.   [*Side Note.*]

And al to proue who doth him loue and who wil be vnkynd, *a*
Thou hast in led layde him abed, this trow I in my mynd;
For this we trow, and thou dost know, as thy might is most,
That him to dye, to lowe and hye it were to grete a lost.

And he be dede, this knowe I very right;
Thou saw, Lorde, this erth corrupt with fals adulacyon,
And thought it place vnmete for Jaspar thy knyght;
Wherfore of body and soule thou made seperacyon, *b*
Preantedate seynge by pure predestynacyon
Whan his lyfe here shulde fyne and consum;
Wherfore, Lorde, thus ende I my dolorous exclamacyon,
Thy godenes knewe what was beste to be done.

As a prynce penytente and ful of contricion,
So dyed he, we his seruauntes can recorde: *c*
And that he may haue euerlastynge fruicyon,
We the beseche, gloryous kynge and lorde!
For the laste leson that he dyd recorde,
To thy power he it aplyed, saynge *tibi omnes*,
As a hye knyghte in fidelyte fermely moryd,
Angeli celi et potestates;
Wherwith payne to the hert him boryd,
And lyfe him lefte, gyuynge deth entres.

Whiche lyfe, in comparyson of thyne,
Is as poynt in lyne, or as instant in tyme;
For thou were and arte and shal be of tyme,
In thy silfe reynynge by power diuyne,
Makynge gerarcyüs thre and orders nyne,
The to deifye:
Wherfore we crye,
Suffer nat Jaspar to dye,

---

a C. neugacio. [*Side Note.*]
b C. excusacio. [*Side Note.*]
c M. xvii. C. conclusio. [*Side Note.*]

But to lyue;
For eternally that he shal lyue
Is oure byleue.

And than [?] moste craftely dyd combyne
Another heuen, called cristalline,
ᵃ So the thyrde stellyferal to shyne
Aboue the skye:
Wherfore we crye,
Suffer nat Jaspar to dye,
But to lyue;
For eternally that he shal lyue
Is oure byleue.

Moreouer in a zodiake pure and fyne
Synys xii. thou set for a tyme,
And them nexte, in cercle and lyne,
Saturne thou set, Iupiter, and Mars citryne,
Contect and drye:
Wherfore we crye,
Suffer nat Jaspar to dye,
But to lyue;
For eternally that he shal lyue
Is oure byleue.

Than, to peryssh, thorouthryll, and myne
The mystes blake and cloudes tetryne,
Tytan thou set clerely to shyne,
The worldes iye:
Wherfore we crye, *vt supra.*

Yet in their epycercles to tril and twyne,
Retrograte, stacyoner, directe, as a syne,
Uenus thou set, Marcury, and the Mone masseline;
Nexte fyre and ayre, so sotyl of engyne,

---

a M. xix. C. prolongacio. [*Side Note.*]

The to gloryfye:
Wherfore we crye,
Suffer nat Jaspar to dye,
But to lyue;
For eternally that he shal lyue
Is oure byleue.

Water, and erth with braunch and vine;
And so, thy werkes to ende and fyne,
Man to make thou dyd determyne,
Of whome cam I:
Wherfore I cry and the supplye,
Suffer nat Jaspar to dye,
But to lyue;
For eternally that he shal lyue
Is oure byleue.

With him, to comford at all tyme,
Thou ioyned the sex than of frayle femynyne,
Which by temptacyon serpentyne
Theyre hole sequele broughte to ruyne
By ouergrete folye:
Wherfore we crye,
Suffer not Jaspar to dye,
But to lyue;
For eternally that he shal lyue
Is oure byleue.

Than, of thy godenes, thou dyd enclyne
Flessh to take of thy moder and virgyne,
And vs amonge, in payne and famyne,
Dwalte, and taughte thy holy doctryne
Uulgarly:
Wherfore we crye,
Suffer nat Jaspar to dye,
But to lyue;
For eternally that he shal lyue
Is oure byleue.

Tyl a traytoure, by false couyne,
To Pylat accused the at pryme;
So taken, slayne, and buryed at complyne,
Rose agayne, of Adam redemynge the lyne
By thy infynyte mercy:
For whych mercy,
Incessantly we crye,
And the supplye,
Suffer nat our lorde to dye,
But to lyue;
For eternally that he shal lyue
Is oure byleue.

Kynges, prynces, remembre, whyle ye may,
a Do for yoursilfe, for that shal ye fynde
Executours often maketh delay,
The bodye buryed, the soule sone oute of mynde;
Marke this wel, and graue it in youre mynde,
Howe many grete estates gone are before,
And howe after ye shal folowe by course of kynde:
Wherfore do for youresilfe; I can say no more.

Though ye be gouernours, moste precious in kynde,
Caste downe your crounes and costely appareyle,
Endored with golde and precyous stones of Ynde,
For al in the ende lytyl shal auayle;
Whan youre estates Deth lyketh to assayle,
Your bodyes bulgynge with a blyster sore,
Than withstande shal neyther plate ne mayle:
Wherfore do for youresilfe; I can say no more.

There is a vertue that moost is auaunsed,
Pure perseueraunce called on the porayle,
By whome al vertues are enhaunsed,
Which is not wonne but by diligente trauayle:

---

a M. xx. [*Side Note.*]

Ware in the ende; for and that vertue fayle,
Body and soule than are ye forlore:
Wherfore, if ye folowe wyll holsom counsayle,
Do for youresilfe; I can say no more.

Kynges, prynces, moste souerayne of renoune,
Remembre oure maister that gone is byfore:
This worlde is casual, nowe vp, nowe downe;
Wherfore do for ycursilfe; I can say no more.

Amen.

Honor tibi, Deus, gloria, et laus!

Smerte, *maister de ses ouzeaus.*

ELEGY ON KING HENRY THE SEVENTH.*

. . . . orlde all wrapped in wretchydnes,
. . . . hy pompes so gay and gloryous,
. . . . easures and all thy ryches
. . . . y be but transytoryous;
. . . . to moche pyteous,
. . . . e that eche man whylom dred,
. . . . by naturall lyne and cours,
. . . . s, alas, lyeth dede!

. . . . ryall a kynge,
. . . . ιaner the prudent Salamon;
. . . . sse and in euery thynge,
. . . . 10 Crysten regyon,
. . . . not longe agone,
. . . . his name by fame spr[e]de;
. . . . te nowe destytute alone,
. . . . as, alas, lyeth dede!

---

* From an imperfect broadside in the Douce Collection, now in the Bodleian Library, Oxford. This unique piece formerly belonged to Dr. Farmer, who has written on it, " Qu. the author of this Elegy? Per *J. Skelton*, tho' not in his works?" to which Douce has added, " The Doctor is probably right in what he says concerning the Elegy on Henry the Seventh, which is a singular curiosity."

At the top of the original is a woodcut, representing the dead king, lying on a bed or bier, crowned and holding his sceptre; on one side the royal arms, on the other the crown resting on a full-blown rose, which has the king's initials in its centre.

Henry died April 21st, 1509: see note, vol. iii. p. 170.

. . . . ater we wretchyd creatures,
. . . . es and tryumphaunt maiestye,
. . . . pastymes and pleasures,
. . . . thcuten remedye;
. . . . o wyll the myserable bodye
. . . . n heuy lede,
. . . . lde but vanyte and all vanytye,
. . . . h alas, alas, lyeth dede!

. . . . is subgectes and make lamentacyon
. . . . o noble a gouernoure;
. . . . ayers make we exclamacyon,
. . . . de to his supernall toure:
. . . . dly rose floure,
. . . . yally all aboute spred,
. . . . lated where is his power?
. . . . alas, alas, lyeth dede!

Of this moost Crysten kynge in vs it lyeth not,
    His tyme passed honour suffycyent to prayse;
But yet though that that thyng envalue we may not,
Our prayers of suertye he shall haue alwayes;
    And though that Atropose hathe ended his dayes,
His name and fame shall euer be dred
As fer as Phebus spredes his golden rayes,
    Though Henry the Seuenth, alas, alas, lyeth dede!

But nowe what remedye? he is vncouerable,
    Touchyd by the handes of God that is moost just;
But yet agayne a cause moost confortable
    We haue, wherin of ryght reioys we must,
    His sone on lyue in beaute, force, and lust,
In honour lykely Traianus to shede;
    Wherfore in hym put we our hope and trust,
Syth Henry his fader, alas, alas, lyeth dede!

And nowe, for conclusyon, aboute his herse
    Let this be grauyd for endeles memorye,

With sorowfull tunes of Thesyphenes verse;
  Here lyeth the puyssaunt and myghty Henry,
  Hector in batayll, Vlyxes in polecy,
Salamon in wysdome, the noble rose rede,
  Creses in rychesse, Julyus in glory,
Henry the Seuenth ingraued here lyeth dede!

VOX POPULI, VOX DEI.*

Mr. Skeltone, poete.

To the Kinges moste Exellent Maiestie.

I PRAY yow, be not wrothe
For tellyng of the trothe;
For this the worlde yt gothe
Bothe to lyffe and lothe,
As God hymselffe he knothe;
And, as all men vndrestandes,
Both lordeshipes and landes
Are nowe in fewe mens handes;
Both substance and bandes
Of all the hole realme
As most men exteame,
Are nowe consumyd cleane

---

* *Vox Populi, Vox Dei*] From *MS.* 2567 in the Cambridge
Public Library, collated with *MS. Harl.* 367, fol. 130. The
latter, though it contains a very considerable number of lines
which are not found in the former, and which I have placed
between brackets, is on the whole the inferior MS., its text
being greatly disfigured by provincialisms.

This poem, which is assigned to Skelton only in the Cam-
bridge MS., was evidently composed by some very clumsy
imitator of his style. The subject, however, renders it far
from uninteresting.

From the fermour and the poore
To the towne and the towre;
Whiche makyth theym to lower,
To see that in theire flower
Ys nother malte nor meale,
Bacor, beffe, nor veale,
Crocke mylke nor kele,
But readye for to steale
For very pure neade.
Your comons saye indeade,
Thei be not able to feade
In theire stable scant a steade,
To brynge vp nor to breade,
Ye, scant able to brynge
To the marckytt eny thynge
Towardes theire housekeping;
And scant have a cowe,
Nor to kepe a poore sowe:
This the worlde is nowe.
And to heare the relacyon
Of the poore mens communycacion,
Vndre what sorte and fashyon
Thei make theire exclamacyon,
You wolde have compassion.
Thus goythe theire protestacion,
Sayeng that suche and suche,
That of late are made riche,
Have to, to, to myche
By grasyng and regratinge,
By poulyng and debatynge,
By roulyng and by dating,
By checke and checkematynge,
[With delays and debatynge,
With cowstomes and tallynges,
Forfayttes and forestallynges];
So that your comons saye,
Thei styll paye, paye
Most willyngly allwaye,
But yet thei see no staye

Of this outrage araye:
Vox populi, vox Dei;
O most noble kynge,
Consydre well this thynge!

2.

And thus the voyce doth multyplye
Amonge your graces commonaltye:
Thei are in suche greate penvry
That thei can nother sell nor bye,
Suche is theire extreame povertye;
Experyence dothe yt verefye,
As trothe itselffe dothe testefye.
This is a marveilous myserye:
And trewe thei saye, it is no lye;
For grasyers and regraters,
Withe to many shepemasters,
That of erable grounde make pastures,
Are thei that be these wasters
That wyll vndoo your lande,
Yf thei contynewe and stande,
As ye shall vnderstand
By this lytle boke:
Yf you yt overloke,
And overloke agayne,
Yt wyll tell you playne
The tenour and the trothe,
Howe nowe the worlde yt gothe
Withe my neighbour and my noste,[1]
In every countre, towne, and coste,
Within the circumvisions
Of your graces domynyons;
And why the poore men wepe
For storyng of suche shepe,
For that so many do kepe

---

[1] *my noste*] i. e. mine host.

Suche nombre and suche store
As never was seene before:
[What wolde ye any more?]
The encrease was never more.
Thus goythe the voyce and rore:
And truthe yt is indeade;
For all men nowe do breade
Which can ketche any lande
Out of the poore mans hande;
For who ys so greate a grasyer
As the landlorde and the laweare?
For at every drawing daye
The bucher more must paye
For his fatting ware,
To be the redyare
Another tyme to crave,
When he more shepe wold have;
And, to elevate the pryce,
Somewhate he must ryce
Withe a sinque or a sice,
So that the bucher cannot spare,
Towardes his charges and his fare,
To sell the very carcas bare ·
Vnder xij⁸ or a marke,
[Wiche is a pytyfull werke,]
Besyde the offall and the flece,[1]
The flece and the fell:
Thus he dothe yt sell.
Alas, alas, alas,
This is a pitious case!
What poore man nowe is able
To have meate on his table?
An oxe at foure pounde,
Yf he be any thynge rounde,
Or cum not in theire grounde,

---

[1] *the flece*] A line, which rhymed with this, has dropt out.

Suche laboure for to waste:
This ys the newe caste,
The newe cast from the olde;
This comon pryce thei holde;
Whiche is a very ruthe,
Yf men myght saye the truthe.
The comons thus dothe saye,
They are not able to paye,
But *miserere mei:*
Vox populi, vox Dei;
O most noble kyng,
Consydre well this thynge!

3.

Howe saye you to this, my lordes?
Are not these playne recordes?
Ye knowe as well as I,
This makes the comons crye,
This makes theym crye and wepe,
Myssevsing so theire shepe,
Theire shepe, and eke theire beves,
As yll or wourse then theaves:
Vnto·a comonwealthe
This ys a very stealthe.
But you that welthe this bete,
You landlordes that be grete,
You wolde not pay so for your meate,
Excepte your grasing ware so sweate,
Or elles I feare me I,
Ye wold fynde remeadye,
And that right shortlye.
But yet this extremytie,
None feles yt but the comynaltie:
Alas, is there no remedye,
To helpe theym of this myserye?
Yf there shuld come a rayne,
To make a dearthe of grayne,
As God may. send yt playne
For our covetous and disdayne,

I wold knowe, among vs all,
What ware he that shuld not fall
And sorowe as he went,
For Godes ponyshment?
Alas, th:s were a plage [1]
For poverties pocession,
Towardes theire suppression,
For the greate mens transgression!
Alas, my lordes, foresee
There may be remeadye!
For the comons saye,
Thei have no more to paye:
Vox populi, vox Dei;
O most noble kyng,
Consydre well this thyng!

4.

And yet not long agoo
Was preachers on or twoo,
That spake yt playne inowe
To you, to you, and to you,
Hygh tyme for to repent
This dyvelishe entent
[Of covi:is the convente]:
From Scotland into Kent
This preaching was bysprent;
And from the easte frount
Vnto Saynct Myghelles Mount,
This sayeng dyd surmount
Abrode to all mens eares,
And to your graces peeres,
That from piller vnto post
The powr man he was tost;
I meane the labouring man,
I meane the husbandman,
I meane the ploughman,

---

[1] *plage*] A line wanting to rhyme with this.

I meane the playne true man,
I meane the handecrafteman,
I meane the victualing man,
Also the good yeman,
That some tyme in this realme
Had plentye of kye and creame,
[Butter, egges, and chesse,
Hony, vax, and besse]:
But now, alacke, alacke,
All theise men goo to wracke,
That are the bodye and the staye
Of yóur graces realme allwaye!
Allwaye and at leinghe
Thei must be your streinghe,
Your streinghe and your teme,
For to defende your realme.
Then yf theise men appall,
And lacke when you do call,
Which way may you or shall
Resist your enemyes all,
That over raging streames
Will vade from forreyn reames?
For me to make judiciall,
This matter is to mystycall;
Judge you, my lordes, for me you shall,
Yours ys the charge that governes all;
For *vox populi* me thei call,
That makith but reherssall
De parvo,[1] but not *de* totall,
De locis, but not locall:
Therfore you must not blame
The wight that wrot the same;
For the comons of this land
Have sowen this in theire sande,
Plowing yt withe theire hande;
I founde it wheare I stande;

---

[1] *parvo*] *MS. C.* "paruie." *MS. Harl.* "parvū." **Qy.**
"parvis?"

And I am but the hayne
That wryttes yt newe agayne,
The coppye for to see,
That also learneth me
To take therby good hede
My shepe howe for to fede;
For I a shepherd am,
A sorye poore man;
Yet wolde I wyshe, my lordes,
This myght be your recordes,
And make of yt no dreame,
For yt ys a worthy realme,
A realme that in tymes past
Hath made the prowdest agast.
Therfore, my lordes all,
Note this in especiall,
And have it in memoryall
[With youre wysse vnyversall,
That nether faver nor effection,
Yowe grawnt youre protection
To suche as hath [1] by election
Shall rewle by erection,
And doth gett the perfection
Of the powre menes refection;
Wiche ys a.grett innormyte
Vnto youre grasys commynalte;
For thay that of latt did supe
Owtt of an aschyn cuppe,
Are wonderfully sprowng vpe;
That nowght was worth of latt,
Hath now a cubborde of platt,
His tabell furnyscheyd tooe,
With platt besett inowe,
Persell gylte and sownde,
Well worth towo thousande pounde.

---

[1] *To suche as hath, &c.*] There appears to be some corruption here.

With castinge cownteres and ther pen,
Thes are the vpstart gentylmen;
Thes are thay that dewowre
All the goodes of the pawre,
And makes them dotysche davys,
Vnder the cowler of the kenges lawys.
And yett annother decaye
To youre grasys seetes alwaye;
For the statte of all youre marchantmen
Vndo most parte of youre gentyllmen,
And wrape them in suche bandes
That thay haue halle ther landes,
And payeth but halfe in hande,
Tyll thay more vnderstownde
Of the profett of there lande,
And for the other halfe
He shalbe mayd a calfe,
Excepte he haue gud frendes
Wiche well cane waye bothe endes;
And yet with frendes tooe
He shall haue mvche to doe;
Wiche ys a grett innormyte
To youre grasys regallyte.
Lett marchantmen goe sayle
For that ys ther trwe waylle;
For of one c. ye haue not ten
That now be marchantes ventring men,
That occupi grett inawnderes,
Forther then into Flanderes,
Flawnderes or into France,
For fere of some myschance,
But lyeth at home, and standes
By morgage and purchasse of landes
Owtt of all gentyllmenes handes,
Wiche showld serve alwaye your grace
With horse and men in chasse;
Wiche ys a grett dewowre
Vnto youre regall pawre.
What presydente cane they shewe,
That fowre skore yeres agooe,

That[1] any marchant here,
Above all charges clere,
In landes myght lett to hyre
To thowsant markes by yere?
Other where shall ye fynde
A gentyllman by kynde,
But that thay wyll ly in the wynde,
To breng hyme fer behynde,
Or elles thay wyll haue all,
Yf nedes thay hyme forstall?
Wiche ys the hole decaye
Of your marchantmen, I saye,
And hynderes youre grasys costome
By the yere a thowsant pawnde,
And so marryth, the more petye,
The comonwelth of yche sytte,
And vndoth the cowntre,
As prosse [?] doth make propertie:
This matter most spesyally
Wolde be loked one quiclye.
Yett for ther recreation,
In pastime and procreation,
In tempore necessitatis,
I wysche thay myght haue grattis
Lysens to compownde,
To purchasse fortie pownde
Or fyfte at the moste,
By fyne or wrytte of post;
And yf any marchantman,
To lyve his occupieng then,
Wolde purchasse any more,
Lett hyme forfett it therfore.
Then showld ye se the trade
That marchantmen frist mayde,
Whyche wysse men dyd marshall,
For a welth vnyversall,

---

[1] *That*] Qy. *dele?*

Yche man this lawe to lerne,
And trewly his goodes to yerne,
The landlord with his terme,
The plowghtman with his ferme,
The kneght wyth his fare,
The marchant with his ware,
Then showld increse the helth
Of yche comonwelthe],
And be not withe mé wrothe
For tellyng you the trothe;
For I do heare yt everye daye,
How the comons thus do saye,
Yf thei hadde yt, thei wold paye:
Vox populi, vox Dei;
O most noble kyng,
Consydre well this thyng!

5.

But, howe, Robyn, howe!
Whiche waye dothe the wynde blowe?
Herke! hercke! hercke!
Ys not here a pytious werke,
The grounde and the cheiffe
Of all this hole myscheiffe?
For our covetous lordes
Dothe mynde no nother [1] recordes,
But framyng fynes for fermes,
Withe to myche, as some termes,
Withe rentes and remaynders,
Withe surveye and surrenders,
Withe comons and comon ingenders,
Withe inclosyers and extenders,
Withe horde vp, but no spenders;
For a comonwealthe
Whiche is a verye stealthe.

---

[1] *no nother*] i. e. none other. *MS. Harl.* " *noe* other."

Prove it who shall
To make therof tryall,
Thus goithe theire dyall:
I knowe not whates a clocke,
But by the countre cocke,
The mone [1] nor yet the pryme,
Vntyll the sonne do shyne;
Or els I coulde tell
Howe all thynges shulde be well.
The compas may stand awrye,
But the carde wyll not lye:
Hale in your mayne shete,
This tempest is to grete.
[For pawre men dayly sees
How officers takes their fees,
Summe yll, and some yet worse,
As good right as to pike there purse:
Deservethe this not Godes curse?
There consyenes ys sooe grett,
Thaye fere not to dischare,[2]
Yf it were as moche more,
Soe thay maye haue the stowre.
Thus is oure we[l]the vndone
By synguler commodome;
For we are in dyvision,
Bothe for reght and religion;
And, as some saythe,
We stagger in our faythe:
But excepte in shortt tyme
We drawe by one lyne,
And agre with one accorde,
Bothe the plowghman and the lorde,
We shall sore rewe
That ever this statte we knewe.]

---

1 *mone*] So both *MSS.* But qy. " none? "
2 *dischare*] There is some error here; and perhaps a line or more has dropt out.

The comons so do saye,
Yf thei had yt, thei wold paye:
Vox populi, vox Dei ;
O most noble kyng,
Consydre well this thynge!

6.

Thus runnes this rumour about
Amongest the hole route;
Thei can not bryng aboute
How this thyng shuld be,
Yt hathe suche high degree:
The coyne yt is so scante,
That every man dothe wante,
And some thincke not so scace,
But even as myche to base.
Our merchauntmen do saye,
Thei fynde it day by daye
To be a matter straunge,
When thei shulde make exchaunge
On the other side the sea,
Thei are dryven to theire plea;
For where oure pounde somtyme
Was better then theires by nyne,
Nowe ours, when yt comes forthe,
No better then theires is worthe,
No, nor scant soo good;
Thei saye so, by the roode.
Howe maye the merchauntman
Be able to occupye than,
Excepte, when he comes heare,
He sell his ware to deare?
He neades must have a lyveng,
Or elles, fye on hys wynneng!
This coyne by alteracion
Hathe brought this desolacyon,
Whiche is not yet all knowen
What myscheiffe it hathe sowen.

Thei saye, Woo worthe that man
That first that coyne began,
To put in any hedde
The mynde to suche a rede,
To come to suche a hiere
For covetous desyre!
I knowe not what it meanethe;
But this thei saye and deamythe,
Væ illi per quem scandalum venit!
For this wyll axe greate payne
Before it be well agayne,
Greate payne and sore
To make it as it was before.
The comons thus do saye,
Yf thei hadde yt, thei would paye:
Vox populi, vox Dei;
O most noble kynge,
Consydre well this thinge!

7.

This matter is to trewe,
That many man dothe rewe
Theise sorowes doo ensue;
For poore men thei doo crye,
And saye it is awrye;
Thei saye thei can not be herde,
But styll from daye defferde,
When thei have any sute,
Thei maye goo blowe theire flute:
This goithe the comon brute.
The riche man wyll come in;
For he is sure to wynne,
For he can make his waye,
With hande in hande to paye,
Bothe to thicke and thynne; [1]

---

[1] *thynne*] A line, or perhaps more, has dropt out here.

Or els to knowe theire pleasure,
My lorde is not at leysure; [1]
The poore man at the durre
Standes lyke an Island curre,
And dares not ons to sturre,'
Excepte he goo his waye,
And come another daye;
And then the matter is made,
That the poore man with his spade
Must no more his farme invade,
But must vse some other trade;
For yt is so agreed
That my ladye mesteres Mede [2]
Shall hym expulce with all spede,
And our master the landlorde
Shall have yt all at his accorde,
His house and farme agayne,
To make therof his vttermost gayne;
For his vantage wylbe more,
With shepe and cattell it to store,
And not to ploughe his grounde no more,
Excepte the fermour wyll aryere
The rent hyere by a hole yeare:
Yet must he have a fyne too,
The bargayne he may better knowe;
Which makes the marcket now so deare
That there be fewe that makes good cheare;
For the fermour must sell his goose,
As he may be able to paye for his house,
Or els, for non payeng the rent,
Avoyde at our Lady daye in Lent:
Thus the poore man shalbe shent;

---

[1] *My lorde is not at leysure*] A line borrowed from Skelton's
Why come ye nat to Courte, v. 622. vol. ii. 297.

[2] *mesteres Mede*] The writer, perhaps, recollected that Skelton had mentioned " mayden Meed " in . *Ware the Hauke*, v. 149. vol. i. 178.

And then he and his wyffe,
With theire children, all theire lyffe,
Doth crye oute and ban
Vpon this covetous man.
I sweare by God omnypotent,
I feare me that this presedent
Wyll make vs all for to be shent.
Trowe you, my lordes that be,
That God dothe not see
This riche mans charitie
Per speculum œnigmatœ ?
Yes, yes, you riche lordes,
Yt is wrytten in Cristes recordes,
That Dives laye in the fyere
With Belsabub his sire,
And Pauper he above satte
In the seate of Habrahams lappe,
And was taken from thys Troye,
To lyve allwaye with God in ioye
The comons thus do saye,
Yf thei had yt, thei wold paye:
Vox populi, vox Dei ;
O most noble kyng,
Consydre well this thynge!

8.

The prayse no les is worthe,
Godes worde is well sett forthe:
Yt never was more preached,
Nor never so playnlye teached;
Yt never was so hallowed,
Nor never so lytle followed
Bothe of highe and lowe,
As many a man dothe trowe;
For this ys a playne perscripcion,
We have banyshed superstycion,
But styll we kepe ambycion;
We have sent awaye all cloysterers,
But styll we kepe extorcyoners;

We have taken theire landes for theire abuse,
But we convert theym to a wourse vse.
Yf this tale be no lye,
My lordes, this goythe awrye;
Awrye, awrye ye goo,
With many thinges moo, .
Quyte from the highe waye.
The comons thus do saye,
Yff thei hadd yt, thei wold paye:
Vox populi, vox Dei;
O most noble kyng,
Consydre well this thinge!

9.

Off all this sequell
The faute I can not tell:
Put you together and spell,
My lordes of the councell.
I feare all be not well,
Ambycion so dothe swell,
As gothe by reporte,
Amonge the greatest sorte;
A wonderfull sorte of selles,
That *vox populi* telles,
Of those bottomlesse welles,
That are este, weast, and so furthe,
Bothe by southe, and also northe,
Withe riche, riche, and riche,
Withe riche, and to myche,
The poore men to begyle,
Withe sacke and packe to fyle,
[With suche as we compownd
For an offys ij thowsant pownde:
Howe maye suche men do reght,
Youre pawre men to requytt
Owtt of there trowbell and payne,
But thay most gett it agayne
By craft or such coarsyon,
By bryberey and playne exstorsyon?]

With many ferrelys moo,
That I could truly shewe:
There never was suche myserye,
Nor never so myche vserye.
The comons so do saye,
Yf we had ytt, we wold paye:
Vox populi, vox Dei;
O most noble kynge,
Consydre well this thynge!

10.

And thus this ile of Brutes,
Most plentyfull of frutes,
Ys sodenlye decayede;
Poore men allmost dysmayde,
Thei are so overlayed:
I feare and am afrayde
Of the stroke of God,
Whiche ys a perelous rodde.
Praye, praye, praye,
We never se that daye;
For yf that daye do come,
We shall dyssever and ronne,
The father agaynst the sonne,
And one agaynst another.
By Godes blessed mother,
Or thei begynne to hugger,
For Godes sake looke aboute,
And staye betymes this route,
For feare thei doo come oute.
I put you out of doubte,
There ys no greate trust,
Yf trothe shuld be discuste:
Therfore, my lordes, take heade
That this gere do not brede
At chesse to playe a mate,
For then yt is to late:
We may well prove a checke,
But thei wyll have the neke;

Yt is not to be wondered,
For thei are not to be nombred.
This the poore men saye,
Yf thei hadde yt, thei wolde paye:
Vox populi, vox Dei;
O most noble kyng,
Consydre well this thinge!

11.

Yt is not one alone
That this dothe gronte and grone,
And make this pytyous mone;
For yt is more then wonder,
To heare the infynyte nombre
Of poore men that dothe shewe
By reason yt must be soo.
Thei wishe and do coniector
That my lordes grace and protector,
That cheiffe is nowe erector
And formost of the rynge,
Vnder our noble kynge,
That he wold se redresse
Of this moste greate excesse,
For yt stondes on hym no lesse;
For he is calde doubteles
A man of greate prowesse,
And so dothe beare the fame,
And dothe desyre the same;
His mynde thei saye is good,
Yf all wold followe his moode.
Nowe for to sett the frame,
To kepe styll this good name,
He must delaye all excuses,
And ponnyshe these greate abuses
Of these fynes and newe vses,
That have so many muses;
And first and pryncipallye
Suppresse this shamfull vsurye,

Comonlye called husbondrye;
For y^t there be no remeadye
In tyme and that right shortlye,
Yt wyll breade to a pluresye,
Whiche is a greate innormytie
To all the kynges comynaltye;
For there is no smale nombre
That this faute dothe incombre:
Yt is a wordly wondre.
The comons thus do saye,
Yf thei had yt, thei wolde paye:
Vox populi, vox Dei;
O most noble kyng,
Consydre well this thynge!

12.

Nowe, at your graces leysour,
Yf you wyll see the seisor
Of all the cheffe treasure,
Heapyd without measure,
Of the substance of your realme,
As yt were in a dreame,
I wyll make an esteame,
In the handes of a fewe,
The trothe you to showe,
Howe this matter dothe goo;
For I wyll not spare
The trothe to declare;
For trothe trulye ment
Was never yet shent,
Nor never shent shalbe;
Note this text of me,
Yt may a tyme be framed
For feare some shuld be blamed,
But yt wyll not be shamed;
Yt is of suche a streinghe,
Yt wyll overcome at leinghe.
Yff nowe I shall not fayne,
The trothe to tell you playne

Of all those that do holde
The substance and the golde
And the treasure of this realme; [1]
And shortlye to call,
Allmost thei have all;
Att least thei have the trade
Of all that may be made:
And fyrst to declare
By a bryeffe what thei are,
To make shorte rehersall,
As well spyrytuall as temporall;
The laweare and the landelorde,
The greate reave and the recorde,—
The recorde I meane is he
That hathe office or els ffee,
To serve our noble kyng
In his accomptes or recknyng
Of his treasure surmonttynge,—
Lorde chauncellour and chauncellours,
Masters of myntes and monyers,
Secondaryes and surveyours,
Auditors and receivours,
Customers and comptrollers,
Purvyours and prollers,
Marchauntes of greate sailes,
With the master [2] of woodsales,
With grasyers and regraters,
With Master Williams of shepe masters,
And suche lyke comonwelthe wasters,
That of erable groundes make pasters,
[And payemasters suche as bythe
With Trappes your golden smythe,]

---

[1] *realme*] A line wanting, to rhyme with this.

[2] *master*] *MS. Harl.* " maisteres: " but perhaps some particular individual is alluded to; compare the second line after.

With iij or iiij greate clothiars,
And the hole lybell of lawyars:
Withe theise and theire trayne,
To be bryeffe and playne,
Of theire to, to myche gayne
That thei take for theire payne,
Yt is knowen by ceirten sterres
That thei may mayntayne your graces warres
By space of a hole yeare,
Be yt good chepe or deare,
Thou3he we shulde withstande
Both Fraunce and Scotlande,
And yet to leave ynough
Of money, ware, and stuffe,
Both in cattell and corne,
To more then thei were borne,
By patrymonye or bloode
To enherytte so myche goode.
By cause thei be so base,
Thei wylbe neadye and scace;
For *quod natura dedit*
From gentle blode them ledyth;
And to force a chorlishe best
Nemo attollere potest :
Yet rather then thei wold goo before,
Thei wolde helpe your grace with somwhat
                more,
For thei be they that have the store;
Those be they wyll warraunt ye,
Though you toke never a penye
Of your poore comynaltie.
This is trewe vndoubtelye,
I dare affyrme it certeynlye;
For yf this world do holde,
Of force you must be bolde
To borowe theire fyne golde;
For thei have all the store;
For your comons have no more;

Ye may it call to lyght,
For yt is your awne right,
Yf that your grace have neade:
Beleve this as your Creade.
The poore men so do saye,
Yf thei had yt, thei wold paye
With a better wyll then thei:
Vox populi, vox Dei ;
O most noble kyng,
Consyder well this thynge!

13.

O worthiest protectour,
Be herin corrector!
And you, my lordes all,
Let not your honor appall,
But knocke betymes and call
For theise greate vsurers all;
Ye knowe the pryncypall:
What neadith more rehersall?
Yf you do not redresse
By tyme this coveteousnes,
My hed I hold and gage,
There wylbe greate outrage;
Suche rage as never was seene
In any olde mans tyme.
Also for this perplexyte,
Of these that are most welthye,
Yt ware a deade of charyte
To helpe theym of this pluresie:
Yt comes by suche greate fyttes
That it takes awaye theire wyttes,
Bothe in theire treasure tellynge,
Or els in byeng and sellynge.
Yf thei of this weare eased,
Your grace shuld be well pleased,
And thei but lytle deseased
Of this covetous dropsye,
That brynges theym to thys pluresie,

Bothe the pluresye and goute,
Vncurable to be holpe [out],
Excepte your grace for pytie
Provyde this foresaid remeadye;
As doctors holde opynyon,
Both Ambros and Tertulian,
Withe the Swepestake and the Mynyon,
The Herte and the Swallowe,
And all the rest that followe,
Withe the Gallye and the Roo
That so swyffte do goo,
Goo, and that apase,
By the Henry Grace,
The Herrye and the Edwarde,—
God sende theym all well forwarde,
Withe all the hole fleete!
Whose councell complete
Saithe it is full mete
That greate heddes and dyscreate
Shulde loke well to theire feate.
Amen, I saye, so be ytt!
As all your comons praye
For your long healthe allwaye.
Yf thei hadde yt, thei wold paye
[With a better wyll then thay]:
Vox populi, vox Dei,
Thus dothe wrytte, and thus doth saye,
With this psalme, *Miserere mei;*
O most noble kyng,
Consyder well this thynge!

ffinis quothe Mr. Skelton, Poete Lawriate.[1]

---

[1] *ffinis quothe Mr. Skelton, Poete Lawriate*] Instead of these words. *MS. Harl.* has,

" God saue the kenge
Finis quod vox populi vox dei."

THE IMAGE OF IPOCRYSY.*

Vpon . . . .
Of the cruell clergy[?],
And the proude prelacy[?],
That now doo looke so hie,
As though that by and by
They wold clymbe and fflye
Vp to the clowdy skye:
Wher all men may espye,
By fals hipocrysye
Thei long haue blered the eye
Of all the world well nye;
Comytting apostacie
Against that verytye
Whch thei can not denye:

In which how shamlessly
They do . . . . . and aye
Ther concyens testyfye
The poppe[!] . . . . . .
Curte[?] . . . .
The rest of B . . . . .
    markes,
That be heresyarkes,
Which do com[yt?] ther
    warkes,
As one that in the darke ys,
And wotes not wher the
    marke ys,
Do take the kites for larkes.

---

* *The Image of Ipocrysy*] Is now printed from *MS. Lans-down* 794. The original has very considerable alterations and additions by a different hand: the first page is here and there illegible, partly from the paleness of the ink, and partly from the notes which Peter Le Neve (the possessor of the MS. in 1724) has unmercifully scribbled over it. I give the title here as it stands at the end of the First Part.

Hearne and others have attributed this remarkable pro-duction to Skelton. The poem, however, contains decisive evidence that he was not its author: to say nothing of other passages,—the mention of certain writings of Sir Thomas More and of "the mayde of Kent" (Elizabeth Barton), which occurs in the Third Part, would alone be sufficient to prove that it was the composition of some writer posterior to his time.

Suche be owr primates,
Our bisshopps and prelates,
Our parsons and curates,[1]
With other like estates
That were shaven pates;
As monkes white and blacke,
And channons that cane
    chatte,
Glottons ffayre and fatt,
. With ffriers of the sacke,
And brothers of the bagg,
As nymble as a nagg,
That cane bothe prate and
    bragg,
To make the pulpett wagge
With twenty thousand lyes,
Do make the blind eate flyes,
And blere our symple eyes,
To make vs to beleve
God morowe is god eve;
For pleynly to be breve, .
So nye they do vs dreve,
That we, to our great greve,
Must sey that white is blacke,
Or elles they sey we smacke,
And smell we wote not what:
But then beware the catt;
For yf they smell a ratt,
They grisely chide and chatt,
And, Haue him by the jack,
A fagott for his backe,
Or, Take him to the racke,
And drowne hyme in a sacke,
Or burne hyme on a stake!

Lo, thus they vndertake
The trothe false to make!
Alas, for Christ his sake!
Is the sonnelight darke,
Or ignoraunc[e] a clarke,
Bycawse that thei hath powre
To sende men to the Towre,
The simple to devowre?
If they lyst to lowre,
Ys suger therfor sowre?
Dothe five and three make
    ffour?
As well I durst be bolde
To sey the ffier were colde.
But yet they worke muche
    worse,
When they for blissinge
    cowrse;
For Father Friska jolly,
And *Pater* Pecke a lolly,
That be all full of folly,
Doo fayne them seem holy,
For ther monopoly,
And ther private welthe,
That they haue take by
    stelthe;
And in the churche they
    lurke,
As ill as any Turke,
So proudely they vsurpe,
Besyde the spritt of Christ,
The office of a pryste
In any wise to take,
As thoughe it were a iape,

---

[1] *Our parsons cnd curates*] This line (now pasted over in the MS.) has been obtained from a transcript of the poem made by Thomas Martin of Palgrave.

To runne in att the rove;
For some of them do prove
To clyme vpp ere they knowe
The doore from the wyndowe;
They may not stoope alowe,
But backe bend as a bowe;
They make an owtwarde
    showe,
And so forthe one a rowe,
As dapper as a crowe,
And perte as any pye,
And lighte as any ffly.
At borde and at table
They be full servysable,
Sober and demure,
Acquayntans to allure,
Wher they may be sure [1]
By any craft or trayne
To fyshe for any gayne,[2]
Or wayt for any wynnyng,—
A prestly begynnynge!
For many a hyerlinge,
With a wilde fyerlinge,
Whan his credyte is most,
With mikell brag and bost
Shall pryck owt as a post,
Chafyng lyke myne hoste,
As hott as any toste,
And ride from cost to cost,
And then shall rule the rost.

And some avaunced be
For ther auncente,
Thoughe ther antiquitye
Be all innequitye;
Yett be they called
To the charge of the fald,
Because they be balled,
And be for bisshopps stalled.
And some kepe ther stations
In owtwarde straunge na-
    tyons,
Lernynge invocatyons,
And craftye incantatyons;
And so by inchantement
Gette theyr avauncement.
And some by fayned favour
For honour or for havour,
By voyses boughte and solde,
For sylver and for golde,
For lande, for rente or free,
Or by authoritye
Of menn of hye degree,
Or for some qualitye,
As many of them bee,
For ther actyvitee,
Ther practyse and industrye,
Sleyght, craft, and knavery,
In matters of bawdery,
Or by helpe of kynne,
An easy liffe to wynne.

---

1 *Wher they may be sure*] Followed by a deleted line, now partly illegible,—

    " . . . . wayte to haue wynnynge."

2 *To fyshe for any gayne*] Followed by a deleted line which seems to have been,—

    " With shotinge or with singinge."

I swere by Saincte Mary,
He that thus dothe cary
Is a mercenary,
Yea, a sangunary,
A pastore for to pull
Of bothe skynne and wolle.
Thoughe Christ be the doer,
They force not of his looer,
They sett therby no stoore;
Ther stody is for moore:
And I tell youe therfore
That they ther tyme temper
With a provisoo *semper*
An other wey to enter,
For love of wordsly good,
Not forcinge of the fllode
Of hyme that bledd the roode;
It is not for ther moode.
They make deambulacyons
With great ostentations,
And loke for salutations
On every mannes face,
As in the merkett place
To saye, God saue your
   grace!
Thus in churche and che-
   pinge,
Wher they may haue me-
   tinge
With lordes and with ladyes,
To be called Rabyes:
Nowe God saue these dadyes,
And all ther yonge babyes!
The holy worde of God

Is by these men forbod;
Pater noster and Creede
They vtterly forbeede
To be said or songe
In our vulgar tonge.
Ohe Lorde, thou hast great
   wronge
Of these that shoulde be
   trustye,
Whiche sey the breade is
   musty,
And with ther lawe vnlusty
Make it rusty and dusty!
But I do thinke it rustye.
For lacke of exercyse:
Wherfore they be vnwise
That will the lawe despise,
And daylye newe devyse,
So dyvers and so straunge,
Which [1] chaunge and re-
   chaunge
Of fastinges and of feestes,
Of bowes [2] and behestes,
With many of ther [3] iestes,
As thoughe lay men wer
   bestes;
As many of vs bee,
That may and will not see,
Nor ones cast vpp an eye,
These jugglinges to espye;
For this that nowe is vsed
Is efte ageyne refused,
Chaunged or mysvsed,
That we be still abused:

---

[1] *Which*] Qy. " With ? "
[2] *bowes*] Qy. " vowes ? "
[3] *of ther*] Qy. " other ? "

The lawe that servethe nowe,
Ageyne they disalowe.
Thus forthe and backe,[1]
With bryve and with bull
They dayly plucke and pull,
And yett be never ffull;
For wher one bull makes,
An other bull forsakes;
The thyrde yett vndertakes
To alter all of newe:
Thus none will other sue.
Wherfore, by swete Jesu,
I thinke they be vntrewe
That iuggle tyme and tyme
To gett thyne and myne;
Yea, thoughe the worlde
        pynne,
No man wyll they spare,
So they ther pelfe prefarre,
The lawes to make and marre,
To bynde vs nere and farre;
Wherto may be no barre
In peace tyme nor in warre;
For none ther is that darre
Replye ageyne or speake,
This daunce of thers to
        breake;
The trouthe it is so weeke:
They make all men cry
        creake,
Or fry them to a steake,—
Adieu, Sir Huddypeake!
Lo, Peters barge is leake,
And redy for to synke!
Beware yett least youe
        drinke;

God dothe not slepe nor
        wynke,
But sethe lande and brynke;
And yf ye take the chynke,
I feare me ye will stynke,
And corrupt your vnctyon
With an iniunctyon;
Your pride and presumption,
In abvsing your functyon,
Will breade a consumtion,
And make a resumption,
To bringe youe to compunc-
        tion;
Youre lawes falsely grounded,
That hath the world sur-
        ounded,
By trouthe shalbe confounded.
Thoughe ye be lordes digne,
Ye shoulde no man maligne,
But ever be benyngne;
And namely in suche case
Wher God his gyfte or grace
Lyst to plante or place:
The poore man, or the riche,
Is to his pleasure lyche;
For Christ, our derest Lorde,
That made the full accorde,
As Scripture dothe recorde,
Betwyxt God and man,
Suppressynge Sattan
And all his kingdom, whan
Vpon the holy roodd
He shadd his blissed bloode,
As muche for one as other,
Exceptinge not his mother,
Made every man his brother,

---

1 *backe*] Something wanting here.

As many as ther bee
In faythe and charitee.
But nowe by fals abvsyon,
The clergy by collation,
Without good conclution,
Haue broughte vs to confu-
tion,
And made an illution:
By great inyquytie,
Avaunt themselfes to be
No lesse then godes, yee,
Of equall authorytye;
Whiche, by ipocrysye,
To exalt ther dignytye,
Call vs the leudd lay ffee,
Men of temporalitee;
But they pretend to bee
A people eternall,
Of powr supernall:
I fere me, infernall;
For they that be carnall,
Idolaters to Baall,
And nothinge gostely at all,
Be named spirituall;
Fo so we must them calle,
As we aye do and shall,
What happe soever falle.
Ther successyon may not dye,
But lyve eternallye;
For, without question,
Perpetuall succession
They haue from one to other,
As childer of ther mother;

Yea, they kepe all in store
That other hadd afore,
And daylye gather more.
Lo, thus the people rore,
As on a fistred sore
Of matter most vnpure,
That thei ar dryven to indure
Tyll God himself send cure!
That as you be possessors,
So be yee successors
Vnto your predecessors:
And yet ye be questors,
And hoorders vppe of testers;
Ye daylye cache and gather
Of mother and of father,
And of no man rather
Then of your poore brother,
And of euery other;
Yea, all that comes is gayne,
You passe of no mans payne,
Whiche ye allwey reteyne,
Who ever grudge or playne,
It may not out agayne;
Noughte may be remitted
That to youe is commytted;
Ye be not so lighte witted.
The people thinke it true
That ye possession sue
To haue an easy life,
Without debate or strife,
To lyve without a wife,
Lordely [1] and at ease,
Without payne or disease,

---

[1] *Lordely, &c.*] On the outer margin of the MS., opposite
this verse, are the following lines, partly cut off by the binder;
     " Thes be the knavysh
      knackes that ever w . . .
             o . . .
    ffor Javelles and for J[ackes]."

Your belly god to please,
And worldly welth to haue:
Ye do your heeades shave,
To make youe sure and save
In every wind and wave,
That wolde as sone rave
As ones to chippe [1] an heare
So farre aboue your eare,
Or suche an habite weare,
With a polled heade,
To fayne yourselves deade;
But for possessions sake
That ye suche rules take,
And bynde youe to the brake,
That ye maye not forsake
Durynge all your lyves:
So well is he that thrives.
Thus be youe spirituall;
And yett ye do vs call
But lewde and temporall;
And that is for that we
So weake and simple be,
To put oure possession
From oure succession
And heires lyniall
Or kynne collaterall,
That be menn temporall,
And so from lyne to lyne;
For ech man for his tyme
Sayes, While it is myne,
I will give while I maye,
That, when I am away,
They shall both singe and
    saye,
And for my soules helthe
    pray,

Tyll it be domes day:
So, after this array,
Alake and well away!
We oure landes straye,
And other goodes decay;
Wherat ye laughe and play:
And natheles allwey
We dayly pay and pay,
To haue youe to go gaye
With wonderfull araye,
As dysardes in a play.
God wolde it were inprented,
Written and indentyd,
What youe haue invented!'
So great diversyte
Nowe in your garmentes be,
That wonder is to se;
Your triple cappe and crowne,
Curtle, cope, and gowne,
More worthe then halfe a
    towne,
With golde and perle sett,
And stones well iffrett;
Ther can be no bett;
And for no price ye lett,
How far of they be fett.
Oh ye kynde of vipers,
Ye beestly bellyters,
With Raynes and Cipres,
That haue so many miters!
And yett ye be but mychers.
Youe weere littell hattes,
Myters, and square capps,
Decked with flye flappes,
With many pretty knackes,
Like Turkes of Tartary,

---

[1] *chippe*] Qy. " clippe ? "

Moores, or men of Moscovye,
Or lyke bugges of Arraby,
With ouches and bosses,
With staves and crosses,
With pillers and posses,
With standers and banners,
Without good life or manners:
Then haue youe gay gloves,
That with your hand moves,
Wroughte with true loves,
And made well, for the nones,
With golde and precious
    stones:
Ye blisse vs with your bones,
And with your riche ringes,
That quenes and kinges,
At your offringes,
Shall kisse with knelinges;
Which your mynykyns
And mynyon babbes,
Your   closse chambred
    drabbes,
When masse and all is done,[1]
Shall were at afternone:
Your curtells be of sylke,
With rochetes white as
    mylke;
Your bootes of righte sattyne,
Or velvett crymosyne;

Your shoes wroughte with
    gold,
To tredd vpon the molde;
Wandring, as Vandals,
In sylke and in sandals,
Ye kepe your holy rules,
As asses and mules;
For on your cloven cules
Will ye never sytt
But on a rich carpett;
And nowe and then a fitt,
After the rule of Bennett,
With, dythmunia vennett,
A gaye a vott gennett,
With Gill or with Jennyt,
Wyth Cycely or Sare;
Yf thei come wher they are,
Thei lay one and not spare,
And never look behind them,
Wher soever they ffynd them;
For whan that thei be hett,
And Asmodeus grett,
They take, as thei can gett,
All fyshe that comes to nett,
For lust fyndes no lett [2]
Tyll hys poyson be spett;
Be she fyne or feat,
Be she white or jett,
Long or short sett,

---

[1] *When masse and all is done*] Followed by a deleted line;
      "The paynes to release."

[2] *For lust fyndes no lett*] Occupies the place of the following
three deleted lines;
      "be she ffayre or fowle
      for vnderneth an amys
      alyke ther hart is."

Do she smyle or skowle,
Be she ffayr or fowle,
Or owgly as an owle;
For vnderneth a cowle,
A surplyse or an amys,
Can no man do amys;
Ye halse them from harmes
With blessinges and charmes,
While the water warmes,
In your holy armes,
Broging in ther barmes,
Devoutly to clipe it,
To caste her with a tryppytt,
With, lusty Sir John, whip it
Vnderneth your tippitt,
Prætextu pietatis,
Quam contaminatis
Sub jugo castitatis,
Your burning heate to cease,
And expell your disease,
Vnder pretens of pease,
The paynes to release
Of poore sely sowles,
That hide be in holes
As hote as any coles.
Ye cappes haue and capes,
With many other iapes,
To cover with your pates;
As hoodes and cowles,
Like horned owles,
With skapplers and cootes,
Courtbies and copes,
White knottyd ropes,
With other instrumentes,
Straunge habilimentes,
And wanton vestementes,
And other implementes,
As tyrantes haue in tentes:
But what therby ment is,

Or what they signifye,
I cane not tell, not I,
Nor you vndowtedlye
Can shew no reason whie.
Ye make it herisy
And treason to the kinge,
Yf we speke any thinge
That is not to your lykynge;
The truth may not be spoken,
But ye will be wroken:
Yett marke and note this
    token;
Yf Gods worde ones open,
Which wyll er long perdye,
Then shall we here and se
In Cristianitye,
Whether youe or we
The very traytours be.
But, by the Trynite,
It wonder is to me
To se your charite
And hospitalite
So littell to the poore;
And yet vpon a hoore
Ye passe for non expence,
As thoughte it non offence
Were in the sighte of God;
Youe fray not of his rod;
Youe loue your bely cod;
For them that haue no nede
Ye dayly feest and fede:
I thinke it be to dreede
Lest here you haue your
    mede.
Ye drawe and cast lottes,
In hattes and in pottes,
For tottes and for quottes,
And blere vs with your
    blottes,

And with your mery poppes:
Thus you make vs sottes,
And play with vs boopepe,
With other gambaldes like,
To pill oure Lordes sheepe,
Your honour for to kepe,
Vsinge great excesse,
Which I pray God represse,
And soone to sende redresse!
For no man can expresse
The wo and wretchednesse
Youe on oure neckes do lye,
By your grett tyrannye,
Your pride and surquedrye,
That ye do openlye:
But that youe secretly
Practyse pryvylye,
May not be tolde,—and why?
Lest it be herysye,
And than by and by
To make a faggott ffrye.
For we can not deny,
And treuth doth playne dys-
    crye,
And all wysemen espye
That all the falt doth lye
Vpon oure owne foly,
That ye be so iolye,
For with oure owne goodes

We fether vppe oure [1] hoodes.
Youe sanguinolently,
Your mony is so plenty,
That youe make no deynty
Of twenty pound and twenty,
So youe may haue entry;
And then youe laughe and
    skorne
To se vs were the horne,
Ridinge here and hether,
Goinge ther and thether,
Lyke cokold foles together,
In colde, wynde, and in
    wether,
For woll, for ledd, and lether;
And yet do not consydre
We wer an oxes fether:
This is a prety bob,
Oure hedes for to gnob [2]
With suche a gentill job:
And we oure selves rob
Of landes temporall,
And jvelles great and smalle,
To give youe parte of all
In almes perpetuall,
To make our heyres thrall
For your hye promotyon,
Through our blynde devo-
    tion

---

1 *oure*] Qy. " youre?" but compare 6th line of next column.
In the following line, "*sanguinolently*" should perhaps be
printed as Latin,—"*sanguinolenti.*"

2 *Oure hedes for to gnob*] Followed by two deleted lines;
" And make vs soch a lob
To vse one lyke a lob."

And small [1] intellygens,
But that our censcyens,
Laden with offens,
And you vs so incense,
When we be going hens,
To make soch recompens,
By gyvyng [2] yowe our pens,
Our land, goodes, and rentes,
For that holy pretens,
Havyng ffull confydens
That be a safe defens:
So do we styll dyspens

With all remorse and sens
Of harty penytens.
This cane not be denyed:
Your jugglynge is espied,
Your mayster is vntyed,
Which is the prince of pride;
For you on neyther syde
Can suffre or abyde
To here the troth tryed,
Which ye intend to hide
With vehement desyre,
As hote as any ffire.

Thus endeth the ffirst parte of this present treatyse, called
the Image of Ipocrysy.

Alake, for Christes might,
These thinges go not arighte!
Oure lanterns give no lighte,
All bisshopps be not brighte:
They be so full of spyte,
They care not whom they
byte,

Both frend and foo they
smyte
Wyth prison, deth, and
flighte;
So dayly they do fyght
To overturne the ryght:
So we be in the plyte,

And small, &c.

. . . . . .

To make soch recompens]

This passage is substituted for two deleted lines;

" To your possessyon
Without discretion."

By gyvyng, &c.

. . . . . .

Of harty penytens]

This passage is substituted for three deleted lines;

" S . . . fonde affection
To cure correccion
Without protection."

That, losing of oure sight,
We know not black from
    whyght,
And be thus blinded quyte,
We know not day from nyght.
But, by my syres soule,
The true Apostell Paule
Wrott, as we may see
In Tyte and Tymothe,
Who should a bisshoppe be:
A man of holy liffe,
The husbonde of one wiffe;
That vseth not to strife,
Or strike with sworde or
    knyff,
Nor that at any tyme
Suspected is of cryme,
But wise and provident,
Colde and contynent,
But never vynolent;
That when he eat cr drinke,
Slepe, awake, or winke,
Doth styll on measure thinke,
And therof vse a messe,
To put away excesse,
Kepe hyme lowe and chast;
That he make no wast
By prodigalite
Or sensualytye,
A waster for to be,
But, after his degree,
With liberallite
Kepe hospitallite;
He must be sadd and sage,
Vsinge non outrage,
But soberly with reason
To spende in tyme 'and season,
And so to kepe his meason;
He may in no wise streke,

But suffer and be meke,
Shamefast and discrete,
Temperat, dulce, and swete,
Not speakinge angerly,
But soft and manerly;
And, in any wise,
Beware of covetyse,
The rote of all ill vice;
He must be liberall,
And thanke oure Lorde of all;
And, as a heerde his sheepe,
His childer must he kepe,
And all his family
In vertu edyfy,
Vnder disciplyne
Of holsome doctryne,
With dew subiection,
That non obiection
Be made vnto his heste
Of most or of leste;
For thus he doth conclude,
As by simylitude,
Howe he that cane not skill
His housholde at his will
To governe, rule, and teche,
Within his power and reach,
Oughte to haue no speache
Of cure and diligence,
Of suche premynence,
Within the churche of God;
And eke it is forbode
That he no novice be,
Lest with superbite
He do presume to hye,
And consequently
Fall vnhappely
Into the frenesy
Of pride and of evyll,
Lyke Lucyfer, the devyll;

For he playnly writes,
That of these neophites,
And pevishe proselites,
Springe vpp ipocrites;
A bisshoppe eke must haue,
His honesty to save,
Of all men such a name,
That his outwarde fame
Be clene from any blame,
Impeched with no shame,
To draw all people in,
They may repent of synne,
And so he may them wynne,
That thei fall not vnware
Into the devils snare.
Thus Paule, as ye may se,
Taughte Tyte and Tymothe,
Who should a bisshoppe be:
And Christ oure maister dere,
While he lyved here,
Full poorly did appere,
Mekely borne and bredd;
The bare earth was his bedd,
For where to hele his headd,
Or where to lye and rest,
He had no hole nor nest;
But in great poverty
He lyved soberly,
His worde to multyply;
And thus did edifye

His churche that is so holy,
Suppressinge synne and foly:
But not with friska ioly,
As somme do nowe a dayes,
That haue so many wayes
All maner [1] gaynes to reape,
Ther tresures one a heap
To gather and to kepe,
By pillinge of his shepe,
Not forsyng who do wepe,
And to his flocke repayre
As it were to a ffayre;
To sit in Peters chayer
With pride and ambition,
Sowyng great sedition;
And by superstition
Blinde vs with remission,
By bulles vnder led,
To serve both quicke and
        dead;
And by that way pretend
To clyme vpp and ascend
That Lucifer did discend.
I thinke that suche frykars
Be not Christes vickars,
But crafty intrycars,
And pryvy purse pykars;
For they that be sekars
Of stores newe and olde,
May perceyve and beholde

---

[1] *All maner, &c.*

. . . . . .

To gather and to kepe]

These three lines substituted for two deleted lines;

" *To gather and to kepe*
Treasure in *a hepe.*"

Howe euery thinge is solde
For sylver and for golde:
The craft can not be told,
What is and hath bene done
By Antychryst of Rome;
For thens the sourdes springe
Of every naughty thinge,
Hide vnderneth the whynge
Of the Sire of Synne;
At whom I will begynn
Somwhat for to speake,
And playnly to intreate
Of this farly freake,
That sitteth in his seat,
Devouringe synne as meatte,
Whiche he and his do eate
As they may catch and
    geate: [1]
They spare not to devower
Cyty, towne, and tower,
Wherat no man may lower;
For be it swete or sower,
Or be it good or yll,
We must be muett still,
The lustes to fulfill
Of that cocodryll,
Which at his only will
May ech man save or spyll.
This wicked man of warr
So hault is that he darr,
As he lyste, make and marr,
His owne lawe to prefarr
Aboue the worde of God;
It passeth Godes forbod
That ever it should be;

A man to clyme so hy,
By reason of his see,
To clayme auctoritye
Aboue the Deyte,
It is to hy a bost,
And synne one of the most
Ageynst the Holy Gost,
That is not remissable:
For as for the Bible,
He taketh it for a ridle,
Or as a lawles lible,
Which, to the hy offence
Of his conscience,
He dare therwith dispence,
And alter the sentence;
For wher God do prohibitt,
He doth leve exhibite,
And at his lust inhybyte;
And wher God doth com-
    maunde,
Ther he doth countermaunde;
After his owne purpose
The best text to turne and
    glose,
Like a Welshe manes hose,
Or lyke a waxen nose:
But wyse men do suppose
That truth shall judge and
    trye,
For lyars can but lye.
He is so hault and taunt,
That he dare hyme avaunt
All erthly men to daunt;
And faynes to give and
    graunt,

---

[1] *geate*] Followed by a deleted line;
    " Be it by colde or heate."

In heaven above or hell,
A place wherin to dwell,
As all his lyars tell,
Which he doth dayly sell,
After his devise,
If men come to his prise;
It is his marchaundyse;
For, as ye will demaunde,
He can and may commaunde
A·thowsande, in a bande,
Of angells out of heaven,
To come throughe the leven,
And make all thinge even,
His biddinges to obey,
Which beares the greatist
    swaye,
Your soules to convey
Frome all decaye
Out of the fendes wey;
But provided alwey,
That ye first mony paye;
At the appoynted daye
Ye present, if it maye;
Then, vnder thi petycion,
Thou gettest true remyssion,
From synnes the absolution,
By this his owne commyssion,
By bryve or els by bull,
To fill his coffers full;
Ye may aske what ye wull.
Alas, ye be to dull
To se this lorde of losse,
The fo of Christes crosse,
This hoore of Babilon,
And seede of Zabulon,
The enemy of Christ,
The devels holy pryst,
And very Antechrist,
To revell and to ride,

Like the prince of pride,
That of euery syde
Warres the worlde wyde,
Whom no strenghe may
    abide—
The devill be his guyde!
For loke in his decrees,
And ye shall finde out lyes,
As thik as swarme of byes,
That throughe the worlde
    flyes,
Making parsemonyes
Of Peters patrimonyes,
But great mercymonyes
Of his seremonyes,
To smodder vs with smoke:
For, when he wilbe wroke,
No man may bere his stroke;
So hevy is his yoke,
To Christes full vnlike,
That saide his yoke is swete,
His burthen lighte and meete
For all men that be meke,
To suffer and to bere,
Without drede or fere:
But Popes afterwarde,
That never had regard
Which ende shoulde go fore-
    warde,
Haue drawen vs bakwarde,
And made the yoke so harde
By false invented lawes,
As thoughe lay men were
    dawes,
And dome as any stone,
With sivile and canon
To serve God and Mammon;
Righte and wronge is one.
Serche his decretalles

And bulles papalles,
Et, inter alia,
Loke in his *palia*
And *Bacchanalia,*[1]
With his extravagantes
And wayes *vagarantes :*
His lawes *arrogantes*
Be made by truwantes
That frame his finctions
Into distinctions,
With cloutes of clawses,
Questyons and cawses,
With Sext and Clementyne,
And lawes legantyne:
His county pallantyne
Haue coustome colubryne,
With codes viperyne
And sectes serpentyne:
Blinde be his stores
Of interogatores .
And declaratores,
With lapse and relapse,
A wispe and a waspe,
A clispe and a claspe,
And his after clappes;
For his paragraffes
Be no cosmograffes,
But vnhappy graffes,
That wander in the warrayne,
Fruteles and barayne,
To fede that foule carrayne,
And dignite papall;
With judges that scrape all,
And doctours that take all,

By lawes absynthyall
And labirynthyall:
His tabellions
Be rebellions;
His laweres and scribes
Live only by bribes;
His holy advocates
And judges diligates
Haue robbed all estates,
By many inventions
Of sundry suspentions,
Subtile subventions,
Crafty conventions,
Prevy preventions,
And evell exemptions;
So hath his indictions
And his interdictions,
With croked commyssions,
Colde compromyssions,
Cursed conditions,
Hevy traditions,
Elvishe inibitions,
And redy remissions:
Then hathe he inductions
And colde conductions;
His expectatyves
Many a man vnthrives;
By his constitutions
And his subtitutions
He maketh institutions,
And taketh restitutions,
Sellinge absolutions,
And other like pollutions:
His holy actions

---

[1] *palia . . . Bacchanalia*] It would seem from the context that the right reading is " Palilia." The MS. has " Bacchanallia."

Be satisfactions
Of false compactions:
He robbeth all nations
With his fulminations,
And other like vexations;
As with abiurations,
Excomunycations,
Aggravations,
Presentations,
Sequestrations,
Deprivations,
Advocations,
Resignations,
Dilapidations,
Sustentations,
Adminystrations,
Approbations,
Assignations,
Alterations,
Narrations,
Declarations,
Locations,
Collocations,
Revocations,
Dispensations,
Intimations,
Legittimations,
Insinuations,
Pronunttiations,
Demonstrations,
Vacations,
Convocations,
Deputations,
Donations,
Condonations,
Commynations,
Excusations,
Declamations,
Visitations,

Acceptations,
Arrendations,
Publications,
Renunttiations,
Fatigations,
False fundations,
And dissimulations,
With like abbominations
Of a thowsand fasshions:
His holy vnions
Be no communyons:
His trialitees
And pluralytyes
Be full of qualitees;
His tottes and quottes
Be full of blottes:
With quibes and quaryes
Of inventataries,
Of testamentaries,
And of mortuaries,
By sutes of appeales,
And by his ofte repeales,
He oure mony steales.
I speake not of his sessions,
Nor of his confessions
Olde and avricular,
Colde and caniculer;
Howe the cubiculer,
In the capitular,
With his pylde spitler,
Playde the knavyculer
Vnderneth a wall:
I may not tell youe all,
In termes speciall,
Of pardon nor of pall,
Nor of confessionall;
For I feare, yf he call
The sentence generall,
I mighte so take a fall,

And haue his bitter curse,
And yett be not the wurse,
Save only in my purse,
Because I shoulde be fayne
To by my state agayne
Ex leno vel ex lena,
Aut pellice obscæna,
Res certe inamœna:
Papisticorum scena,
Malorum semper plena;
For all the worlde rounde
He falsely doth confounde
By lawes made and founde,
By thyr devyse vnsownde,
With no steadfast grounde,
But with fayned visions
And develyshe devisions,
With basterde religions:
Thus this cursed elfe,
To avaunce his pelfe,
Falsely fayne[s] hymeself
To be *semideus:*
No, youe Asmeodeus,
Ye are Amoreus,
The sonne of Chanaan;
O thou monstrous man,
And childe of cursed Chan,
Arte thou halfe god, halfe
        man?
Gup, leviathan,
And sonne of Sattan,
The worme *letophagus,*
And sire to Symonde Magus!
O porter Cerberus,
Thou arte so monstrous,
Soo made and myschevous,
Proude and surquedrous,
And as lecherous
As Heliogabalus

Or Sardanapalus!
Hatefull vnto God,
And father of all falsehoode,
The poyson of prestoode,
And deth of good knight-
        hoode,
The robber of riche men,
And murderer of meke men,
The turment of true men
That named be newe men,
The prince of periury,
And Christes enemy,
Vnhappy as Achab,
And naughty as Nadab,
As crafty as Caball,
And dronken as Naball,
The hope of Ismaell,
And false Achitofell,
The blissinge of Bell,
And advocate of hell;
Thou hunter Nembroth,
And Judas Iscarioth,
Thou bloody Belyall,
And sacrifise of Ball,
Thou elvishe ipocrite,
And naughty neophite,
Thou pevishe proselite,
And synefull Sodymite,
Thou gredy Gomorrite,
And galefull Gabaonite,
Tho[u] hermofrodite,
Thou arte a wicked sprite,
A naughty seismatike,
And an heritike,
A beestely bogorian,
And devill meridian,
The patrone of proctors,
And dethe of trewe doctours,
The founder of faytors,

And trust of all traytours,
The shender of sawes,
And breaker of lawes,
The syre of serdoners,
And prince of pardoners,
The kinge of questors,
And rule of regestors,
The eater of frogges,
And maker of goddes,
The brother of brothells,
And lorde of all losells,
The sturrur of stoores,
And keper of hoores
With gloriouse gawdes,
Amonge trusty bawdes,
The father ef foles,
And ignoraunce of scoles,
The helper of harlettes,
And captayne of verlettes,
The cloke of all vnthriftes,
And captayne of all cay-
    tifes,
The leader of truwantes,
And chefe of all tyrauntes,.
As hinde as an hogge,
And kinde as any dogge,
The shipwrake of Noye,—
Christ saue the and Sainct
    Loy!
Arte thou the hiest pryst,
And vicar vnto Christ?
No, no, I say, thou lyest:
Thou arte a cursed crekar,
A crafty vppcrepar;
Thou arte the devils vicar,
A privye purse pikar,
By lawes and by rites
For sowles and for sprites:
O lorde of ipocrites,

Nowe shut vpp your wick-
    ettes,
And clape to your click-
    ettes,—
A farewell, kinge of crek-
    ettes!
For nowe the tyme falles
To speake of cardinalles,
That kepe ther holy halles
With towres and walles:
Be they not carnalles,
And lordes infernalles?
Yea, gredy carmalles,
As any carmarante;
With ther coppentaute
They loke adutante:
For soth, men say they be
Full of iniquite,
Lyvinge in habundance
Of all worldly substance,
Wherin they lodge and ly,
And wallowe beasteally,
As hogges do in a stye,
Servinge ther god, ther belly,
With chuettes and with gelly,
With venyson and with tartes,
With confytes and with fartes,
To ease ther holy hartes.
They take ther stations,
And make dyambulations
Into all nations,
For ther visitations,
Callinge convocations,
Sellinge dispensations,
Givinge condonasions,
Makinge permutations,
And of excomunycations
Sell they relaxations;
For they, in ther progresse,

With Katern, Mawde, and
    Besse,
Will vse full great excesse,
Withowt any redresse;
And all men they oppresse
In syty, towne, and village;
From olde and yong of age
They robbe and make pyllage,
Thyr lusts for to aswage,
Which they extorte by mighte
As in the churches righte;
They may not lese a fether:
But God, that lyveth ever,
Graunt that they never
Haue power to come hether!
For wher they ones arive,
So cleane they do vs shryve,
That I swere ty my life,
The contry ther shall thrive
Yeres tenn and ffive
After them the worse:
Men give them Godes curse
To shute within ther purse;
Both lernyd and lewde
Wolde they were beshrewed,
They never mighte come nere
For to visitt here,

Altho they haue sotch chere
As they cann well desyre,
And as they will requier;
For why, it doth appere,
The hartes ar sett on fyer
Of chanon, monke, and fryer,
That daylye dothe aspyre,[1]
By bulles vnder ledd,
How they should be fedd;
It is therfore greÃt skill
That every Jacke and Gyll
Performe the Popes will,
Hys purse and panch to ffill;
For, as I erst haue tolde,
There lyves not suche a
    scolde
That dare ons be so bold,
From shorne ne yet from
    polde,
Nor monye, meate, nor golde,
From soch men [2] to withholde,
Ther favour boughte and
    solde,
That take a thowsand ffolde
More then that Judas did:
The trouth can not be hid;
For it is playnly kid

---

[1] *aspyre*] Followed by a deleted line (inserted above with
a slight variation);

    " Thyr hartes ar so on fyer."

[2] *soch men*] Originally " them." This line is followed by
three deleted lines (inserted above,—the first two slightly
altered);

    " Mony meat or golde
    But be they shorne or polde
    Ther lyves not suche a scolde."

Judas for his dispense
Sold Christ for thirty pense,
And did a foule offence,
His Lorde God so to tray;
And they in likewise say,
After Judas way,
What will ye give and pay,
As the matter falles,
For pardonnes and for palles,
And for confessionalles?
We may have absolucions
Without restytutyons,
And at oure owne election
Passe without correction,
Besydes Christes passion
To make satisfaction;
We feare for non offence,
So they haue recompence:
By great audacitees
They graunt capacitees;
For heaven and for hell
They mony take and tell:
So thus they by and sell,
And take therof no shame,
But laughe and haue good
          game,
To all oure souls bane:
God helpe, we be to blame
Sutch lordes to defame;
Yett, by the common fame,
Some bisshops vse the same,
In Christes holy name
Soules to sell and bye:
My mynde is not to lye,
But to write playnlye

Ageynst ipocresye
In bisshopp or in other,
Yea, thoughe it were my
          brother,
My father or my mother,
My syster or my sonne;
For, as I haue begonne,
I will, as I haue donne,
Disclose the great outrage
That is in this Image;
For he that feles the pricke,
And theron groweth sycke,
May with the gald horse kike;
For, as I erst haue said,
Oure bishops at a brayd
Ar growne so sore afrayde,
And in the world so wide
Do vse sutch pompe and
          pride,
And rule on euery syde,
That none may them abide:
Of no prince, lord, nor duke,
They take will a rebuke;
All lay men they surmount,
Makinge non accompte,
Nor caste no reckonynge
Scarcely of a kinge:
This is a wonder thinge;
They stande so suer and
          fast,
And be nothinge agast;[1]
For that blody judge
And mighty sanguisuge,
The Pope that is so huge,
Is ever ther refuge;

----

[1] *agast*] Followed by a deleted line;
    " But fede whilst they do brast."

So be the cardinalles
Ther suer defence and walles,
With whom they stifly stande
By water and by lande,
To gett the overhande
Of all the world rounde,
Wher profitt may be founde:
They be so many legions,
That they oppresse regions
With boke, bell, and candell,
Any kinge to handell,
As they haue many one:
For triall herevpon
I take of good Kinge John,
Whom by the bitinge
Of ther subtill smytinge,
First by acytinge,
And after interditinge,
By fulmynatious
Of excommunications;
For by ther holy poores
They stored vpp stoores,
And kepte suche stvrre with
hores,
And shut vpp all churche
doores
For ther princely pleasure,
They lyve so owt of measure,
Till they might haue leasure,
Ther lieg lorde and kinge
So base and lowe to bringe;
Which was a pyttevs thyng,
That he with wepinge yees,
Bowinge backe and thies,
And knelinge on his knees,
Must render vpp his fees,
With kingly dignytees,
Septer, crowne, and landes,
Into ther holy handes:

Alas, howe mighte it be
That oure nobilitee
Could then no better se?
For theyrs was the fault
Oure prelates were so haulte;
Their strength then was to
seke
Ther liege lorde to kepe;
They durst not fight ne strike,
They feared of a gleke,
That, no day in the weke,
For any good or cattell,
Durst they go to battell,
Nor entre churche ne chap-
pell
In syxe or seven yere,
Before Christ to appere,
And devine seruice here
In any hallowed place,
For lacke of ther good grace;
Ther was no tyme nor space
To do to God seruice,
But as they wolde devise;
Their lawes be so sinystre,
That no man durst minystre
The holy sacrementes
Till they hadd ther intentes
Of landes and of rentes,
By lawes and by lyes;
To inriche ther sees,
The blind men eat vpp flees;
For by ther constitutions
They toke restitutions
Of cyties and of castells,
Of townes and bastells,
And make ther prince pike
wastells,
Till they rang out the belles,
And did as they wold elles,

Like traytours and rebelles,
As the story telles.
But Jesu Christ hymeself,
Nor his appostells twelffe,
Vnto that cvrsyd elfe
Did never teach hym so
In any wise to do,
For lucre or advayle,
Ageynst thyr kyng to rayle,
And lieg lorde to assayle,
Within his owne lande
To put hym vnder bande,
And take brede of his hande:
The Lorde saue sutch a flock
That so could mowe and mock
To make ther kinge a block,
And eke ther laughinge
    stocke!
They blered hym with a
    lurche,
And said that he must wurche
By counsell of the churche;
Wherby they ment nothinge
But to wrest and wringe,
Only for to bringe
Ther liege lorde and kinge
To be· ther vnderlinge:
Alas, who euer sawe
A kinge vnder awe,
Ageynst all Gods lawe,
All righte and consience,
For doinge non offence
To make sutch recompence?
They gave ther lorde a laske,
To purge withall his caske,
And putt hym to no taske,
But as they wold hyme aske:

This was a midday maske,
A kinge so to enforce
With pacyence perforce.
Take hede therfore and
    watche,
All ye that knowe this tatche,
Ye make not sutch a matche;
Loke forth, beware the
    katche,
Ye fall not in the snatche
Of that vngratiovs pacthe,
Before the rope hym racthe,
Or Tyburne dothe hym
    strache.
But who so preache or pra·e,
I warne youe, rathe and late
To loke vpp and awake,
That ye do never make
Your maister nor your mate
To sytt withowt your gate;
Take hede, for Christes sake,
And knowe your owne estate,
Or ye be tardy take;
Yea, lest it be to late
To trust on hadd I wist,
Imasked in a myst,—
As good to ly bypist;
For these hie primates,
Bysshops and prelates,
And popeholy legates,
With ther pild pates,
Dare conquer all estates:
They do but as they will;
For, be it good or ill,
We must be muett still:
Why lay men can not se,
It is the more pite.

Thus endeth the Seconde Parte of this present treatyse,
called the Image of Ipocresy.

Of prechers nowe adayes
Be many Fariseyes,
That leue the Lordes layes,
And preche ther owne wayes;
Wherof nowe of late
Hathe risen great debate;
For some champe and chaffe
As hogges do in draffe,
And some cry out apase
As houndes at a chase,
Whiche for lacke of grace
The playne truthe wold de-
        fase.
So busely they barke,
An other in the darke,
That is a busarde starke,
And cane not se the marke,
Wondereth at this warke,
And therfore taketh carke
Bycause he is no clarke.
Some be soft and still
As clappes in a mill,
And some cry and yell
As sprites do in hell;
Some be here and ther,
And some I wote not wher;
Some holde vpp, yea and nay,
And some forsake ther lay;
Some be still and stey,
And hope to haue a daye;
Some wote not what to say,
But dout whether they may
Abide or rune away;
Ther wittes be so weake,
They say they dare not
        speake,
They be afrayd of heate;

Some be sycke and sadd,
For sorrowe almost madd;
I tell youe veryly,
Ther wittes be awry,
They peyne themselves
        greatly
To haue the trouth go by;
Some on bokes dayly prye,
And yett perceyve not reason
        whie;
Tho some affirme, some do
        deny,
With nowe a trouth and then
        a ly,
To say one thinge openly,
And an other prively;—
Here be but youe and I;
Say to me your mynd playn-
        lye,
Is it not open heresy?
Thus say they secretly,
Whisperinge with sorrowe
That they deny to morowe.
Ther tales be so dobble,
That many be in trobble,
And doubt which way to take,
Themselves sure to make:
A lorde, it makes me shake!
For pyty that I quake.
They be so colde and horse,
That they haue no forse,
So they be prefarred,
Tho all the rest were marred.
Thus the people smatter,
That dayly talke and clatter,
Oure preachers do but flatter,
To make themselves the fatter,

And care not thoughe the
    matter
Were clerely layde a watter.
Douse men chatt and chide it,
For they may not abid it;
The Thomistes wold hide it,
For *littera occidit.*
Thus these sysmatickes,
And lowsy lunatickes,
With spurres and prickes
Call true men heretickes.
They finger ther fidles,
And cry in quinibles,
Away these bibles,
For they be but ridles!
And give them Robyn Whode,
To red howe he stode
In mery grene wode,
When he gathered good,
Before Noyes ffloodd!
For the Testamentes
To them, they sey, sente is,
To gather vpp ther rentes,
After ther intentes:
Wherby it by them ment is,
That lay men be but lowtes;
They may not knowe the
    clowtes,
Nor dispute of the doubtes,
That is in Christes lawe;
For why, they never sawe
The bagg nor the bottell
Of oure Arrestotle,
Nor knowe not the toyes
Of Doctore Averroyes;
It is no play for boyes,

Neyther for lay men;
But only for schole men,
For they be witty men,
As wise as any wrenne,
And holy as an henne.
For Doctoure Bullatus,
Though *parum literatus,*
Will brable and prate thus;
Howe Doctoure Pomaunder,
As wise as a gander,
Wotes not wher to wander,
Whether to Meander,
Or vnto Menander;
For of Alexander,
Irrefragable Hales,
He cane tell many tales,
Of many parke pales,
Of butgettes and of males,
Of Candy and of Cales,
And of West Wales.
But Doctoure Dorbellous
Doth openly tell vs
Howe they by and sell vs:
And Doctoure Sym Sotus
Cann goostely grope vs;
For he hathe rad Scotus,
And so the dawe dotus
Of Doctour Subtyles;
Yea, three hundreth myles,
With sutch crafty wyles
He many men begiles,
That never knewe an vnce
At full of Master Dunce.
Then Doctoure Bonbardus
Can skill of Lombardus;
He wonnes at Malepardus,[1]

---

[1] *Malepardus*]. The abode of Reynard according to the
famous old romance: "reynart had many a dwellyng place,

With Father Festino,
And Doctoure Attamino,
Dudum de camino,
With ther *consobrino,*
Cupite equino
Et corde asinino ;
Hi latent in limo
Et in profundo fimo,
Cubantes in culino
Cum Thoma de Aquino,
Tractantes in ima
De pelle canina
Et lana caprina.
Then Doctoure Chekmate
Hath his pardoned pate,
A man yll educate;
His harte is indurate,
His heade eke edentate;
His wittes be obfuscate,
His braynes obumbrate,
Oure questions to debate;
For thoughe cam but late,
His cause is explicate
With termes intricate,
I note wherof conflate;
And therfore must he make
His bull and antedate.
Then Doctour Tom-to-bold
Is neyther whote nor colde,
Till his coles be solde;
His name may not be tolde

For syluer nor for golde;
But he is sutch a scolde,
That no play may hym holde
For anger vnbepyst,
Yf his name were wist;
Ye may judge as ye liste;
He is no Acquiniste,
Nor non Occanist,[1]
But a mockaniste;
This man may not be myste,
He is a suer sophiste,
And an olde papist.
But nowe we haue a knighte:[2]
That is a man of mighte,
All armed for to fighte,
To put the trouthe to flighte
By Bowbell pollecy,
With his poetry
And his sophestry;
To mocke and make a ly,
With quod he and quod I;
And his appologye,
Made for the prelacy,
Ther hugy pompe and pride
To coloure and to hide;
He maketh no nobbes,
But with his diologges
To prove oure prelates goddes,
And lay men very lobbes,
Betinge they[m] with bobbes,
And with ther ow[n]e roddes;

---

but the castel of *maleperduys* was the beste and the fastest burgh that he had, ther laye he inne whan he had nede and was in ony drece or fere."   Sig. a 8. ed. 1481.

1 *Occanist*] So written, it would seem, for the rhyme, properly " Occamist."

2 *a knighte*] i. e. Sir Thomas More.

Thus he taketh payne
To fable and to fayne,
Ther myscheff to mayntayne,
And to haue them rayne
Over hill and playne,
Yea, over heaven and hell,
And wheras sprites dwell,
In purgatorye holles,
With whote ffier and coles,
To singe for sely soules,
With a supplication,
And a confutation,
Without replication,
Havinge delectation
To make exclamation,
By way of declamation,
In his Debellation,[1]
With a popishe fasshion
To subvert oure nation:
But this daucok doctoure
And purgatory proctoure
Waketh nowe for wages,
And, as a man that rages
Or overcome with ages,[2]
Disputith *per ambages,*
To helpe these parasites
And naughty ipocrites,
With legendes of lyes,
Fayned fantasies,
And very vanyties,
Called veryties,
Vnwritten and vnknowen,
But as they be blowne

From lyer to lyer,
Inventyd by a ffryer
In magna copia,
Brought out of Vtopia
Vnto the mayde of Kent,[3]
Nowe from the devill sent,
A virgyne ffayre and gent,
That hath our yees blent:
Alas, we be myswent!
For yf the false intent
Were knowen of this witche,
It passeth dogg and bitche:
I pray God, do so mutche
To fret her on the itche,
And open her in tyme!
For this manly myne
Is a darke devyne,
With his poetry,
And her iugglery,
By conspiracy
To helpe our prelacy,
She by ypocresye,
And he by tyranny,
That causeth cruelly
The simple men to dye
For fayned herisye:
He saythe that this nody
Shall brenne, soule and body,
Or singe his palanody,
With feare till he pant,
To make hym recreante
His sayinges to recante,
So as he shalbe skante

---

[1] *his Debellation*] i. e. Sir Thomas More's *Debellacyon of Salem vnd Byzance.*

[2] *ages*] i. e. age is.

[3] *the mayde of Kent*] i. e. Elizabeth Barton.

Able for to loke
In writinge or in booke,
That treatithe of the rote
Or of the base and fote
Of ther abhomynation:
He vsethe sutche a fasshion,
To send a man in station
With an evill passion
To his egression,
Before the procession
Slylye for to stalke,
And solempeny to walke,
To here the preacher talke,
Howe he hath made a balke;
And so the innocent,
For feare to be brent,
Must suffer checke and checke,
His faccott on his necke,
Not for his life to quecke,
But stande vpp, like a bosse,
In sighte at Paules crosse,
To the vtter losse
Of his goode name and fame:
Thus with great payne and shame
He kepethe men in bandes,
Confiskinge goods and landes,
And then to hete ther handes
With faccottes and with brandes,
Or make them be abjure:
These thinges be in vre;
Youe leade vs with the lure
Of your persecution
And cruell execution,
That the fyry fume
Oure lyves shall consume
By three, by two, and one;

Men say ye will spare none
Of hye nor lowe degre,
That will be eneme
To your ipocrese,
Or to your god the bele;
For who dare speake so felle
That clerkes should be simple,
Without spott or wrinkell?
Yett nathelesse alwey
I do protest and saye,
And shall do while I may,
I never will deny,
But confesse openly,
That punnysshement should be,
In every degre,
Done with equite;
When any doth offende,
Then oughte youe to attende
To cause hyme to amend,
Awaytinge tyme and place,
As God may give youe grace,
To haue hyme fase to fase,
His fautes to deface,
With hope to reconcyle hyme;
But not for to begile hym,
Or vtterly to revile hyme,
As thoughe ye wold excile hyme;
For then, the trouth to tell,
Men thinke ye do not well.
Ye call that poore man wretch,
As thoughe ye hadd no retche,
Or havinge no regarde,
Whiche ende should go for-warde:
Ye be so sterne and harde,

Ye rather drawe backwarde,
Your brother so to blinde,
To grope and sertche his
   mynde,
As thoughe youe were his
   frinde,
Some worde to pike and
   finde,
Wherby ye may hyme blinde;
With your popishe lawe
To kepe vs vnder awe,
By captious storyes
Of interrogatoryes:
Thus do ye full vnkindly,
To feyne yourselves frindley,
And be nothinge but fyndly.
I tell youe, men be lothe
To se youe wode and wrothe,
And then for to be bothe
Th' accuser and the judge:
Then farewell all refuge,
And welcom sanguisuge!
When ye be madd and angry,
And an expresse enemy,
It is ageynst all equitye
Ye shoulde be judge and
   partye:
Therfore the kinges grace
Your lawes muste deface;
For before his face
Youe should your playntes
   bringe,
As to your lorde and kinge
And judge in euery thinge,
That, by Godes worde,
Hathe power of the sworde,
As kinge and only lorde,
So scripture doth recorde;
For her within his lande

Should be no counterband,
But holy at his hande
We shoulde all be and
   stande,
Both clerkes spirituall,
And lay men temporall:
But youe make lawe at will,
The poore to plucke and pill,
And some that do no yll,
Your appetites to ffill,
Ye do distroy and kill.
Lett Godes worde try them,
And then ye shall not frye
   them;
Yea, lett the worde of God
Be euery mannes rode,
And the kinges the lawe
To kepe them vnder awe,
To fray the rest with ter-
   roure,
They may revoke ther er-
   roure:
And thus, I say agayne,
The people wolde be fayne
Ye prelates wolde take
   payne
To preache the gospell
   playne;
For otherwise certayne
Your laboure is in vayne;
For all your crueltye,
I knowe that you and we
Shall never well agree·
Ye may in no wise se
Sutch as disposed be
Of ther charitye
To preach the verytye;
Ye stope them with decrees,
And with your veritees,

Vnwritten, as ye saye;
Thus ye make them stay:
But God, that all do may,
I do desire and pray,
To open vs the day,
Which is the very kaye
Of knowledge of his way,
That ye haue stolen awaye!
And then, my lordes, perfay,
For all your popishe play,
Not all your gold so gay,
Nor all your riche araye,
Shall serve youe to delaye
But some shall go astraye,
And lerne to swyme or sinke;
For truly I do thinke,
Ye may well wake or wynke,
For any meat cr drinke
Ye geitt, without ye swynke.
But that wold make youe
    wrothe;
For, I trowe, ye be lothe
To do eyther of both,
That is, yourself to cloth
With laboure and with
    sweate
And faste till youe eate
But that youe erne and
    geate;
Like verlettes and pages,
To leve your parsonages,
Your denns and your cages,
And by [1] dayly wages:
God blesse vs, and Sainct
    Blase!
This were a hevy case,

A chaunce of ambesase,
To se youe broughte so base,
To playe without a place:
Now God send better grace!
And loke ye lerne apase
To tripe in trouthes trace,
And seke some better chaunce
Yourselves to avaunce,
With sise synke or synnes;
For he laughe[s] that wynnes,
As ye haue hetherto,
And may hereafter do;
Yf ye the gospell preche,
As Christ hymself did teche,
And in non other wise
But after his devise,
Ye may with good advyse
Kepe your benefise
And all your dignite,
Without malignite,
In Christes name, for me;
I gladely shall agre
It ever may so be.
But this I say and shall,
What happ soeuer fall,
I pray and call
The Kinge celestiall,
Ones to give youe grace
To se his worde haue place;
And then within shorte space
We shall perceyve and se
Howe euery degre
Hath his auctorite
By the lawe of Christ,
The lay man and the prest,
The poore man and the lorde;

---

[1] *by*] i. e. buy,—acquire, earn.

For of that monocorde
The scripture doth recorde;
And then with good accorde,
In love and in concorde
We shall together holde;
Or elles ye may be bolde,
For heate or colde
Say ye what ye will,
Yt were as good be still;

For thoughe ye glose and frase
Till your eyes dase,
Men holde it but a mase
Till Godes worde haue place,
That doth include more grace
Then all erthly men
Could ever knowe or ken.

Thuse endith the thirde parte of this present treatise called
the Image of Ypocresye.

Nowe with sondry sectes
The world sore infectes,
As in Christes dayes
Amonge the Pharisees,
In clothinge and in names;
For some were Rhodyans,
And Samaritans,
Some were Publicanes,
Some were Nazarenes,
Bisshops and Essenes,
Preestes and Pharisees;
And so of Saducees,
Prophetes and preachers,
Doctours and teachers,
Tribunes and tribes,
Lawers and scribes,
Deacons and levytes,
With many ipocrites;
And so be nowe also,
With twenty tymes mo
Then were in Christes dayes
Amonge the Pharisees:
The Pope, whom first they call
Ther lorde and principall,
The patriarke withall;

And then the Cardinall
With tytles all of pride,
As legates of the side,
And some be cutt and shorne
That they be legates borne;
Then archebisshops bold,
And bisshops for the folde,
They metropolitannes,
And these diocysanyes,
That haue ther suffraganyes
To blesse the prophanyes;
Then be ther curtisanes
As ill as Arrianes
Or Domicianes,
Riall residentes,
And prudent presidentes;
So be their sensors,
Doughty dispensors,
Crafty inventors,
And prevy precentors,
With chaplaynes of honour
That kepe the Popes bower;
Then allmoners and deanes,
That geit by ther meanes

The rule of all reames;
Yett be ther subdeanes,
With treasorers of trust,
And chauncelours iniust,
To scoure of scab and rust,
With vicars generalls,
And ther officialles,
Chanons and chaunters,
That be great avaunters;
So be ther subchaunters,
Sextons and archedeakons,
Deakons and subdeakons,
That be ypodeakons,
Parsonnes and vicars,
Surveyors and sikers,
Prevy pursepikers,
Provostes and preachers,
Readers and teachers,
With bachilers and maysters,
Spenders and wasters;
So be ther proctors,
With many dull doctors,
Proude prebendaryes,
Colde commissaries,
Synfull secundaries,
Sturdy stipendaries,
With olde ordinaryes,
And penytencyaryes,
That kepe the sanctuaries;
So be ther notaries,
And prothonotaries,
Lawers and scribes,
With many quibibes,
Redy regesters,
Pardoners and questers,
Maskers and mummers,
Deanes and sumners,
Apparatoryes preste
To ride est and weste;

Then be ther advocates,
And *parum* litterates,
That eate vpp all estates,
With wyly visitors,
And crafty inquisitors,
Worse then Mamalokes,
That catche vs with ther
  crokes,
And brenne vs and oure
  bokes;
Then be ther annivolors,
And smalle benivolers,
With chauntry chapleynes,
Oure Ladyes chamberleynes;
And some be Jesu Christes,
As be oure servinge pristes,
And prestes that haue cure
Which haue ther lyvinge
  sure,
With clerkes and queresters,
And other smale mynisters,
As reders and singers,
Bedemen and bellringers,
That laboure with ther lippes
Ther pittaunce out of pittes,
With Bennet and Collet,
That bere bagg and wallett;
These wretches be full wely,
They eate and drinke frely,
Withe *salve, stella cœli*,
And ther *de profundis;*
They lye with *immundis*,
And walke with vacabundis,
At good ale and at wynne
As dronke as any swynne;
Then be ther grosse abbottes,
That observe ther sabbottes,
Fayer, ffatt, and ffull,
As gredy as a gull,

And ranke as any bull,
With priors of like place,[1]
Some blacke and some
    white,
As channons be and monkes,
Great lobyes and lompes,
With Bonhomes and brothers,
Fathers and mothers,
Systers and nonnes,
And littell prety bonnes,
With lictors and lectors,
Mynisters and rectors,
Custos and correctors,
With papall collectors,
And popishe predagoges,[2]
Mockinge mystagoges,
In straunge array and robes,
Within ther sinagoges;
With sectes many mo,
An hundreth in a throo
I thinke to name by roo,
As they come to my mynde,
Whom, thoughe they be vn-
    kind,
The lay mens labor finde;
For some be Benedictes
With many maledictes;
Some be Cluny,
And some be Plumy,
With *Cistercyences,*
Grandimontences,
Camaldulences,
Premonstratences,
Theutonycences,
Clarrivallences,

And *Basiliences;*
Some be Paulines,
Some be Antonynes,
Some be Bernardines,
Some be Celestines,
Some be Flamynes
Some be Fuligines,
Some be Columbines,
Some be Gilbertines,
Some be Disciplines,
Some be Clarines,
And many Augustines,
Some Clarissites,
Some be Accolites,
Some be Sklavemytes,
Some be Nycolites,
Some be Heremytes,
Some be Lazarites,
Some be Ninivites,
Some be Johannytes,
Some be Josephites,
Some be Jesuytes,
Servi and Servytes,
And sondry Jacobites;
Then be ther Helenytes,
Hierosolymites,
Magdalynites,
Hieronimytes
Anacorites,
And Scenobites;
So be ther Sophrans,
Constantinopolitanes,
Holy Hungarians,
Purgatorians,
Chalomerians,

---

[1] *place*] Should perhaps be " plite "—or there may be some
omission in the MS. after this line.

[2] *predagoges*] Qy. " pædagoges ? "

And Ambrosians;
Then be ther Indianes,
And Escocyanes,
Lucifrans,
Chartusyanes,
Collectanes,
Capusianes,
Hispanians,
Honofrianes,
Gregorianes,
Vnprosianes,
Winceslanes,
With Ruffianes,
And with Rhodianes;
Some be Templers,
And Exemplers,
Some be Spitlers,
And some be Vitlers,
Some be Scapelers,
And some Cubiculers,
Some be Tercyaris,
And some be of St. Marys,
Some be Hostiaris,
And of St. Johns frarys,
Some be Stelliers,
And some be Ensefers,
Some Lucifers.
And some be Crucyfers,
Some haue signe of sheres,
And some were shurtes of
    heres,
Some be of the spone,
And some be crossed to
    Rome,
Some daunte and daly
In Sophathes valley,
And in the blak alley
Wheras it ever darke is,
And some be of St. Markis

Mo then be good clarkes,
Some be Mysiricordes,
Mighty men and lordes,
And some of Godes house
That kepe the poore souse,
Minimi and Mymes,
And other blak devines,
With Virgins and Vestalles,
Monkes and Monyalles,
That be conventualles,
Like frogges and todes;
And some be of the Rhodes,
Swordemen and knightes,
That for the [faith] fightes
With sise, sinke, and quatter.
But nowe never the latter
I intend to clatter
Of a mangye matter,
That smelles of the smatter,
Openly to tell
What they do in hell,
Wheras oure ffryers dwell
Everich in his sell,
The phane and the prophane,
The croked and the lame,
The mad, the wild, and tame,
Every one by name:
The formest of them all
Is ther Generall;
And the next they call
Ther hie Provincyall,
With Cvstos and Wardyn
That lye next the gardeyn;
Then oure father Prior,
With his Subprior
That with the covent comes
To gather vpp the cromes;
Then oure fryer Douche
Goeth by a crouche,

And slouthfull ffryer Slouche
That bereth Judas pouche;
Then ffryer Domynike
And ffryer Demonyke,
Fryer Cordiler
And ffryer Bordiler,
Fryer Jacobine,
Fryer Augustyne,
And ffryer Incubyne
And ffryer Succubine,
Fryer Carmelyte
And ffryer Hermelite,
Fryer Mynorite
And ffryer Ipocrite,
Frier ffranciscane
And ffrier Damiane,
Frier Precher
And ffrier Lecher,
Frier Crusifer
And ffrier Lusifer,
Frier Purcifer
And ffrier *Furcifer*,
Frier Ferdifer
And ffrier *Merdifer*,
Fryer Sacheler
And ffryer Bacheler,
Fryer Cloysterer
And ffrier Floysterer,
Frier *Pallax*
And ffrier *Fallax*,
Frier *Fugax*
And ffrier *Nugax*,
Frier *Rapax*
And ffrier *Capax*,
Frier *Lendax*
And ffrier *Mendax*,
Frier *Vorax*
And ffrier *Nycticorax*,
Fryer *Japax*,

Frier Furderer
And ffrier Murderer,
Frier Tottiface
And ffrier Sottiface,
Frier Pottiface
And frier Pockyface,
Frier Trottapace
And ffrier Topiace,
Frier Futton
And ffrier Glotton,
Frier Galiard
And ffrier Paliard,
Frier Goliard
And ffrier Foliard,
Frier Goddard
And ffrier Foddard,
Frier Ballard
And ffrier Skallard,
Frier Crowsy
And ffrier Lowsy,
Frier Sloboll
And ffrier Bloboll,
Frier Toddypoll
And ffrier Noddypoll,
Frier fflaphole
And ffrier Claphole,
Frier Kispott
And ffrier Pispott,
Frier Chipchop
And ffrier Likpott,
Frier Clatterer
And ffrier fflatterer,
Frier Bib, ffrier Bob,
Frier Lib, ffrier Lob,
Frier Fear, ffrier Fonde,
Frier Beare, ffrier Bonde,
Frier Rooke, ffrier Py,
Frier Flooke, ffrier Flye,
Frier Spitt, ffrier Spy,

Frier Lik, ffrier Ly,
With ffrier We-he
Found by the Trinytye,
And frier Fandigo,
With an hundred mo
Could I name by ro,
Ne were for losse of tyme,
To make to longe a ryme:
O squalidi laudati,
Fœdi effeminati,
Falsi falsati,
Fuci fucati,
Culi cacati,
Balbi braccati,
Mimi merdati,
Larvi larvati,
Crassi cathaphi,[1]
Calvi cucullati,
Curvi curvati,
Skurvi knavati,
Spurci spoliati,
Hirci armati,
Vagi devastati,
Devii debellati,
Surdi sustentati,
Squalidi laudati,
Tardi terminati,
Mali subligati,
Inpii conjurati,
Profusi profugi,
Lapsi lubrici,
Et parum pudici !
Oth ye drane bees,
Ye bloody flesheflees,
Ye spitefull spittle spyes,

And grounde of herisees,
That dayly without sweat
Do but drinke and eate,
And murther meat and meat,
Ut fures et latrones !
Ye be *incubiones,*[2]
But no *spadones,*
Ye haue your *culiones ;*
Ye be *histriones,*
Beastely *balatrones,*
Grandes thrasones,
Magni nebulones,
And *cacodæmones,*
That [eat] vs fleshe and
  bones
With teeth more harde then
  stones;
Youe make hevy mones,
As it were for the nones,
With great and grevous
  grones,
By sightes and by sobbes
To blinde vs with bobbes;
Oh ye false faytours,
Youe theves be and tratours,
The devils dayly wayters!
Oh mesell Mendicantes,
And mangy Obseruauntes,
Ye be *vagarantes !*
As persers *penitrantes,*
Of mischef *ministrantes,*
In pillinge *postulantes,*
In preachinge *petulantes,*
Of many *sycophanies,*
That gather, as do antes,

---

1 *cathaphi*] Qy. " cataphagi " (voraces)?
2 *incubiones*] Properly " incubones."

In places wher ye go,
With *in principio*
Runnynge to and ffro,
Ye cause mikle woo
With hie and with loo;
Wher youe do resorte,
Ye fayne and make reporte
Of that youe never harde,
To make foles aferde
With visions and dremes,[1]
Howe they do in hevens,
And in other remes
Beyonde the great stremes
Of Tyger and of Gange,
Where tame devils range,
And in the black grange,
Thre myle out of hell,
Where sely sowles dwell,
In paynes wher they lye,
Howe they lament and cry
Vnto youe, holy lyars,
And false fflatteringe ffriers,
For *Dirige* and masses;
Wherwith, like very asses,
We maynteyn youe and your
　　lasses;
But in especiall
Ye say, the sowles call
For the great trentall;
For some sely sowles
So depe ly in holes
Of ffier and brennyng coles,
That top and tayle is hid;
For whom to pray and bid

Thens to haue them rid,
Ye thinke it but a foly;
Althoughe the masse be holy,
The fendes be wyly;
Till masse of *scale cœli*,
At Bathe or at Ely,
Be by a ffrier saide
That is a virgine mayde,
These sowles may not away,
As all yow ffriers say;
So trowe I without doubte
These sowles shall never out;
For it is *rara avis*,
Ye be so many knaves;
I swere by crosses ten,
That fewe be honest men;
So many of youe be
Full of skurrilite,
That throughly to be sought
The multitude is noughte:
Ye be nothinge denty;
Ye come among vs plenty
By coples in a peire,
As sprites in the heire,
Or dogges in the ffayre;
Where yow do repayre,
Ye ever ride and rune,
As swifte as any gune,
With nowe to go and come,
As motes in the sonne,
To shrive my lady nonne,
With humlery hum,
Dominus vobiscum !
God knoweth all and some,

---

[1] *dremes*] I suspect the author wrote " *swevens*," and that
" *dremes*," a gloss on the word, crept by mistake into the
text.

What is and hath bene done,
Syns the world begone,
Of russett, gray, and white,
That sett ther hole delighte
In lust and lechery,
In thefte and trecherey,
In lowsy lewdenes,
In synne and shrodenes,
In crokednes acurst,
Of all people the worste,
Marmosettes and apes,
That with your pild pates
Mock vs with your iapes:
Ye holy caterpillers,
Ye helpe your wellwillers
With prayers and psalmes,
To devoure the almes
That Christians should give
To meynteyne and releve
The people poore and nedy;
But youe be gredy,
And so great a number,
That, like the ffier of thunder,
The worlde ye incomber:
But hereof do I wonder,
Howe ye preache in prose,
And shape therto a glose,
Like a shipmans hose,
To fayne yourse[l]ves ded,
Whiche nathelesse be fed,
And dayly eate oure bred,
That ye amonge vs beg,
And gett it spite of oure hede:
It wonder is to me,
Howe ye maye fathers be
Your sede to multiply,

But yf yow be *incubi*,
That gender gobolynes:
Be we not bobolynes,
Sutch lesinges to beleve,
Whiche ye amonge vs
  dry[ve]?
Because ye do vs shrive,
Ye say we must youe call
Fathers seraphicall
And angelicall,
That be fantasticall,
Brute and bestiall,
Yea, diabolicall,
The babes of Beliall,
The sacrifise of Ball,
The dregges of all durte,
Fast bounde and girte
Vnder the devils skyrte;
For *pater* Priapus,
And *frater* Polpatus,
With *doctor* Dulpatus,
Suffultus fullatus,[1]
Pappus paralyticus,
And *pastor improvidus*,
Be false and frivolus,
Proude and pestiferous,
Pold and pediculous,
Ranke and ridiculous,
Madd and meticulous,
Ever invidious,
Never religious,
In preachinge prestigious,
In walkinge prodigious,
In talkinge sedicious,
In doctrine parnicious,
Haute and ambicious,

---

[1] *fullatus*] Qy. " fulcratus ? "

Fonde and supersticious,
In lodginge prostibulus,
In beddinge promiscuous,
In councells myschevous,
In musters monstrous,
In skulkinge insidicious,
Vnchast and lecherous,
In excesse outragious,
As sicknesse contagious,
The wurst kind of edders,
And stronge sturdy beggers:
Wher one stande and teaches,
An other prate and preches,
Like holy horseleches:
So this rusty rable
At bourd and at table
Shall fayne and fable,
With bible and with bable,
To make all thinge stable, ·
By lowringe and by lokinge,
By powrynge and by potinge,
By standinge and by stop-
    inge,
By handinge and by ffotinge,
By corsy and by crokinge,
With their owne pelf promo-
    tinge,
With ther eyes alweyes to-
    tinge
Wher they may haue sho-
    tinge
Ther and here ageyne:
Thus the people seyne,

With wordes true and playne,
Howe they jest and ioll
With ther nody poll,
With rownynge and rollinge,
With bowsinge and bollinge,
With lillinge and lollinge,
With knyllinge and knollinge,
With tillinge and tollinge,
With shavinge and pollinge,
With snyppinge and snatch-
    inge,
With itchinge and cratchinge,
With kepinge and katchinge,
With wepinge and watchinge,
With takinge and catchinge,
With peltinge and patchinge,
With findinge and fatchinge,
With scriblinge and scratch-
    inge,
With ynkinge and blatchinge;
That no man can matche
    them,
Till the devill fatche them,
And so to go together
Vnto their denne for ever,
Wher hens as they never
Hereafter shall dissever,
But dy eternally,
That lyve so carnally;
For that wilbe ther ende,
But yf God them sende
His grace here to amend:
And thus I make an ende.

Thus endeth the ffourthe and laste parte of this treatise,
called the Image of Ypocresy.

The grudge of ypocrites conceyved ageynst the auctor of this treatise.

These be as knappishe knackes
As ever man made,
For javells and for iackes,
A jymiam for a iade.

Well were we, yf we wist
What a wight he were

That sturred vpp this myst,
To do vs all this dere:

Oh, yf we could attayne hym,
He mighte be fast and sure
We should not spare to payne hym,
While we mighte indure!

The awnswer of the auctor.

Ego sum qui sum,
My name may not be told;
But where ye go or come,
Ye may not be to bold:

For I am, is, and was,
And ever truste to be,
Neyther more nor las
Then asketh charite.

This longe tale to tell
Hathe made me almost horse:

I trowe and knowe right well
That God is full of force,

And able make the dome
And defe men heare and speake,
And stronge men overcome
By feble men and weke:

So thus I say my name is;
Ye geit no more of me,
Because I wilbe blameles,
And live in charite.

Thuse endith this boke called the Image of Ypocresye.

THE MANER OF THE WORLD NOW A DAYES.*

So many poynted caps
Lased with double flaps,
And so gay felted hats,
    Sawe I never:
So many good lessons,
So many good sermons,
And so few devocions,
    Sawe I never.

So many gardes worne,
Jagged and al to-torne,   10
And so many falsely forsworne,
    Sawe I never:
So few good polycies
In townes and cytyes
For kepinge of blinde hostryes
    Sawe I never.

So many good warkes,
So few wel lerned clarkes,
And so few that goodnes markes,
    Sawe I never: 20

---

* Was *Imprinted at London in Flete Strete at the signe of the Rose Garland by W. Copland*, n. d.   This piece (of the original impression of which I have not been able to procure a sight) is now given from *Old Ballads*, 1840, edited by J. P. Collier, Esq., for the Percy Society.

Such pranked cotes and sleves,
So few yonge men that preves,
And such encrease of theves,
    Sawe I never.

So many garded hose,
Such cornede shoes,
And so many envious foes,
    Sawe I never:
So many questes sytte
With men of smale wit,   30
And so many falsely quitte,
    Sawe I never.

So many gay swordes,
So many altered wordes,
And so few covered bordes,
    Sawe I never:
So many empti purses,
So few good horses,
And so many curses,
    Sawe I never.   40

Such bosters and braggers,
So newe fashyoned daggers,
And so many beggers,
    Sawe I never:
So many propre knyves,
So well apparrelled wyves
And so yll of theyr lyves,
    Saw I never.

So many cockolde makers,
So many crakers,
And so many peace breakers,   50
    Saw I never:
So much vayne clothing
With cultyng and jagging,
And so much bragginge,
    Saw I never.

So many newes and knackes,
So many naughty packes,
And so many that mony lackes,
    Saw I never: 60
So many maidens with child
And wylfully begylde,
And so many places untilde,
    Sawe I never.

So many women blamed
And rightuously defaimed,
And so lytle ashamed,
    Sawe I never:
Widowes so sone wed
After their husbandes be deade,   70
Having such hast to bed,
    Sawe I never.

So much strivinge
For goodes and for wivinge,
And so lytle thryvynge,
    Sawe I never:
So many capacities,
Offices and pluralites,
And chaunging of dignities,
    Sawe I never.   80

So many lawes to use
The truth to refuse,
Suche falshead to excuse,
    Sawe I never:
Executers havinge the ware,
Taking so littel care
Howe the soule doth fare,
    Sawe I never.

Amonge them that are riche
No frendshyp is to kepe tuche,   90
And such fayre glosing speche
    Sawe I never:

So many pore
In every bordoure,
And so small soccoure,
    Saw I never.

So proude and so gaye,
So riche in araye,
And so skant of money,
    Saw I never: 100
So many bowyers,
So many fletchers,
And so few good archers,
    Saw I never.

So many chepers,
So fewe biers,
And so many borowers,
    Sawe I never:
So many alle sellers
In baudy holes and sellers,   110
Of yonge folkes yll counsellers,
    Sawe I never.

So many pinkers,
So many thinkers,
And so many good ale drinkers,
    Sawe I never:
So many wronges,
So few mery songes,
And so many yll tonges,
    Sawe I never.   120

So many a vacabounde
Through al this londe,
And so many in pryson bonde,
    I sawe never:
So many citacions,
So fewe oblacions,
And so many newe facions,
    Sawe I never.

So many fleyng tales,
Pickers of purses and males,   180
And so many sales,
    Saw I never:
So much preachinge,
Speaking fayre and teaching,
And so ill belevinge,
    Saw I never.

So much wrath and envy,
Covetous and glottony,
And so litle charitie,
    Sawe I never: 140
So many carders,
Revelers and dicers,
And so many yl ticers,
    Sawe I never.

So many lollers,
So few true tollers,
So many baudes and pollers,
    Sawe I never:
Such treachery,
Simony and usury,   150
Poverty and lechery,
    Saw I never.

So many avayles,
So many geales,
And so many fals baylies,¹
    Sawe I never:
By fals and subtyll wayes
All England decayes,
For more envy and lyers ²
    Sawe I never.   160

---

1 *baylies*] Qy. " bayles ? "
2 *lyers*] Qy. " lyes ? "

So new facioned jackes
With brode Happes in the neckes,
And so gay new partlettes,
Sawe I never:
So many slutteshe cookes,
So new facioned tucking hookes,
And so few biers of bookes,
Saw I never.

Sometime we song of myrth and play,
But now our joy is gone away, 170
For so many fal in decay
Sawe I never:
Whither is the welth of England gon?
The spirituall saith they have none,
And so many wrongfully undone
Saw I never.

It is great pitie that every day
So many prybors go by the way,
And so many extorcioners in eche cuntrey
Sawe I never. 180
To theé, Lord, I make my mone,
For thou maist heápe us everichone:
Alas, the people is so wo begone,
Worse was it never!
Amendment
Were convenient,
But it may not be;
We have exiled veritie.
God is neither dead nor sicke;
He may amend al yet, 190
And trowe ye so in dede,
As ye beleve ye shal have mede.
After better I hope ever,
For worse was it never.

Finis.*   J. S.

* [The above poem] may, after all, be Skelton's; but, at

any rate, it is only a *rifacimento* of the following verses,—
found in *MS. Sloane, 747.* fol. 88, and very difficult to decipher:

" So propre cappes
So lytle hattes
And so false hartes
    Saw y never.

So wyde gownes
In cytees and townes
And so many sellers of bromys
    Say I never.

Suche garded huoes [hose]
Suche playted shoes
And suche a pose
    Say y never.

Dowbletes not[?] syde
The syde so wyde
And so moche pride
    Was never.

So many ryuen shertes
So well appareld chyrches
And so many lewed clerkes
    Say I never.

So fayre coursers
So godely trappers
And so fewe folners
    Say y never.

So many fayere suerdes
So lusty knyghtes and lordes
And so fewe covered bordes
    Say I never.

So joly garded clokes
So many clyppers of grotes
And go vntyde be the throtes
    Say I never.

So many wyde pur[r]ces
And so fewe gode horses
And so many curses
    Say y never.

Suche bosters and braggers
And suche newe facyshyont daggers
And so many cursers
    Say I never.

So many propere knyffes
So well apparelld wyfes
And so evyll of there lyfes
    Say I never.

The stretes so swepynge
With wemen clothynge
And so moche sweryuge
    Say I never.

Suche blendynge of legges
In townes and hegges
And so many plegges
    Say I never.

Of wymen kynde
Lased be hynde
So lyke the fende
    Say I never.

So many spyes
So many lyes
And so many thevys
    Say I never.

So many wronges
So few mery songes
And so many ivel tonges
    Say I neuer.

So moche trechery
Symony and vsery
Poverte and lechery
                Say I never.

So fewe sayles
So lytle avayles
And so many jayles
                Sawe y never.

So many esterlynges
Lombardes and flemynges
To bere awey our wynynges
                Sawe I never.

Be there sotyll weys
Al Englande decays
For suche false Januayes
                Sawe I neuer.

Amonge the ryche
Where frenship ys to seche
But so fayre glosynge speche
                Sawe I never.

So many poore
Comynge to the dore
And so litle socour
                Sawe I never.

So prowde and say [gay?]
So joly in aray
And so litle money
                Sawe I never.

So many sellers
So fewe byers
And so many marchaunt taylors
                Sawe I never.

Executores hauynge mony and ware
Than hauynge so litle care
Howe the pore sowle shall fare
    Sawe I never.

So many lawers vse
The truthe to refuse
And suche falsehed excuse
    Sawe I never.

Whan a man ys dede
His wiffe so shortely wed
And hauynge suche hast to bed
    Sawe I neuer.

So many maydens blamed
Wrongefully not defamed
And beyenge so lytle ashamyd
    Sawe I never.

Relygiouse in cloystere closyd
And prestes and large 1 losed
Beyenge so evyll disposyd
    Sawe I never.

God saue our sovereygne lord the kynge
And alle his royal sprynge
For so noble a prince reyny[n]ge
    Sawe I never."

---

1 *and large*] Qy. " at large ? " but it is by no means certain that " large " is the reading of the MS.

END OF VOL. II.

Printed in Great Britain by
Amazon.co.uk, Ltd.,
Marston Gate.